CW01082041

A
CONTINUAL
FAREWELL

MY LIFE IN LETTERS WITH TONY WILSON

A
CONTINUAL
FAREWELL

MY LIFE IN LETTERS WITH TONY WILSON

Lindsay Reade

OMNIBUS PRESS
London / New York / Paris / Sydney / Copenhagen / Berlin / Madrid / Tokyo

Contents

A Sort of Foreword   7

Introduction   11

Chapter 1: So It Goes   17

Chapter 2: A Dangerous Woman   39

Chapter 3: Bitten by Rabid (and Punk)   67

Chapter 4: The Darkening of the Light   99

Chapter 5: Acts of Creation and Destruction   117

Chapter 6: To Broadway (Or Not)   141

Chapter 7: The Sweet Cheat Gone   181

Chapter 8: The Eastern Mystic and the Western Hustler   193

Chapter 9: How Love Fled   209

Chapter 10: That's the Deal   233

Chapter 11: Is You Is Or Is You Ain't (My Baby)?   235

Chapter 12: A Horse to Water   273

Chapter 13: On the Factory Floor   287

Chapter 14: Shown the Factory Door   297

Chapter 15: Phoenix and Ashes   321

Chapter 16: 'Nice Boys' Were Never My Cup of Poison   339

Acknowledgements   351

A SORT OF FOREWORD

Anyone who was around when Factory Records started will remember the complex, interconnected forces that shaped the label and the bands it launched. If you weren't around, it was like this: there was a post-industrial city facing grim times, but there were plenty of cheap, ramshackle spaces to play in, and to play with. There was a television company, Granada, with a big red sign on the roof of their building, glowing for the region. There was Tony Wilson, who worked for that TV company – a smart man, with smart taste and many connections. He was reading the news one minute and presenting his own arts programme the next.

Granada film crews shot spotty, snot-dripping bands in horrid holes and some famous names occasionally called in at the studios. *So It Goes* got away with it; captured something of the zeitgeist, but motivated many more beyond the city. It was 'part-networked'. Not shown all over the country, just in some regions at different times.

Spluttering, misfiring cultural expressions like these encouraged provincial evolution, while the government of the day had no idea what to do with the north other than ravage the region's working classes. But Manchester and Liverpool didn't become rustbelt wreckage. They regenerated, and part of the reason why this happened is down to Factory and the Haçienda.

Other record labels came and went. Factory had identity and kept going, perhaps against common sense. It had bands and voices that stuck with you, got into your head: Joy Division, then New Order, ACR, Happy Mondays and others. They had their time. Some still have it. Their various personalities, personal ticks, reputations, that have lasted, and aged a bit, maybe.

And in the middle of this, you have what's in this book: a love affair. You have the real Tony Wilson and the woman he fell for, Lindsay Reade. And she for him. You have the way their lives were swept up in the beginnings and endings of what wasn't just a record label but a sort of kick in the head for a lot of people. You've got Wilson's letters, written by hand, or typed out like he typed his scripts – fast thinking, making quick associations, sometimes pretentious, often funny, always clever. Even when things go wrong – which they did. You will read this through Lindsay's eyes, and like her you will have to make sense of the bad times and what happens when marriages break down, and when people also break. The extent to which this book documents how a culturally significant body of work, like Factory's numbered series of releases, which included buildings and objects as well as music, cannot be separated from its emotional core: the lives of the people who made it happen.

Bob Dickinson
May 2024

INTRODUCTION

The book you are about to read came about after I was approached in December 2019 by Jan Hicks, archives manager from the Science and Industry Museum in Manchester. Jan was organising an exhibition about Factory Records to follow on from the *Use Hearing Protection* retrospective in London, held to celebrate the fortieth anniversary of Factory Records. Jan's idea was to present me as one of five key women to balance with the five male directors, Tony Wilson, Alan Erasmus, Rob Gretton, Martin Hannett and Peter Saville. The other women to be featured alongside myself were Gillian Gilbert (New Order), artist Linder Sterling, office manager Lesley Gilbert and artist and singer Ann Quigley.

Jan asked each of us to provide some sort of exhibit that would represent us. I couldn't find very much in the way of Factory paraphernalia, hence the decision was made to include the sleeve of a record I made with Vini Reilly/The Durutti Column – a cover version of 'I Get Along Without You Very Well.' But while looking through the things I'd kept, I discovered a whole tranche of correspondence from Tony, mostly on very thin Factory notepaper. Upon reading through, I remembered what a fine letter writer Tony was. Certainly, the letters were worthy of interest and needed preserving, especially as I'm now of an age when one's death is no longer just a rumour.

Tony and Factory have haunted me for most of my life, like a shadow you can't shake off. This book, with its scanned letters and documents, is a raw and truthful exposure and I question why I would want to reveal such intimate detail. Other than a way of preserving Tony's letters, it's also partly because personal relationships have always been more important to me than other things in life. I suspect this is true of many women, more so than men. Despite failing spectacularly at relationships, perhaps the account of my marriage downfall, related within, could possibly be of benefit to someone else in their own personal life.

Tony was an important man and his letters, along with associated items, provide a record of a significant time. Along with my narrative, the letters give another slant on his life, his TV presenting, his first marriage, his skill with words and the early beginnings of Factory Records.

I'm not a Catholic, as Tony was, but there's one part of Catholic practice which appeals to me, and that is confession. I think there's also an element of that in this work. A confession and an apology.

The Haçienda name is drawing more crowds than Factory ever did. Following the plethora of books, films, merchandising and concerts under this banner, the Factory Records story looked, with the exhibition, to be reducing to an archive. On visiting the aforementioned homage to Factory in June 2021, I noted a different flavour from preceding tributes (books, films, etc.), it being an actual archive of the posters, records and ephemera from the early Factory catalogue – from 1-50 – along with various other exhibits.

This book, then, is my own final archiving.

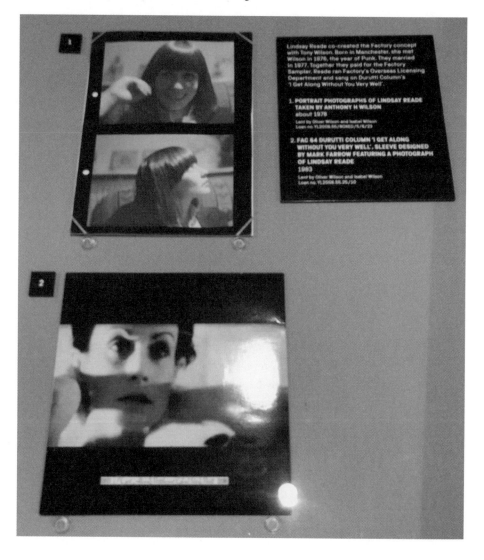

On the page opposite is a snapshot of my own inclusion at the exhibition. Jan thought I'd be moved that Tony had kept, all his life, two photographs he'd taken of me; these had been contributed to the exhibition by his children. But when I saw them, I felt somewhat underwhelmed – is that all my offering amounted to? Photographs? The Durutti Column cover was another photograph – a still Tony took from a video that he'd filmed of me. Afterwards, driving home, it seemed apt when Ringo Starr's song 'Photograph' was on the radio. All I've got is a photograph, indeed.

I was amused to see a note in my own handwriting at the exhibition, also donated by Tony's children. I'd jotted down that John Brierley, who ran Cargo Studios in Rochdale, and also Malcolm McLaren had called. It illustrates how often I answered the busy phone at our little cottage on Town Lane, Charlesworth; Factory Records didn't just begin at 86 Palatine Road. There were no mobiles of course, so, other than Granada Studios, this was then the main point of contact for Tony. It also demonstrates how much time Tony spent away from home: why else would I have written that 'John Brierley rang Sunday'?

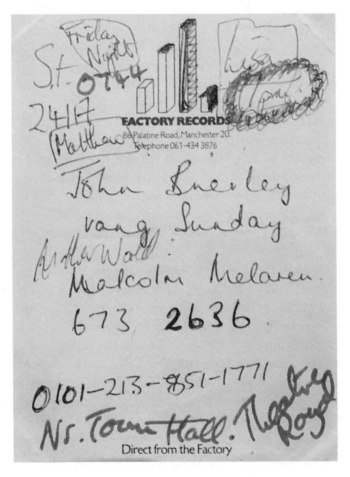

Tony probably kept this note because Malcolm McLaren, a person he admired and sought out, had actually telephoned him. They were similar types in some ways, both out to make history and both believing that the band Malcolm managed and Tony put on TV, the Sex Pistols, were doing just that. Tony and many others credit this band's gig at Manchester's Lesser Free Trade Hall in 1976 as critical to the wave of punk, and post-punk, that followed – and Tony worshipped at the shrine of punk (unlike me). Tony gave the Pistols their debut TV performance on the first series of his show, *So It Goes,* and begged McLaren, in vain, to put them on again in the second series or, better still, devote a whole show to them. McLaren, it seemed, feared that a repeat appearance might compromise the band.

Both McLaren and Wilson were drawn, in their different expressions, to the Situationist movement, which focused on creating 'situations' capable of smashing the spectacle of capitalism and consumerism. McLaren demonstrated on the streets and shocked people with his bands and his fetish, risqué fashion shop SEX on the King's Road, the name emblazoned in huge, pillowed, red lettering. Nowadays, that would seem a bit naff but in the seventies such actions were unheard of. Tony's expressions were more artistically subtle: names for bands such as The Durutti Column (named after an anarchist column led by Buenaventura Durruti during the Spanish Civil War), sandpaper album sleeves that destroyed the records placed next to them, bars named after spies, such as Kim Philby. That sort of thing.

John Brierley, the other caller immortalised on the note, originally met Tony at Granada while working there as a cameraman in 1976 but his Rochdale recording studio, Cargo, became Tony's go-to studio in the early days when the budget was too tight for Strawberry Studios in Stockport. Joy Division's first tracks for the Factory Sample ('Digital' and 'Glass') were recorded there in 1978. Tony and I spent many a night in Rochdale – Orchestral Manoeuvres in the Dark recorded 'Electricity' there and, probably the most important of all tracks – Joy Division's 'Atmosphere' – was also put down there.

The other scribble on the notepad is in Tony's handwriting. He'd noted down 'Matthew' and above it 'St' and 'Friday night'. It's possible this was a reference to Eric's club, run by Roger Eagle on Mathew St in Liverpool (opposite where the Cavern Club had hosted The Beatles). Roger had been the resident DJ at The Twisted Wheel in Manchester and then started a club nearby called The Magic Village before running Eric's in Liverpool. Tony has also jotted down 'Nr. Town Hall', and this is actually situated quite close to Mathew St. Perhaps it refers to a meeting place near Eric's. It's difficult to date this note: it could be 1978 (given the references) or 1979; Factory stationery officially came out in 1979. Tony and I went to Eric's quite a lot during 1978 and 1979, and the Factory record label very nearly became a joint venture between Tony and Roger (or Factory and Eric's).

Roger Eagle (left) with partner Pete Fulwell at Eric's, Liverpool.

The long telephone number was for Los Angeles. Tony had his sights on America throughout his life; he first visited as a young university student, then in later years we went to California for our honeymoon and, at the last, he made a perilous trip from his sick bed to his beloved New York only a few weeks before his untimely death, aged just 57.

The most vivid dream I've had about Tony (and there've been many) followed his death in 2007. It was so powerful that I woke up crying as if I had really been with him. He clearly said to me the following:

'See it as a good memory and move on.'

This hasn't always been easy, given our volatile history, the regrets and the persistent reminders. But writing things down generally helps, which is why a diary, or a book such as this can be beneficial to the processing of life events. Overall, having recounted the memories, both happy and sad, I am left feeling grateful to have lived through them. Certainly Tony, with his indomitably optimistic outlook, never failed to embrace the ups and downs of his life as ultimately good. After all, how else would there be a story?

CHAPTER 1
So It Goes

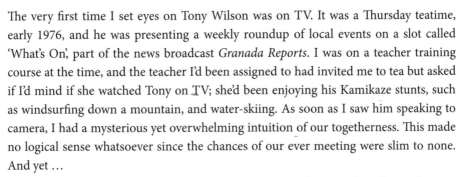

The very first time I set eyes on Tony Wilson was on TV. It was a Thursday teatime, early 1976, and he was presenting a weekly roundup of local events on a slot called 'What's On', part of the news broadcast *Granada Reports*. I was on a teacher training course at the time, and the teacher I'd been assigned to had invited me to tea but asked if I'd mind if she watched Tony on TV; she'd been enjoying his Kamikaze stunts, such as windsurfing down a mountain, and water-skiing. As soon as I saw him speaking to camera, I had a mysterious yet overwhelming intuition of our togetherness. This made no logical sense whatsoever since the chances of our ever meeting were slim to none. And yet ...

Only weeks later he walked into a party I was attending in Altrincham; this was near where my boyfriend lived – and nowhere near where Tony lived. Like many love stories, ours began with a sighting across a crowded room. We were both with other people, but it didn't matter, merely a glance foretold something important between us. Our eyes locked for a second or two, but he was with his girlfriend and so remained aloof, gentleman that he was. Also with him was a male friend called Nick, who got chatting with me. It was nothing romantic, but I met Nick later at Lyme Park one sunny afternoon and we smoked some Thai grass I'd procured. Fresh and woven onto a stick, it was better than anything I've ever smoked before or since. It was unlike the mind-numbing skunk you get today; this was so mind-expanding that I'd bought quite a lot of it. I wanted my friends to experience it. Nick told me his friend Tony would doubtless want to try it and suggested I call him. When he gave me Tony's phone number, I sensed our fate was sealed.

It was on 15 May 1976 that I met Tony in the car park of the Ram's Head pub in Disley. I climbed into his Ford Escort RS 2000 and we drove a short way up the hill whereupon we shared a joint of this amazing grass. Even at this early stage, we both knew we would share a significant partnership. Tony later described the intensity of that meeting in a letter, which read: 'The certainty I felt that sunny afternoon was quite searing. Few things in the world are definite but I knew that afternoon that the irrevocable had happened. I had met the wife of my years and the mother of my children. Such knowledge is not changing or mutable. Facts like that merely exist.' For my part, the pattern of events and the immediate familiarity I felt with him ignited in me a belief in the machinations of fate, and even reincarnation.

I drove away from that meeting with Tony knowing it was already over with my boyfriend Mike. I'd cared for Mike and it'd never crossed my mind to leave him, but I knew categorically my future now lay elsewhere. I was fairly ruthless about ending it with him and wasted no time over it.

Tony told me his girlfriend June was going to India and said it would be less hurtful to her if we waited until after she'd gone. I couldn't understand this – his relationship had only lasted a few months, whereas Mike and I had been together for nearly two years. It seemed somewhat duplicitous, but I preferred to take the view that Tony was being kind (rather than cowardly). I heartily objected to his plan, feeling an unnerving mistrust, but felt consoled when he said he'd write to me every day in the meantime. We intended to go to Thailand once he was free (probably because of the Thai grass ostensibly bringing us together) although for some reason neither he, nor I, ever did. In the event, we actually got together within two or three weeks and I moved into his two-up two-down in Charlesworth, Derbyshire, within two months.

Tony's correspondence over the next thirteen years reflects the changing landscape of our feelings for one another; from love to hate and back again.

His first letter mentions Thelma McGough, with whom Tony had had an important two-year relationship prior to June. Thelma had an interesting dating history, previously having had an intense six-month relationship with John Lennon while at The Liverpool College of Art. After Thelma ditched him, he moved on to Cynthia Powell. Three years later, Thelma briefly dated Paul McCartney, but Tony was more impressed that she'd had a relationship with the writer Tom Wolfe, who'd sent her thirty-three love letters. He was known as a journalist more than a novelist at that time. Thelma was a creative woman, a painter of Op-Art canvases and a designer of fashion-forward clothes. Later she came to work at Granada as a researcher on *The Krypton Factor* before producing a BAFTA award-winning series *Blind Date*. By the time Tony met Thelma, she was married to the Liverpool poet Roger McGough and had two children with him, as well as a son, Nathan, from a former relationship.

Tony initially kept calling at her house because he was keen to speak to Roger. He was never there, and Tony ended up falling in love with Thelma. Their relationship really began the afternoon he asked her to go with him to the Walker Art Gallery to explain a painting that he intended to feature on 'What's On'. For almost the entire duration of her relationship with Tony, Roger was living away from home, as he was based at Loughborough University as Poet in Residence. Tony was able therefore to spend time

Tony with Thelma's boys

with Thelma's children, and he had an enduringly close relationship with her teenage son, Nathan, who subsequently stayed with us regularly – he remembers me giving him driving lessons. Nathan would later go on to manage Happy Mondays.

Tony's mother Doris was a devout Catholic and Tony, having been raised in the faith, was sentimental about the church and his days as an altar boy. Thelma, who called Tony 'Anthony', told me she questioned how, as Catholics, his affair with a married woman played out with their conscience. His answer, and Doris's, was that love and happiness triumphed above all else. Doris liked Thelma; she made her Tony happy and that was all that mattered to her. The three of them even took a holiday together in Paris. Doris died suddenly in 1975 so I never met her, but she clearly knew Tony – and his weaknesses – well. She always told him that women would be the ruin of him. I suspect she meant that he lacked common sense, with him being a sucker for beauty, and with him having opportunities denied to other men.

The catalyst for the split between Tony and Thelma came when Roger McGough eventually wrote to Tony, appealing to him as a gentleman and a fellow Catholic, to return his wife to him. It was Thelma who first picked the letter from the mat at Tony's small cottage in Town Lane, Charlesworth. She told me: 'Recognising the handwriting, I asked Anthony not to open it, but he did, and cried. Roger's heartfelt plea pricked Anthony's conscience. He asked me "one last time" to "come and live here". I told him I couldn't leave my children. "Bring them," he said, as he always had. I stayed the night, both of us in distress. In the morning, he asked again, and my answer was the same. At that point we both knew we couldn't continue.'

'I was angry with them both at the time,' she continued, 'because I believed they were using their Catholicism as an excuse – Roger to have me back and Anthony to let me go if I wasn't going to move in – I felt I had no say. Though in hindsight the choice lay with me. Painful as this realisation was for us both, I knew instinctively he needed to move on without me and find his own wife, and I needed to move on with my husband. I could no longer have both. Of course, as was typical of him, he sought to reference the end as drama, sending me a card with a screenshot of Rick and Ilsa in *Casablanca*. Inside he wrote, "We'll always have Paris," completing the circle, since his first farewell after our first kiss was, "Here's looking at you, kid".'

Tony's last love letter to Thelma was dated 1 March 1976, although he continued to send her books with handwritten inscriptions. Coming so soon after this, his relationship with June was likely a rebound thing. In reality, he'd wanted Thelma to leave Roger for a man 'with a smaller kitchen', which was a jokey reference to a line in Roger's poem 'Summer with Monika' about being left for someone with a bigger kitchen. Tony's kitchen at his house in Charlesworth was a tiny galley-style affair, an add-on to the small cottage.

That summer, Tony took me to Liverpool to meet Thelma at a function there. She displayed no jealousy which I thought was very dignified. She told me that she felt privileged that he'd asked her to meet me and gave Tony her approval because she 'wanted him to be happy just as Doris had done'. She wrote to me: 'When "A" told me he was in love with you but still seeing June – whom he'd said was only a "bridging loan" – I told him to get a grip of himself and face up to reality. I meant that he should stop taking the easy option to avoid confrontation, not for June's sake or yours, but his own.'

I liked Thelma immediately but, in later years, my own jealousy pained me. She was able to keep hold of Tony in a way that I couldn't. She gave him support when I gave him rows. Being once removed, hers was perhaps a more unconditional love than mine, making her a truer confidante and friend. They were also able to meet often at Granada as she'd built a successful career there. My relationship with Tony was different than hers. As his wife and lover more than his friend, I would end up losing so much with him – family, house, career, financial security – and yet still, until his life was cut short, I never ruled out our reunion in older age. Sadly, unconditional love and a reunion only came about when we made our peace four years after an ugly parting of ways, and again much later, when he was dying of cancer.

When Tony embarked on a relationship with the former beauty queen Yvette Livesey in 1990, he and I were then on a friendly footing, so he arranged for me to meet her at a Factory dinner in Scotland. Unfortunately, unlike Thelma with me, I was unable either to give my approval or refrain from displaying any jealousy. For one thing, she was twenty years younger than him and me. I felt it was her youth and beauty that was turning his head but somehow it didn't fit. He was celebrating but I feared for him.

But that was all to come. To return to 1976, 30 May to be exact, Tony typed out his first letter to me and it was, as he predicted, the first of many. His letters were almost always typed; he was often glued to a typewriter, writing scripts and notes to camera and such like.

The letter arrived at the house I was renting at that time; Mike and I had lived there together for several months but he'd moved out as soon as our relationship ended. Tony and I had met a couple of times before the letters began but when I realised he was sticking to his plan of waiting until June went to india before ending things with her, I told him we shouldn't meet until then. Our first 'date' earlier that May was actually to see Slaughter & the Dogs, a punk band the producer Martin Hannett had told Tony about. This band was on the Rabid record label based in Withington, Manchester, and Martin was one of the three directors, along with Tosh Ryan and Lawrence Beedle.

As you can see from the envelope, Tony didn't even know my surname at this point:

Charlesworth,

Sunday, May 30th,76

Darling

The first of many. It's been a strange week, oh yes
and a strange weekend. Late afternoon, I think I have cooled
all my problems out, mind looks clearer than the sky anyway. My
plan is correct, I think I know that now. I know you don't think
much to it-your pretty fists were an eloquent dissention- but like
the man sang , "trust in me babe." So for the first few weeks
of this 'could-be-eventful' summer (This is the first summer of
the rest of our lives) I'll write, each day, I'll take the risk of
losing you, I'll wake up as I did this morning trying to imagine
how lovely your sleeping face would look on the pillow, I'll
wake up like that every morning, I'll endure Mrs MCGough's verbal
invective at my weak nature — you shouldn't have found out so
soon little lady -I'll get my show and my thing together as they
say on the west coast of scotland, I'll become a small but
contented gun, oh and I'll also miss you but you already know
that. And don't give me any of that "I don't believe it for one
minute' crap. You know it like I know it, that's why we're acting
so crazy. You can go back to your railing stage now but you know
I know you know. Christ this sounds like bad Laing poems. Which
as any two bit TV lin'man will know is a nice way into another
thing I wanted to say. I've got this poem, which I guess is the
only thing I can give you in the present isolations. It's the
one I mentioned about "Sweetest love I do not go/ for weariness of
thee/Nor in hope the world can show a fitter love for me;/...let
not thy divining heart, forethinke me any ill......."

Anyway it ends with one of the only sentiments /

/ideas/images I've ever found remotely comforting in such troubled times as these,

> "But think that we
> Are but turned aside to sleep;
> They who one another keep
> Alive, ne'r parted be.

It's long time before the dawn Mr D Crosby used to sing, but then again some sunrises can be worth it. Oh and one more lovely quote,I've just been crying my eyes out - yes I'm not as hard as I appear......my dear.......)- while watching David Copperfield on the TV. My love for Dickens and Aunt Betsy can wait for another time but there was one lovely moment, where Mr Micawber was venting on his worries about the future and the difficulties to be faced therein. MRs Micawber turns on him and with a voice that is as loving as it is scolding, says;

> "You are going to a distant country expressly
> in order that you may be fully understood and appreciated
> for the first time.

The Micawbers went to Australia; us, Bangkok.

Yours,
    Anthony

Charlesworth

Sunday, May 30th, 76

Darling

The first of many. It's been a strange week, oh yes and a strange weekend. Late afternoon, I think I have cooled all my problems out, mind looks clearer than the sky anyway. My plan is correct, I think I know that now. I know you don't think much to it-your pretty fists were an eloquent dissension - but like the man sang, "trust in me babe". So for the first few weeks of this 'could-be-eventful' summer (This is the first summer of the rest of our lives) I'll write, each day, I'll take the risk of losing you, I'll wake up as I did this morning trying to imagine how lovely your sleeping face would look on the pillow, I'll wake up like that every morning, I'll endure Mrs McGough's verbal invective at my weak nature - you shouldn't have found out so soon little lady - I'll get my show and my thing together as they say on the west coast of Scotland, I'll become a small but contented gun, oh and I'll also miss you but you already know that. And don't give me any of that "I don't believe it for a minute" crap. You know it like I know it, that's why we're acting so crazy. You can go back to your railing stage now but you know I know you know. Christ this sounds like bad Laing poems. Which as any two bit TV link man will know is a nice way into another thing I wanted to say. I've got this poem, which I guess is the only thing I can give you in the present isolations. It's the one I mentioned about "Sweetest love I do not go for weariness of thee/Nor in the hope the world can show a fitter love for me/let not thy divining heart fore think me any ill......"

Anyway it ends with one of the only sentiments/ideas/images I've ever found remotely comforting in such troubled times as these,

"But think that we

Are but turned aside to sleep;

They who one another keep

Alive, ne'r parted be.

It's a long time before dawn Mr D Crosby used to sing, but then again some sun-rises can be worth it. Oh and one more lovely quote, I've just been crying my eyes out -(yes I'm not as hard as I appear.....my dear.....) - while watching David Copperfield on the TV. My love for Dickens and Aunt Betsy can wait for another time but there was one lovely moment, where Mr Micawber was venting his worries about the future and the difficulties to be faced therein. Mrs Micawber turns on him and with a voice that is as loving as it is scolding, says;

"You are going to a distant country expressly
in order that you may be fully understood and appreciated
for the first time."
The Micawbers went to Australia; us, Bangkok.
Yours,
Anthony

After his initial salutation of 'Darling', Tony refers to me as 'little lady'. When I read his note in 1976, it never occurred to me then that there might be a hint of condescension or patriarchy in this phrase. In February 1976, the first episode of a musical drama entitled *Rock Follies* screened on TV, featuring an all-girl band of three feminist rockers called The Little Ladies. One of the themes of the series was the exploitation of women in the male-dominated music industry. Tony was doubtless aware of *Rock Follies*. Incidentally, it was a headline review of *Rock Follies* in *Time Out* titled 'It's The Buzz, Cock!' which inspired Howard Devoto to name his new band with Pete Shelley, 'Buzzcocks'.

The poem Tony quotes is taken from John Donne's 'Sweetest Love I Do Not Go'. I'd loved Donne's poetry since studying him for A-level at school: I'd found some consolation in his words after breaking up with my first boyfriend. There was little other comfort for an aching heart to be found in lessons at school.

Sweetest love, I do not go
For weariness of thee
Not in the hope the world can show
A fitter love for me ...
Let not thy divining heart
Forethink me any ill;
Destiny may take thy part,
And may thy fears fulfil;
But think that we
Are but turn'd aside to sleep;
They who one another keep
Alive, n'er parted be.

The song Tony refers to in the line, 'it's a long time before dawn' is 'Long Time Gone' by Crosby, Stills and Nash.

ldent to write: '. . . I know very
t I am about and that my skies
been neglected, though they
en failed in execution, no doubt,
over anxiety about them, which
e destroy that easy appearance
ture always has . . .'

these statements contain truths
e Constable we see in the cur-
· exhibition. On the one hand
e's paintings are steeped in the
of formal landscape painting
enre of artists he admired, like
tuisdael, Gainsborough and
und on the other, they are
of Constable's love and obser-
a particular country-side, and
ecially particular skies. Not for
'ormal generalisations—the
tree or the romanticised sky,
i he despised Turner.

nly Constable's care for detail
racy is shown in his documen-
farm machinery and the vari-
tween say a Surrey 'Double
ugh in 1831 and a Worcester-
igh in 1835, which he drew,
ded in his paintings. It does not
ie, however, that Constable was,
med, a 'natural painter', for
of English landscape, though
drawn, has been selected to
highly idealised version of

able was a painter of cultivated
t—a landscape which was being
loughed, reaped and sown. Yet
· the work is always taking place
nce, so that the small bodies of
carts or ploughs are all made to
niously with the general mood
stable, himself, wished to con-
is the mood of the evening sun
indscape to gold, the break
thowers, the baking summer
never the mood of rural
of cold or anxiety, ravaged
I seldom even an actual storm.
able idealised the countryside
which fitted his personal philos-
he comfortably-off son of a
a miller who liked to celebrate
bandry and fresh air.
ow can anyone help being
e by Constable's skies? Take,
tudy: A view at Hampstead' and
f 'Cirrus Clouds' all painted in
i 1822, and we see Constable
i, untrammelled by social con-
—exercising the science of
on and painting.

ate show includes alongside the
rks from foreign collections, a
t of documentary material that
recently come to light, includ-
table's lecture notes and

In addition there is a written
tion to each section so that you
e to buy a catalogue. The
a itself, with colour plates and
tion by Conal Shields, one of
rition organisers, costs £2.75 in
:, £1.75 in paperback. But look
'or the broadsheet containing an
tion to the show, priced 15p.

'ery, Millbank, SW1 (828 1212)
tube. (Admission 50p, school
· students, pensioners 25p).
inlay, Wednesday, Friday,
· 10.00 - 6.00. Tuesday,
v 10.00 - 10.00. Sunday 11.30 -

'It's The Buzz, Cock!'

*'Rock Follies', Thames TV's
series about the life and
hard times of a female rock
group, begins its six-part
run on Tuesday.* Andrew
Nicholds *reports . . .*

Dee: 'It's the buzz, cock. When you sing
the rock music you get this buzz—it
starts in your chest, maybe it's to do
with the amplifiers or the microphones,
I don't know, it's something electric,
something about energy, I don't know,
anyway it starts in your chest and
spreads from there, like when you toss a
pebble in a pond, I mean it ripples only
not gently, in great energy waves, arms,
fingers, groin, knees, toes, throat, mouth,
head, loud, terrifically loud head buzz
and when the gig's over . . . you can't
just turn it off . . . you have to move,
dance, break things, make love . . .'.

The 'Little Ladies' rock group—Dee
Rhodes, Anna Wynd and Nancy Cunard
des Longchamps ('Q')—meet as leading
ladies, in the doomed revival of a '30s
Broadway musical. The show collapses,
the women form a group and hit the
road. The only way they can get
recorded is by contracting to make the
cinema's first soft-core porn musical,
'Hot Neon'. They are extricated by
Greek/Scouse millionaire Stavros Kuklas,
who makes changes: 'We can't go back-
wards to the old Little Ladies. Their
image was locked into the '50s and '60s.
We want to move forward—into the '40s.'
A nightclub—'The Blitz'—is opened, its
stage an Underground platform. In the
middle of the Victory Gals' act there is
a bomb warning . . .

'Rock Follies' is written by Howard
Schuman, who also wrote the lyrics; the
music is by Andy Mackay from Roxy
Music. Schuman came over here in 1968,
with a film-script but no work permit
—like the surf freak 'Q' lives with and
supports. Hawking his plays around the
television companies brought only glowing rejections, plus the comment from
Thames TV's management of the time
that 'we only do plays for Joe Bloggs'.
Success came with 'Verite', in which a
New York film-maker disastrously tries

to immerse himself in English culture
and society; Schuman admits he himself
finds England 'a total turn-on'. Next
came 'Captain Video's Story', 'Censored
Scenes from King Kong'—recorded but
resolutely untransmitted by the BBC—
and, a few weeks ago, 'Amazing Stories'
(about the residents of Wimbledon
mutating into carrots).

In light of these early struggles, and
those of Schuman's friends who were
trying to make it in the business at the
same time, it isn't surprising that the
Little Ladies story mirrors the setting-up
of the 'Rock Follies' series itself. The
(real) female group Rock Bottom were
originally intended for the parts until
contract wrangles forced a change of
plan. One of the series' characters, an
upper-middle class *Rolling Stone* journalist, was at first given the surname
Norman; this was changed because there
are several journalists with that name,
and who knows what people might
think? Though by this time everyone
was convinced that every theatrical
agent, entrepreneur, hustler etc who
made an appearance was actually meant
to be old so-and-so in the business that
they'd known for years. And the visit to
the set of a notorious ex-alcoholic
journalist is reflected in a character
called Mark Jeffries 'with great colour
supplement connections . . .'

But aren't we in danger of getting a
little esoteric here? Will 'Rock Follies'
be understood by anyone north of
Hendon or south of Croydon? What,
after all, about Joe Bloggs? Schuman
recognises the dangers of creating too
specialised a world bounded by the
Bermuda Triangle of Kensington,
Denmark Street and NW1. But it should
be apparent to everyone that if the
minor characters are in fact caricatures,
this is of their own making. The horren-

dous commune Dee lives in ('In a small
way, we're trying to create a new kind
of human being in Camden Town') uses
jargon like barricades—as rooted in
possession as the world outside, it
succumbs to the pressures of sex and the
power of the Landlord.

Dee is the key to all the levels of
exploitation, and her reactions should
be the audience's (as played by Julie
Covington she is the strongest member
of the group, physically and vocally).
She holds out longest against the world
of entrepreneur Kuklas, but at the same
time she lets herself be screwed in every
sense by boyfriend Spike, Schuman is
confident that his meanings will come
across, however minority-taste the
trappings may seem.

Plus there is the music. Whether
parody or comment, the production
numbers both augment the action and
put the icing on the cake. To put it
patly, rock is all that Dee finally has left
to stand on—so the irony is complete
when Anna rounds on her in the last
episode:

'You have this pathetic illusion that
there's a distinction between Capitalism
and your ideal of Rock Music. But Rock
is a *celebration* of Capitalism. The pulse
is pure jungle, survival of the fittest—and
thousands of bands do struggle to
survive, struggle for the bread to pay for
all that capitalist-produced technology;
amplifiers, electronic equipment, the
apparatus of the recording studio . . .
Rock is Capitalist music . . .'

And so it seems to prove: the 'Rock
Follies' album is planned for the end of
the month, and T-shirts to go with it.
When the ladies at Thames TV were
discussing further ways to promote the
series, and Schuman jestingly suggested
'Rock Follies' candy bars, their faces
positively lit up. Full circle, Ha-tcha!

Review of *Rock Follies*

To write every day was a tall order for a busy man like Tony, which probably explains why he subsequently took to sending me postcards, all with the capital letter A cut out of them. I was impressed he'd found such artistic cards although, with hindsight, it could be seen as vain. In one of them, he added *Anthony Enterprises Ltd* to the A, shades of things to come. His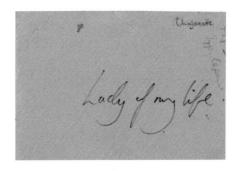

vanity didn't trouble me until much later on. Initially, I didn't see it that way, more that he was an outgoing, clever and confident young man. Both versions were true, in fact.

And inside:

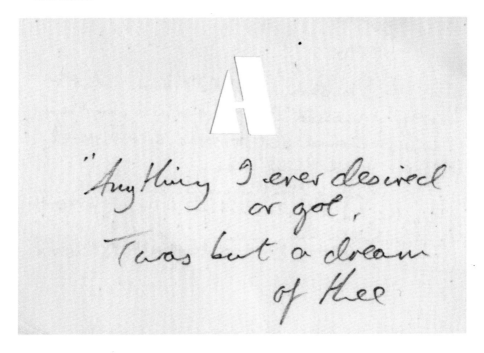

'Anything I ever desired or got, T'was but a dream of thee.'

Yet again Tony is quoting from John Donne, this time from 'The Good Morrow'. This brilliant poem begins: 'I wonder by my troth what thou and I did till we loved? Were we not weaned until then?' The actual line of the verse reads: 'If ever any beauty I did see which I desired or got, 'twas but a dream of thee.'

I don't remember the incident Tony is referring to in the next card (undated but June 1976). Although Mike had left the house we'd shared, he didn't give me up all that lightly, and naturally, there would have been discussions and sightings. I've got a feeling Mike appeared in my local pub in Bramhall and Tony made a rapid exit as soon as he saw him. I remember Mike called at the house once when Tony was present and asked me in a fury what the hell I was doing with 'that poseur'. Oddly enough, Mike eventually came to admire Tony for his achievements and the two of them became friendly many years later (at a time when I'd sadly become more attuned to Mike's original point of view).

D—g,

I'm sorry. I didn't know what to say. I guessed that 'your man' was there and it seemed best to make a cold, quick exit. It didn't feel nice. Before - in the pub - your smile - how long did it last. 2 seconds? The best 2 seconds in this god-forsaken week.

Beginning to need you, lady.

Anthony

xxx

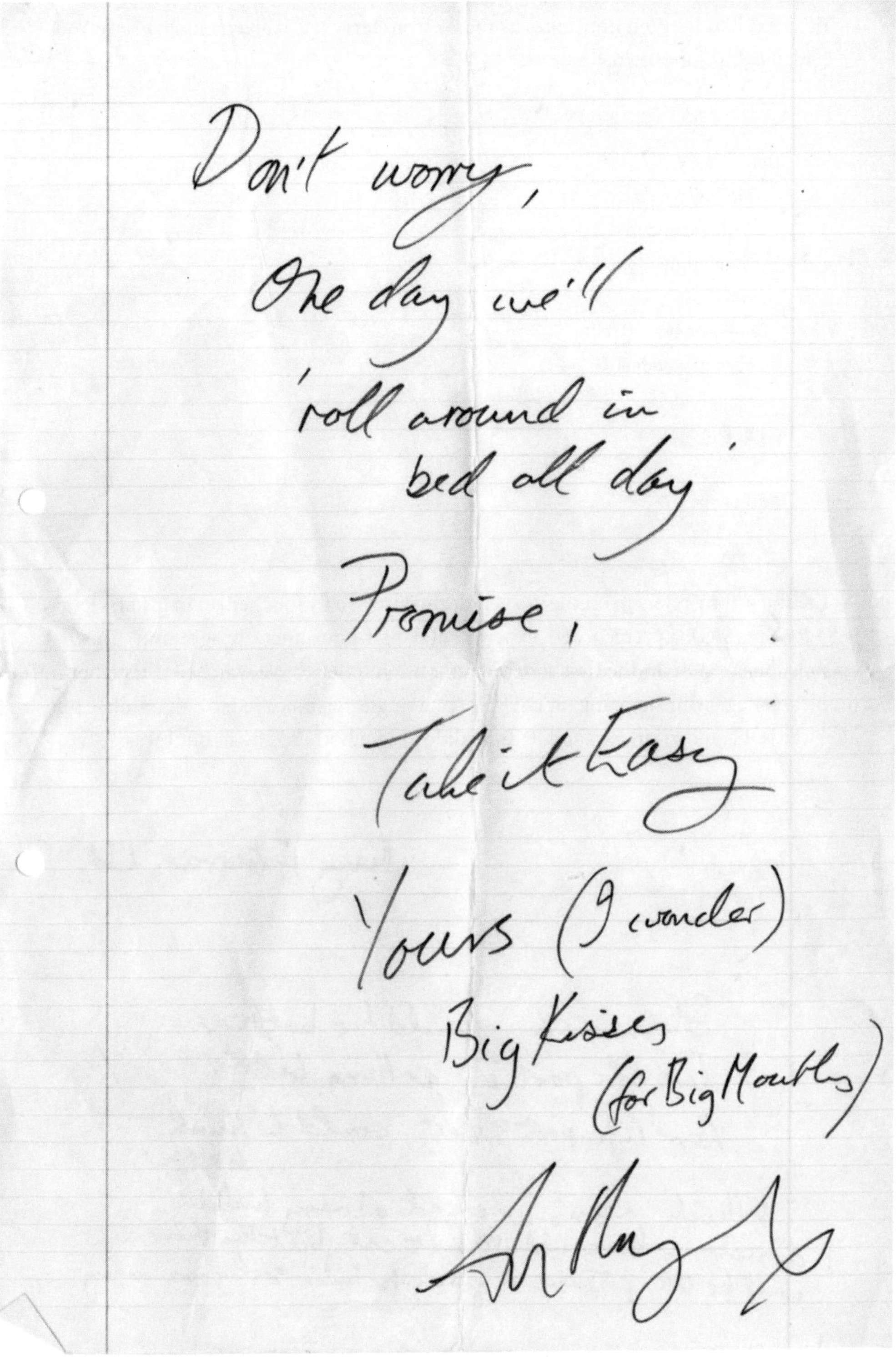

Don't worry,
One day we'll
'roll around in
 bed all day'
Promise,

Take it Easy

Yours (I wonder)
Big Kisses
(for Big Mouths)

This next handwritten note takes its meme from Jerry Jeff Walker's song 'I Love You': Undated, but June 1976.

Don't worry,
   One day we'll
      'roll around in
      bed all day'
   Promise,
   Take it Easy
      Yours (I wonder)
         Big Kisses
      (for Big Mouths)

   Anthony X

The show Tony refers to on the next card, and also briefly touched on in his first letter, is *So It Goes (SIG),* a prerecorded, experimental, half-hour music programme. The first episode, one of nine in the first series, aired on 3 July 1976. We watched it together in his little cottage while tripping on LSD. Not one single person called to congratulate him afterwards. I couldn't understand it. Tony didn't seem bothered by it, but I was.

away — I'd recommend the same for you but you're not the type that takes advice.

The last bit — just my way of saying 'I think of you ———> LOTS

of love,
darling.

Yours
'as this machine is to him'

Anthony

Show O.K., could be better

Love life part 1, getting better

Love life parts 3,4 & 5, could be much better.

 Which means we've got a lousy fuckin director who couldn't shoot cats, but the show will be O.K.; June is going to India early - running away - I'd recommend the same for you but you're but   you're not the type that takes advice.

 The last bit - just my way of saying 'I think of you'

LOTS

_→

of love, darling,

Yours

'as this machine is to him'

Anthony x

SIG was a development on from Tony's 'What's On' slot on *Granada Reports,* with its review of local events and musical acts about to appear in Manchester. Many of them, often relatively unknown at the time, went on to find fame, such as Blondie and Elvis Costello. *SIG* featured studio and live performances, and Clive James was a regular intellect and comic on the show. It seemed that Tony had now found his niche. Still a TV presenter with a penchant for writing clever scripts and with a love of music, he was able to wear his denims and represent a more hippy genre, which was much more who he was than a suit-and-tie guy. He smoked dope virtually every day of his life – apart from in childhood, and the final six months of it. I too was inclined toward a more bohemian outlook, with my long black hair, blue jeans, love of music and dope-smoking. We were simpatico in literature and in the music we listened to, and we fell totally in love. I adored accompanying Tony on his musical adventures. It was something we both would have done for pleasure anyway, and here he was being paid for it.

While interviewing Tony when I was researching a biography of Ian Curtis (*Torn Apart*) in 2005, Tony recalled: 'The night after the first show went out, we were at the Portobello Hotel in London on the way for a week in France and we met up with Leonard Cohen. And Leonard said, "Oh, your show was fucking great, Tony." We had a lovely week in France, got home on the Monday and my father rang and said, "Oh, *The Sun* doesn't like you." I'm wondering why the only thing he says is that one of the critics has got it in for me, but I go to work next day and *every* critic in Britain had it in for me.'

The Daily Express and *Time Out* were also critical of the show, but Elkan Allan, who created and produced *Ready Steady Go!,* described it as 'the best music show on television in the last ten years'. This was high praise indeed coming from the guy who'd conceived such a legendary show. *RSG* featured classic performances of truly great rock artists from 1963 to 1966 and was essential viewing every Friday night with its opening title: 'The weekend starts here!'.

I had the impression at the time that Tony enjoyed every minute of *So It Goes*; why else would he have taken such offence when Martin Hannett described the show in the *New Manchester Review* (a fanzine and listings magazine) as 'Granada's answer to the Five O'Clock Club'? This was a children's TV show. Tony and Martin crossed paths at another Slaughter & the Dogs gig at the Forum, Wythenshawe and after confronting Martin about this review, Tony told him to 'fuck off' before walking away. But throughout the concert, Tony found himself repeatedly approached by kids telling him that Martin wanted to see him in the car park. It made him nervous and he announced we had to leave before the event was over.

Yet Tony himself was intensely critical of the first series. I remember him describing the music as 'complete and utter shite, Be-bop deluxe, John Miles'. When I protested, remembering, for example, Dr Hook & The Medicine Show, he responded, 'Yes, just quite nice pop shlock. It was utter shite.' As time moved on punk rock became more prevalent, and this interested Tony much more. He'd seen the Sex Pistols on 4 June 1976, the first of two gigs that the aforementioned Howard Devoto and Pete Shelley arranged at the Lesser Free Trade Hall in Manchester that summer. Tony dropped in, having just got off a train from London to Manchester Piccadilly. There has been debate over which of the two gigs Tony attended – personally I don't much care, but think it was the first. Devoto clearly remembers speaking to Tony at the first concert when Tony introduced himself to him and he, of all people, would have a clear memory of that night. Tony of course said he was at the first, which isn't the strongest case for someone who always chose the myth over truth. Whichever gig he attended, Tony was seriously impressed, and he booked the Sex Pistols for the last episode of that first series of *SIG* in August, making up for the more bland seventies music he'd aired earlier. Over the next several months, Tony became obsessed, almost possessed, by this new youth culture of punk.

Proto-punk pub rockers Eddie & The Hot Rods also made their first TV appearance on *SIG* in July 1976 and rumblings of the new punk movement had been felt when the Sex Pistols had supported them at the Marquee club earlier that year in February. The ensuing chaos resulted in the Pistols smashing up the Hot Rods' gear on stage, earning them their first ever review in the *NME* on 21 February, entitled, 'Don't look over your shoulder, but the Sex Pistols are coming'. The article made no mention of the Hot Rods at all. The author of said review, Neil Spencer, described seeing 'a chair arcing gracefully through the air, skidding across the stage and thudding contentedly into the PA system, to the obvious nonchalance of the bass drums and guitar'. It was reading this review

that prompted Devoto and Shelley to go to the Sex Pistols' gigs in London, along with friend Richard Boon, further inspiring them to form Buzzcocks and organise the two subsequent summer gigs that brought Sex Pistols and punk to Manchester.

Punk may have been menacing but that last episode of *SIG* at the end of August 1976 rounded off the most beautiful summer of sunshine and love for Tony and me. I don't think we were ever happier.

Tony's reference to 'as this machine is to him' was the first, but not the last, time he used the phrase. He took it from *Hamlet,* a line spoken by Polonius as he reads a love note from Hamlet to Ophelia. An interpretation of the phrase could be something along the lines of 'As long as I live', but Shakespeare says it better. The love note from *Hamlet* reads: 'I have not art to reckon my groans, but that I love thee best, oh, most best, believe it. Adieu. Thine evermore, most dear lady, whilst this machine is to him.'

Regarding Tony's comment about the director: I assume this was Peter Walker. Peter is quoted in David Nolan's book *I Swear I Was There*[1] saying that Tony was 'very much an egocentric sort of presenter, very much involved in what the programme looked like, how he wanted it to be and the music, perhaps at that stage, was secondary to his own career'. While Tony had every right to mind what the programme looked like, I suspect he wouldn't have liked being seen as egocentric, despite the fact that he was. He didn't like it when I later got irritated by that side of him myself, and tried to bring his ego down a peg or two. But it was probably necessary for Tony to have a large ego to do what he did – to perform and fulfil his ambitions. I do think that Tony's interest in, and knowledge of, music was secondary to his near obsession with youth culture and his career.

1 Nolan, David, *I Swear I Was There: The Gig That Changed The World,* John Blake, 2006.

With June's eventual departure, there was now nothing to stand in the way of our being together. I didn't hesitate to move into Tony's cottage in Charlesworth once he invited me. My mum said it was too soon. As always, she was doubtlessly right. My mum probably viewed him as egocentric too, and I sensed a vague unspoken concern that he wasn't who she would want for me.

But I adored the man, so there would have been no stopping me.

I admired how busy Tony was and how focused he was on an interesting career; so few people find a job they love but Tony loved his with a passion. Ironically this was a factor in our undoing later on. I liked the way he scribbled lists of things he had to do every day, often on his hand, but I took the picture below of one of his typical notes. Dated August, I wondered if it was 1977, as that was when XTC played *So It Goes*. But the calendar suggests it was 1978 as the 21st then fell on a Monday. Either way, it clearly concerns his TV work, there's not much sign of Factory getting going just yet, apart from the references to the bank and £15,000, the amount his mother had left him. He seems to be figuring out costs and 1978 was when he used funds for the EP release *A Factory Sample*. There's also mention, in pencil, of Alan Erasmus, his friend who lived in Didsbury.

Besides putting musicians and bands on, Tony would interview all manner of ordinary as well as noteworthy people. I don't remember how I ended up with this sketch in my possession, but I suspect it was drawn by the illustrator, Dennis McLoughlin, who may have appeared on Granada Reports.

Man - Aug 21st.   25,000

2, →

① Sex Pistols - M.U.   2,500
                                          2,000
② Halifax - surveyor   228-1491   ̄ ̄5 ̄

③ Iggy :   phone L.A.

④ Sonny cassetting.   5/   Chapman

⑤ Car - Blake's   £15,000

⑥ Virgin : M.U. membership for XTC : 10

⑦ Berserkeley : J. Richman :

⑧ Colin Bell :   F. Cooper   62
                                    -3103
⑨ Play in a Day   Macclesfield 23163

⑩ BANK   Mr. Johnson :
                              Mr Lucas 63950
⑪ Salford Corporation : £72.19 → Mr   Jeffrey
                 794-4711   Filbert

              £41. + V.A.T.   15.

         Alan Erasmus   10.30
                                            Mr.
                                            Johnson

                    10.00 Thursday

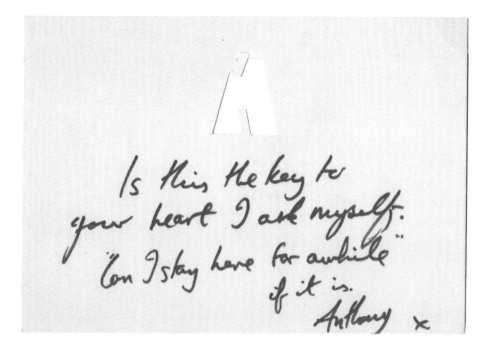

At the end of the long hot summer of 1976, I began teaching a reception class in Gorton. It was quite a distance to travel, and Tony showed me a shop that would still be open on my route back. Big supermarkets were not in evidence then. At the same time he gave me the card above, along with his house key. The key had a red fob and was inscribed with my initials: he was sharing his cottage with me. It may be that Tony had heard the single 'Keys To Your Heart', by Joe Strummer's pre-Clash band The 101ers in 1976. All the same, the note and key meant the world to me.

Is this the key to
your heart I ask myself.
   "Can I stay here for awhile"
if it is.
Anthony X

CHAPTER 2
A Dangerous Woman

Tony proposed to me on Christmas Day, 1976. He was sentimental about Christmas – midnight mass was mandatory at the Catholic church in Marple Bridge he'd attended throughout his boyhood, and he thought it appropriate for us to marry there, a year to the day we'd first met. And so, the date of 14 May was chosen as our wedding day. Tony also liked the idea of a venue as close as possible to where our meeting in Disley had taken place, and he found The Moorhouse Hotel in Higher Disley, just up the road from the Ram's Head car park. We did consider other venues for the reception, and he briefly indulged my idea of a Buddhist wedding, but none of them seemed quite right, so I agreed to his idea even though it was a long way for guests to travel. It wouldn't prevent a hundred of them turning up though – at my dad's expense!

Tony chose a band instead of a D.J.; Dougie James and the Soul Train, a cabaret-soul act often seen performing at Fagin's above the Manchester venue Rafters. They had a big sound that went down well in large, crowded venues like Fagin's but somehow a full-on cabaret band didn't feel quite right in this environment, especially when Tony and I got up for the traditional first dance. Many years later Dougie would tell me that every couple whose wedding reception he played at ended up getting divorced …

Tony also chose the image for our wedding invitation – *Venus and Mars* by Sandro Botticelli; a painting that puts me in mind of the cover of Joy Division's *Closer*, except that this one resonates with sex, the other with death. Experts think the painting may originally have been intended as a wedding gift, encouraging the bride to produce a male heir. Tony and I never had children, but we did give birth to Factory. Either way, in 1977, I saw the picture simply as two lovers and felt that Tony had chosen an artistic and appropriate image. War god Mars seems satiated in the image, perhaps sleeping the 'little death' following orgasm. (I did always wonder why love goddess Venus was fully clothed, while Mars was half naked).

With hindsight, I've seen the Botticelli picture as appropriate in more ways than one, and symbolic of what came to be. It almost foretold our future, much as the image chosen for the cover of Joy Division's *Closer* (a tomb) foretold the death of Ian Curtis. Mars is in a drugged sleep and to the bottom right of the picture is a fruit resembling datura, also known as 'poor man's acid'. Tony and I had several acid trips together, but he had a penchant for drugs way beyond me and, both before and more frequently after we'd gone our separate ways, he added cocaine as a staple to his cannabis use. The goddess Venus had many lovers, as subsequently did I. Not only that but she is having an adulterous affair with Mars himself in the picture, and this also became true of Tony and me. In the story of Mars and Venus, their illicit liaison is publicly exposed by Venus's cuckolded husband, Vulcan, god of fire and forge. The four devilish satyrs in the picture – Factory directors? – mischievously play with Mars's military 'hardware', notably his lance, while wasps hover near Mars's left ear. One of the satyrs is about to blow a conch shell into his right ear to wake him, at which point he's very likely to be stung by a wasp. Tony did indeed get stung, financially at the very least. One example: Tony told me that he and Alan were left out of the ownership of The Haçienda name after Factory went under. There are multiple meanings to be taken from this painting, but it will forever remind me of Tony, and we can, at least, take something positive from it – namely, that love overcomes war – as Venus is pictured alert and watchful while Mars sleeps.

Below are both the wedding invitation and a reproduction of the cover of the album *Closer*. Although the album was released two months after the death of Ian, eerily the cover image had been chosen before his untimely demise.

I'd decided it would be better for Tony and me to have a week apart before our wedding day and so this next, beautifully written letter was sent to my mum's house, where I was staying. Somehow, it didn't seem quite the done thing to leave Charlesworth together to head to a Catholic church in Marple Bridge. Also, I wanted it to feel more special, meeting again at the church after a short absence from one another. During that week apart I took my mum to the Welsh Italianate village of Portmeirion, as this had been the place where Tony and I shared our first magical weekend away together during the blue-skied summer of '76.

*Mr. & Mrs. A. W. Reade request the immense pleasure
of your company at the wedding of their daughter Lindsay
and Mr. Anthony Wilson, at St. Mary's Church,
Marple Bridge, at 3-30 on Saturday the 14th of May
and afterwards at the Moorside Hotel, Higher Disley.*

4, Linksway, Gatley, Cheshire   *R.S.V.P.*

Charlesworth,

The Monday before........

My dearest young wife to be,

"No doubt she was a dangerous woman but I would never be greatly
interested in any woman incapable of harm, in any woman who didn't
threaten me with loss." (Humboldt's Gift, Saul Bellow) Seemed to strike
one of those just right chords. I embrace the days and years to come. The
house......without you ....feels like, I can hardly describe it, most
like the day after good acid when things look bleak, no colour in anything,
washed out and up,.cut yourself and you know the blood would be grey
not red. Without you all is tonal emptiness, right, good job I found out,
you clever little lady........"I'd even like to see her mean old mama"....
...no disrespect to the best Mother-in-law this side of the Euphrates, just
that Mr Parsons is going to that $1,000 wedding on the turntable. So
our little break will teach me the lesson I knew anyway. If you're not
with me, I'm not even with myself. One from one leaves nothing, simple
maths; I've always been god at maths but I've also always been good at
being simple. Didn't you know I knew I couldn't live without you. The
gentleman from Nazareth had problems with people like you. He let one
guy stick his mitt into the wound under his heart. Courtesy of this letter
and the before described loneliness I suppose you're sticking your
moistened fingers into another bleeding heart. Internal bruising anyway,
beautiful lady.

Your letter and notes were delightful.....you have a way of expressing yourself with the written word that is faultless, simple and mostly evocative to the extreme. I envy you. With all my subjunctive structures and surprising adjectives, I can never achieve such direct contact with heart and honest feeling. So i despair of ever showing with these swift flying pieces of metal type any semblance of my devotion and what is more important when your young girl's paranoia creeps into those planet-like eyes, any idea of how fideltiy seems not a chore but a pleasure, a sine qua non (look it up) of my spiritual survival, and just one of the ways I can express my thanks for my Eric Rohmer heroine when words get too stilted to handle.

"With her killer graces

And her secret places

That no boy can fill

With her hands on hern hips

Oh and that smile on her lips

Because she knows that it kills me

With her soft french cream

Standing in that doorway like a dream"

And I can wake up and you're still there. Oh lucky man. Take care of yourself these waiting days. You are all things beautiful to me. And the hymns cool too.

"Oh-oh come take my hand

Riding out tonight to case the promised land"

Marriage is one of those crazy expeditions into wild lands, you choose a partner for a trip like that like choosing a gun. With you, as with no other, my aim is perfect, it will save me from all peril, and the

stock fits so neat and right into my shoulder. Like **it** was made for me.
I felt that about you one year ago. I won't say I've grown surer over
the year. I couldn't. The ceratinty I felt that sunny afternoon was
quite searing. Few things in this world are definite but I knew that
afternoon that the irrevocable had happened. I had met the wife of my
years and the mother of my children. Such knowledge is not changing
or mutable. Facts like that merely exist. Right now I exist merely.
See yah in church baby.........when do I get to kiss the bride.....
sachristy maybe?????....stay cool......be mine.

                    Tony

Undated but 9th May 1977

Charlesworth,

The Monday before......

My dearest young wife to be, "No doubt she was a dangerous woman but I would never be greatly interested in any woman incapable of harm, in any woman who didn't threaten me with loss." (*Humboldt's Gift*, Saul Bellow) Seemed to strike one of those just right chords. I embrace the days and years to come. The house.....without you....feels like, I can hardly describe it, most like the day after good acid when things look bleak, no colour in anything, washed out and up, cut yourself and you know the blood would be grey not red. Without you all is tonal emptiness, right, good job I found out, you clever little lady...... "I'd even like to see her mean old mama".....no disrespect to the best Mother -in-law this side of the Euphrates, just that Mr Parsons is going to that $1,000 wedding on the turntable. So our little break will teach me the lesson I knew anyway. If you're not with me, I'm not even with myself. One from one leaves nothing, simple maths; I've always been good at maths but I've also been good at being simple. Didn't you know I knew I couldn't live without you. The gentleman from Nazareth had problems with people like you. He let one guy stick his mitt into the wound under his heart. Courtesy of this letter and the before described loneliness I suppose you're sticking your moistened fingers into another bleeding heart. Internal bruising anyway, beautiful lady. Your letter and notes were delightful.....you have a way of expressing yourself with the written word that is faultless, simple and mostly evocative to the extreme. I envy you. With all my subjunctive structures and surprising adjectives, I can never achieve such direct contact with heart and honest feeling. So I despair of ever showing with these swift flying pieces of metal type any semblance of my devotion and what is more important when your young girl's paranoia creeps into those planet-like eyes, any idea of how fidelity seems not a chore but a pleasure, a *sine qua non* (look it up) of my spiritual survival, and just one of the ways I can express my thanks for my Eric Rohmer heroine when words get too stilted to handle.

"With her killer graces
And her secret places
That no boy can fill
With her hands on her hips
Oh and that smile on her lips
Because she knows that it kills me

With her soft french cream
Standing in that doorway like a dream" And I can wake up and you're still
there. Oh lucky man. Take care of yourself these waiting days. You are all things
beautiful to me. And the hymn's cool too.
"Oh-oh come take my hand
Riding out tonight to case the promised land"
Marriage is one of those crazy expeditions into wild lands, you choose a
partner for a trip like that like choosing a gun. With you, as with no other, my
aim is perfect, it will save me from all peril, and the stock fits so neat and right
into my shoulder. Like it was made for me. I felt that about you one year ago. I
won't say I've grown surer over the year. I couldn't. The certainty I felt that sunny
afternoon was quite searing. Few things in the world are definite but I knew that
afternoon that the irrevocable had happened. I had met the wife of my years and
the mother of my children. Such knowledge is not changing or mutable. Facts
like that merely exist. Right now I exist merely. See yah in church baby.....when
do I get to kiss the bride....sacristy maybe?????.....stay cool......be mine.
Tony

I feel regret reading his words so many years later; I didn't take them seriously enough at the time and thought him slightly flippant. I probably glossed over some of his crucial lines. His opening lines were prophetic. He was astute to write, 'So I despair of ever showing…. when your young girl's paranoia creeps into those planet-like eyes, any idea of how fidelity seems not a chore but a pleasure, a *sine qua non* of my spiritual survival.' How right to despair and to note my paranoia as shown by later events; I had an innate insecurity and didn't trust him to be faithful.

Tony was so eloquent, and I suppose you'd expect nothing less from a TV journalist with an expertise in writing scripts. But there was a further note of warning even in this most romantic missive. After writing '*sine qua non*', he adds, 'look it up', which was rather patronising. He also refers to me in the letter yet again as 'little lady' (although this time: 'clever little lady'). It saddens me that we didn't cut it, that I didn't keep him from all peril, and that we didn't even have children. Unfortunately, our life together wasn't as easy as a TV script.

The first lyric Tony references from the song playing on his turntable, is taken from the Gram Parsons and Emmylou Harris song '$1,000 Wedding'. Not an auspicious song, it has a sense of doom about it, but Tony clearly loved it. The bride 'went away' when all the invitations had been sent. It isn't clear whether she left him or died. And then he goes off with his friends on a bender and 'it's lucky they survived'. Tony must have been into Gram Parsons from the early seventies onwards, as another of his tracks, 'We'll Sweep Out the

Ashes in the Morning', was one of two songs that he and Thelma had as 'theirs'[1].

Tony must have read *Humboldt's Gift* not long before this letter was written, as it had been published in 1975 and won the Pulitzer Prize the following year. Also in 1975, Saul Bellow won the Nobel Prize in Literature, which may have drawn Tony's attention to it. The plot of *Humboldt's Gift* concerns Bellow's relationship with men; a poet, two writers and a gangster bully concerned with making money. This resonates somewhat with the later Factory battles over money with artists and the disputes between Tony and Rob Gretton, manager of Joy Division and New Order.

Tony always said that Factory was five heterosexual men who were in love with each other. His phrase has a great deal of truth in it. This would explain the male Factory directors' admiration for, and romanticisation of, gangsterism, their use of language (repeatedly using the word 'cunt') and their attraction to pop groups made up mostly of young men. Tony was always enamoured by men and their talents, and while he tended to notice women as objects of physical beauty, the way he surrounded himself with attractive boys (such as those in A Certain Ratio) sometimes made me wonder if he might be bisexual. But whatever Tony's appreciation of and admiration for men, he adored women sexually. Perhaps Tony was fascinated by some pansexual elision, the melting away of fixed sexualities. He often said that I was 'gamine', and I certainly was rather boyish in appearance, as evidenced in the photograph taken in the summer of 1976 by Tony's RS 2000.

1 The other being 'When Will I See You Again?' by The Three Degrees.

The next two lyrics in the letter are both by Bruce Springsteen. 'With her killer graces…' this is a line from 'She's The One' from the album *Born to Run* (1975). The final one, 'Oh-oh come take my hand…' was from an earlier album, *Greetings from Asbury Park, N.J.* (1973); the song was 'Thunder Road'. Tony had become a big fan of Bruce in the early seventies after seeing him play in a tiny venue in America before he became famous.

I'm not sure why Tony referred to me as his 'Eric Rohmer heroine'. I believe it may have been a reference to the French actress Beatrice Romand, who appeared in many of Rohmer's films. When Tony writes 'You are all things beautiful to me. And the hymn's cool too', he's referring to the one concession given to me for a Catholic wedding, my request for the hymn, 'All Things Bright and Beautiful'.

But what a beautiful letter. It makes me wish for the impossible and long to have my time with him again. Then I would, of course, do it all differently.

Tony chose our wedding car as well (of course he did) and here it is (along with me, my dad and the driver).

And certificate.

Like the wedding invitation, the day itself was also alive with symbolism, most of it inauspicious, unfortunately. Tony took his ushers along to show them his dear uncle's grave just before going into church. His bachelor uncle, Edgar Knupfer, lived with Tony's family while he was growing up and Tony always said he felt closer to Edgar than he did to his own father. Without knowing that his father Sydney was gay, Tony disliked his father's effeminate nature from a young age and found himself rejecting him in favour of Edgar, who, although possibly gay himself, was much more manly and Tony identified more with him. Upon visiting the grave of his uncle Edgar, they were all rather taken aback to see, lying directly beside it, the grave of one Lindsay Wilson, the exact spelling of the name I would be taking that day.

Tony had really wanted to be buried with his uncle and I laughed when he told me this because it meant he'd be lying forever next to Lindsay Wilson. However, he changed his mind at the very last because it was too far from the Hidden Gem in central Manchester, which is where he wanted his funeral to be held. The Hidden Gem, officially St Mary's (the same name as the Marple Bridge church) is an old and beautiful Catholic church on Mulberry Street, Manchester. The city of Manchester was always in Tony's heart and the town hall flag flew at half-mast that day as the bells sounded.

This picture was taken many years later; the writing on his uncle's grave is barely legible.

There were other inauspicious symbols. When we came to cut the cake at the reception, the icing was rock hard and, struggling to get the knife through, Tony gently pushed me out of the way so he could do it by himself.

As we left the church, Tony suddenly picked me up and carried me down the path towards the gate, but all the people waiting with confetti were along the other path, so confetti there was none. Confetti is a symbol of fertility, and our barren marriage would bear testimony to the lack of it. I told Tony in the wedding car that it meant we wouldn't have children, to which he said something like 'You do talk bullshit'.

It was a fun moment though, being carried off down the path.

In this snapshot of guests, we can see Tony's dad Sydney, centre frame and looking at the camera. In the left-hand corner is Thelma and to her right, Bob Greaves, the TV presenter with whom Tony usually co-hosted *Granada Reports*. Further to the right we can see a very handsome Nathan McGough, Thelma's eldest son. I've no idea who the others are.

Probably unwisely, Tony and I invited all our close exes. One of mine, Jonathan, an author and persistent diary keeper, recently gave me his diary entry from that day. He judged the reception to be awful, particularly the 'male-chauvinistic, anti-bride' speeches from my dad, from Tony's best man and Tony himself. He wrote, 'Lindsay on view and Lindsay for sale…' My sister Vicki agreed with Jonathan; there should be a best woman to speak for the bride.

The best man's speech was a biography of Tony's life, ignoring me entirely. It wouldn't have been so bad if Tony hadn't reached across me at the end of it and enthusiastically exclaimed, 'Great speech, Charles!' The best man was a doctor, Charles Edmondson. Tony knew him when Charles lived in nearby Stalybridge and Charles's father was Tony's family doctor. They spent time together when they were both based in London and Tony was working at ITN. They lost contact in later years.

It was after Charles's speech and Tony's remark that it suddenly hit me that I'd made a big mistake marrying this egotistical man; I fled to the Ladies so that no one would see my tears. Everything about the day had been planned by Tony and I'd initially imagined

him to be looking out for me but now I saw it all in a different light. The speeches, centring around just him with his approval, along with everything he'd planned, made it feel as if this was his day more than it was ours. This was Tony's personal life plan and I felt almost like a bit part player.

Naturally, the honeymoon, a trip around California, was all planned by Tony. Not that I was complaining; he was the one who could afford it, not me. It should have been wonderful – and was, in parts. The diary my mum gave me to keep a record of the holiday reveals, however, that even in this idyllic climate and location we were having our ups and downs. We stayed in San Francisco for the first week, followed mainly by stays in Motel 6s as we travelled around the Californian Golden Triangle. I was the sole diary author in San Francisco but then, when we set off on Tony's planned expedition, enthusiastic as ever, he also took part and then became the sole author himself. Since this book is an archive of Tony's words, I've included his diary entries. They begin after a week's stay at the delightful El Drisco hotel in San Francisco, seen on the previous page. Tony took the photo of our hotel after he'd just parked our rust-coloured Chevette hire car at the front, ready for our departure.

The day before we left this lovely hotel, we crossed over the Golden Gate Bridge to attend the wedding of someone I neither knew nor remember. It was a moneyed affair, very sumptuous (hence Tony's words in the diary entry about 'American money'). Though keen to travel, I was a bit loathe to leave this gorgeous hotel in a fabulous city in exchange for nights at Motel 6s, but it was time to move on towards the Big Sur coastline.

Saturday May 21st

Tony: 'Reflections on American money: There was a lot of it at our S.F. society wedding. Such opulence - tennis courts through the grove behind the pool etc. - makes me ill at ease, till I remember Chandler's descriptions of such unease as his hero Marlowe waiting in just such dollar palace vestibules - marble cool - to receive work from the hands of the deathly rich. The American hero is not the man in the Hollywood Mediterranean mansion - he's the loser - like Marlowe. Soul rich etc. Lindsay says she doesn't want to be rich - good job, I say and slip out to the tree lined drive to roll another number for the road/ groom.'

Raymond Chandler's fictional character of Philip Marlowe was portrayed by Humphrey Bogart in *The Big Sleep*. Marlowe appears in many of Chandler's novels; other famous examples include *Farewell, My Lovely* and *The Long Goodbye*.

Sunday May 22nd

Tony: 'Missed breakfast - start with the relevant details in my darling's eye that was my big (bad) move of the day. We leave hotel - we also leave one leather coat, one white jacket, one flashy skirt - 75 miles south, en route for Monterey we realise - small discussion ensues. Decide to go on - correct. Hit Santa Cruz - give cafe, shoe shop and bakery a little of our money. Give boardwalk and big dipper a miss. Bel Air Motel in Monterey, basic, but for the 25c a hit pulsating bed. Give me a 25c a hit pulsating woman any day. Ooops I married one - last week - only this evening we're not pulsating. The recommencement of oestrogen ingestion cycle and the blocking of the "true channels of nature" - thanks Vatican II - render madam a mite fidgety. Make contact with local family - friends of Patrick and many others back in England. Very stoned evening - four blocks from Cannery Row - Bob grows his own - by the end we - like his lofty garden - are fluorescent. His 14-year-old daughter cooks Tacos + pumpkin cake - gimme more - and his estranged wife returns in a camper with "a pretty smile" (that's me) and "wild staring eyes" (that's Lins).'

Tony was the first to correctly diagnose PMS syndrome in me. At the time, it irked me that he assumed all my irritation was down to that when, quite often, I felt it was because of him. It's an easy put-down from men, 'Oh, it must be that time of the month again' when women get angry, but which of the sexes is the more responsible for wars? Men murder at ten times the rate to women worldwide. What do we put that down to? That said, Tony was right, I did get a 'mite fidgety', to put it mildly. His reference to Vatican II and the blocking of the 'true channels of nature' must refer in some way to Catholic doctrine. Tony was quite well versed in this, unlike non-religious me.

Monday May 23rd

Tony: 'Left the rather chatty Bel Air and moved on to the south down the coast via a run in with a host of squirrels who enchanted and then bit (and further enchanted) the new Mrs Wilson; via the 17 mile drive around the flat but beautiful Monterey peninsula; via Carmel, old Spanish Mission town established, like the lovely old Mission itself, by catholic refugees from Majorca in 1760 - yes Majorca and yes 1760; via Big Sur, as lovely and un-flat as ever; via the waves, rocks and separate orgasms of Mill Creek where the 23 year old Mr Wilson had spent 10 bored minutes on a previous hitch-hiking hol, but aged 27 remained for 2 hours and was in all, delighted and absorbed; via Hearst Castle, monument to personal greed, and charging $5 a time for a tour - we didn't tour.

'And then we were south, in San Luis Obispo, where Timothy Leary was jailed before snitching on his friends to the FBI. We stay at a quite trippy motel - pink - all over the lampposts even - the Madonna it was called - every room thematically designed and usually pink - a veritable Californian Portmeirion and, as befits this gross land, done with utter lack of taste. The word that best describes this country's greatest lack is "GRACE" - maybe even the people aren't gracious - Dick Nixon isn't gracious that's for sure - and that's the most annoying thing about his Frosties special.

'But it's nice to be gross on occasions - occasions like when you stay in the "morning star" room (the same star we saw crouched on bedroom floor of day 2 in S.F.??) with pink walls - gold chandeliers - and Lindsay Wilson in smilingly athletic frame of mind.

Enjoy.'

Tony had told me a great deal about his hitchhiking holiday in California in 1973, particularly receiving a surprise blowjob from an attractive girl in the back of one of the cars that picked him up when hitchhiking at Mill Creek. He was determined to revisit the beach near where he'd been sitting just before this event took place. It's called on the map, Mill Creek Picnic Area – not to be confused with Mill Creek much further north. This was

Tony in Mill Creek

why I took the photograph of him on the previous page, reflecting the bored 23-year-old that had been sitting in the same spot. Proof, he always said, that you never know what lay around the corner.

Timothy Leary, renowned for his advocacy of psychedelic drugs, did indeed become an FBI informant in order to shorten one of his many prison sentences.

Richard Nixon had been president of the US from 1969 to 1974 but was facing criticism, mainly by the younger generation, for the war in Vietnam. Vast demonstrations and riots were held to put an end to it. Nixon did eventually end the military draft and American involvement in the Vietnam war in 1973. His resignation came in 1974 as a result of the Watergate scandal when he was due to be impeached (something that never worried Trump) for covering up his administration's involvement in the break-in and burglary at the Democratic headquarters in the Watergate building. TV journalist David Frost carried out a series of lengthy interviews with Nixon in 1977. One of these had been broadcast and we watched it in our hotel in San Francisco, although I fell asleep while it was on. Tony was always very keen on politics. He mentions the lack of grace in the country, its people and particularly Nixon. Grace is generally given by God so his words may reflect upon his Catholic background, but I read it rather as a lack of kindness and empathy.

I sent the letter on the next page from the Madonna Inn to my parents – principally for my mum, with the name being appropriate. Tony also mentions our Morning Star room, remembering the first morning of our honeymoon when, jet-lagged, we woke at dawn and watched the sun rise together. I wrote of our drive along Big Sur, a beautiful stretch of scenic road running by the Pacific Ocean, also known as the 'Hippie highway', so named after the heady days of the sixties when the Esalen Institute and other holistic and retreat centres were established there. 'Far out, man' was an expression banded about by hippies in the seventies, akin to 'cool', nowadays. Here it was tongue in cheek.

The American singer Madonna was unheard of in 1977, although she would have approved of the colour scheme of the Madonna Inn.

I began Tuesday May 24th's diary entry writing that we left the pink room and drove to Santa Barbara. I described it being somewhere that seemed a bit like Morecambe and a walk on the pier (bit freaky with stiletto heels) with an evening visit to a drive-in movie. It was Mohammed Ali's life story. I wrote: 'I loved seeing the screen against the open sky, the whole thing was great, even the film had me nearly in tears when his wife got upset about his boxing.'

Tony: 'Some rot about Morecambe; in fact it was called Pismo Beach and marks the cultural beginnings of that phenomenon known as Southern

Madonna Inn
100 MADONNA RD., SAN LUIS OBISPO, CALIF. 93401
AREA CODE 805 543-3000

Just thought we'd drop a note — the name of the hotel seemed appropriate. This is an amazing place — each room is different. We've got one of the most romantic, called "Morning Star" with pink carpets, settee + walls, high beamed cathedral ceiling, gold bed + table + gold + crystal chandelier. And pink notepaper to write to you.

And now we have to leave — dollars don't grow on trees but it was a lovely experience — as is the whole damn thing. Hope Golley is "in the pink" too.

Love + Peace from son No. 3.

We're keeping the diary up to date
+ we'll see you very soon
June 7th
Lots of love Lindsay x x x x x .

P.S. Yesterday we drove down the Big Sur — far out man.

California - this seaside town had the spaced-out buildings of S.Cal for the first time. The towns are not more spacious in terms of intentional aesthetics - rather they are built not to the scale of man - but the car - from place to place, house to house, shop to shop, you always drive, never walk. Town planning by Detroit.'

Wednesday May 25th

Lindsay: 'Woke up & Tony asked why was I in a bad mood? I wasn't, but I soon was. Went into Santa Barbara & had breakfast. I ordered bacon & tomatoes (not wanting lettuce with it) & the girl was confused & I remarked how unimaginative Americans are or something & Tony went mad at me so I went mad at him.'

Tony: 'This is half the recipe for disaster - part two came with a visit to lovely atmospheric S.B. bookstore where occurred the - aagh - disaster - tremble - shake - PURCHASE of *Norma Jean - the Termite Queen*, the new soap opera novel for housewives where the soap stings the eye - 'cause these housewives are depressed, massively.

'Now - you've guessed it - the newly married young lady has found a voice - an empathic spirit. As of lunchtime Wednesday 25th May - the heavens opened.

'We also, went to the beach - reddened our skin on the Pacific shores - and got - specific sores on legs - face the lot - and we got sore at each other. Back at the motel, Lindsay took off on a private expedition in the car - did well - came back with news of bluegrass music in a downtown bar - we sortied out together - decided to get drunk - got drunk - and ended up at Mom's Place - an Italian restaurant - drunk - and had a monster meal - for dessert - a monster row - went home - passed out. The test of strength - nay, friends of the occult - "the darkening of the light" had begun. Moral; Women should never have been given the right to read books - make for an easy life.'

Thursday May 26th

Tony: 'Woke up and the sun was not shining - in our hearts. Of course in Santa Barbara - lots of it. Had breakfast - a B.L.T. - figure it out - in El Paseo - a Spanish courtyard downtown. Thence to the beach for mucho bronzo.

'In the evening went to the beautiful Arlington theatre - Spanish village in the Gods, like a small *chicano* version of the Rainbow - the concert was appalling - Marc Almond + Jesse Colin Young - cheap sentimental lyrics plus efficient workmanlike musicianship less original talent + improvisation. We had a similarly uninspired hamburger which beat the music + our stomachs.

Back at the Motel the cold war got colder and the shoulders got harder. They've also got browner which means at least some things are going to schedule'.

Saturday May 28th

Lindsay: In the hot afternoon we saw *Star Wars* at Grauman's Chinese Theater. Then we had a joint while driving to Universal City - a Hollywood movie lot. While queueing to go on a tour Tony passed out. I wrote: 'His eyes started rolling and his body was giving way. "Don't worry darling," he says. DON'T WORRY! I was feeling weak and worried I might fall on top of him. Must have been a very strong joint. From the tramcar the thing we liked best was a cylindrical tunnel - the car stopped on a platform and the walls whirled round. It felt as if the car was falling over.'

Tony: 'Talking about falling over - I don't think I've ever fainted before - it was wild. Like going under valium except 15' before I collapsed, everything, Lindsay, the wall, the queue - began flashing from grey tones to pure white neon - finally the throbbing reached overexposure like in a picture + I whited out - mucho fun only in retrospect.

'High spot of LA was the beautiful Grauman's Chinese Theatre + the fine film *Star Wars* seen there - oh - the land of movies - 'everyone's a star'.'

Sunday May 29th

Lindsay: We went to Redondo beach and nearly lost our car keys in the sand.

Tony: 'Only nearly - God on our side - we drove 35 miles through industrial Los Angeles; Trafford Park x 10. The FA Cup Final was on the PBS Channel that afternoon and I was hoping to find a bar to watch it in. Eureka. "Happy Days" - a chicano hang-out in a district called Alhambra. Lindsay chatted to the immigrants, I watched the game - we both drank Budweiser. As for Wembley - I didn't miss a thing. Utterly uninspired though our much maligned defence did well. We did well to drive on into the night, out of LA and head into the desert, our heads not a little befuddled by all the beer the Mexicans had thrown at us while watching the football. We end up at a cheaper Motel Six in Barstow - the cicadas at last are in evidence, the night is hot and the desert awaits us - ooooh - heat.'

Tony's beloved Manchester United beat Liverpool 2-1.

Monday May 30th

Tony: 'The desert indeed. We had driven in darkness on Sunday night and although we'd had a bad - hot - night's sleep for the first time - we weren't really aware that the desert was lying all around us - set off for the main drive East in heat and all it did was get hotter. Just a motorway and then desert stretching off either side through grey scrub up to mountains which always seemed to keep their distance - there was one service station 80 miles out - well, a roadside cafe - just one - the Friend's coffee shop - other than that - the old shack and some scorched dry bones - no doubt.

'Finally - our Chevrolet microwave oven arrived at Needles - which we had thought to be just a town in California - instead it's the hottest town in California - as we were told frequently in the coming week - today it was 105*. And that temperature was about par for the rest of the week. Feeling that 'let's get into some cold water' urge which afflicted us throughout our desert days, we turned south at the Arizona border and went 25 miles down the Colorado river to London Bridge - yes indeed - a double decker bus, an English pub - one main street, three motels, 3,500 power boats, and of course, desert. We swam in the lake, filched a small lilo which was drifting downstream and which later became the most important thing in Lindsay's life - well it kept her afloat.

'Lake Havasu City is a tourist trap in the making - now the sand mixes well with the concrete stubble of a yet to be built town and the English ambience harmonizes with the green and blue of grass and lake - all utterly out of place in the middle of this endless desert.

'As life cools down in the evening - 95* man - put a jacket on - we set off into Arizona - 100 miles into Kingsman where I thought we could stop - Lindsay is on for further passage - she drives which is nice for both of us in a role-playing way. As the driver madam seems more fulfilled, therefore happier, therefore me too. Arrive late in Williams - a large village - small town - in fact a big truck stop.'

Interesting to note a friendly power struggle taking place here. I needed and wanted to take control sometimes, but Tony was really only indulging me by letting me drive and letting me take us beyond his planned stop at Kingsman. This, to my mind, meant he was still really in control. Also, his use of the term 'madam' for me is open to interpretation. He often used this term for whoever his current love was. It could be seen as somewhat deferential, as used by shop servers, or maybe even a tad derogatory – as in, 'she's a little madam'. I think he tended to use it when he was 'allowing' his partner to take control.

London Bridge, Arizona

Tony: 'We do like the trucks - at the Grand Motel - very nicely run by a nice old couple. Now of the opinion that Arizonans are the most courteous of Americans. Indian jewellery for sale - must be getting near the reservations - and boy you'd need a reservation.

'$500 for a necklace in turquoise tho he has another name for it. "Squashed" something - must be Indian, Lindsay insists on T. but doesn't buy. We both buy a good night's sleep. We are temporarily in HIGH DESERT. Less low - less hot.

Tuesday May 31st

Tony: 'Drive straight north to the Grand Canyon - just 50 miles. Stop at Fred Flintstone enclosure in middle of forest - kiddies' fun fair - very basic - but we press on for a mediocre breakfast at a sub-mediocre cafe - the owner advises sitting on porches in the shade. We agree and I make second fatal mistake of holiday (remember Norma Jean) - I fail to purchase a MOO-COW MILKER - I'll give you that again - a moo-cow- milker - an extremely tatty plastic milk jug with a brown plastic cow's head which slurps out milk; and yours for only $3.50 at this tourist trap. For Lindsay it is love at first sight. I refuse to pay the inflated price. Will Lindsay ever forgive me.'

Lindsay: I'd finished reading *Norma Jean, the Termite Queen*. Norma Jean is a housewife struggling with her role in the family and in society. She's an artist, yet had to abandon this while caring for house, husband and children. I was struggling with the feminist issues being explored and how women were frequently denied opportunities given freely to men. Tony saw the influence it had on me as unsettling to our relationship. Remember this is nearly fifty years ago, times were different. What I can't understand is why didn't I just buy the milker myself. Did I not have $3.50 to my name? Or did I merely kowtow to what Tony wanted (followed usually by an urge for rebellion)? I had a thing about cows, especially cows with white faces and brown ears. I'd fallen in love with one like that on a camping trip in Ireland; it was in the next field to where our tent was. It was being starved prior to slaughter so I fed it, and, as a result of this encounter, decided to become a vegetarian. This was a difficult lifestyle choice in 1970 and after two years I became malnourished and ill. With Tony I ate meat, but have since mostly chosen vegetarianism as the better way forward.

Tony: 'On to the Canyon. Like Niagara Falls, it is indeed a wonder of the world. Few media acclaimed spectacles live up to their promise - like the smell of coffee - but the Canyon of the Colorado is IT. Lunch at a less than exciting restaurant - real tourist hotel - only one allowed on the crest of the Canyon - good advert for the values of competitive industry.

'Helicopter after dinner - another wonder - in particular pilot accelerates as he approaches lip and drops a little toward the green roof of foliage - sensual effect is that of being shot out into the wilds of the Universe. Lins in front seat, very excited.

'Set off late afternoon to go round the eastern rim of the Canyon and up to the North, something like 250 miles to bring us to the edge of Utah for a drive back to Vegas. It's one of the most out of the way spots in a world of wildernesses but the big pull of the big cliffs means maybe 1,000 people a day and that means this a "tourist desert". Hot - empty of everything but sand, stone and mountains that litter the horizon. In England you measure how far

you drive by the passage of major junctions and lights - here you measure your long, straight line by the range, by the range of mountains whose perspectives pass you by in maybe 20 minutes - to half an hour - and each time there's a new row of peaks, one side or the other which shadow your part of the plain.

'And there are the Indians near the rim and the white man's traffic, every quarter mile a sign saying "Indian Jewellery" another 100 yards and in a patch of flat dust, just spare enough to pull off for a couple of Chevvies, old women, sit, squat position on the floor beneath a cloth laid out with trinkets - they are sitting inside makeshift scrap wood pyramids - only the top section filled with boards to shade them from the sun. The jewellery was blue stone and very, very expensive - aquamarine.

'Away from the holiday in the sun the Indian scene changes. Much more desolate landscape. Every ten miles a village - a few shacks and some wooden eight sided huts with conical tops - teepee of the 20th century + debris, broken old cars + bits of metal - just like the Irish timbers - the cannibals of mechanical trash. As night falls we cross the North rim at a bridge over the canyon called Navajo bridge. What else? It goes dark, we hit the forests + start to run out of gas. This increasingly becomes a feature of the trip. My uncle always refused to buy petrol till the last minute - the last garage - I learnt my ways from him - but in Northern Arizona the next gas station can be a long way away. Much tension - much horrid imaginings of a night in the desert - final

relief as we find a garage just closing. In high spirits we drive on to Fredonia
on the Utah border - small town - 100 buildings - and very Mormon - clean
+ honest - cheap - quite lovely wooden motel room. Have a non-alcoholic
nightcap at a sparkling clean stand-up cafe - spick + span - open smiling but
somewhat empty faces (my anti-religious prejudices) are everywhere. Sets
Lindsay to thinking about mormons, or about the mormon.'

When I was about 14, a Mormon who lived up the road started calling round with
boxes of chocolates and asking me out. I was terribly shy, but agreed to go for a walk
with him. Then, at a nearby park he brazenly suggested making love right there on
a bench. I'd thought such things were against his religion and, besides, I was far too
young and found him very unattractive. He used the first of many seduction techniques
I would hear over the coming years. He said that we might die and never know what
it was like, so we should do it while we could. He was deluded in imagining I'd fall
for this. Tony wrote of his anti-religious prejudices, but presumably they were against
Mormonism rather than Catholicism.

The town of Fredonia felt kind of eerie, the book *Stepford Wives* comes to mind (where
women are brainwashed and compliant) but you couldn't fault how clean everything
was and how friendly people were. It was knowledgeable (as usual) of Tony to be aware
of the connection between Fredonia (or 'Freedonia') and the Marx brothers; it was the
name of a fictional country in which their film *Duck Soup* was set, and this is what he
makes reference to in the following letter.

Wednesday June 1st

Tony: 'Wake up and it's hot. Leave Fre(e)donia - great name - Marx brothers
used it in their films - and head north into Utah. Ahead of us and then beside
us as we turn east towards Nevada the ROCK - MASSIF formations of the Zion
national park. Away in the distances big, rounded, rectangular bare pieces of
rock that are as big as mountains. Wind down from the highlands for a lunch
stop in Hurricane; 2 miles out of town on a boiling hot rock hillside overlooking
the town - pssst - a puncture - we get out and I confidently go for the spare tyre
- and whaddaya know - this is one hire car that hasn't heard about punctures.
No spare. Sometime around the discovery of the negative state of affairs in the
boot Lins + I have a row, can't quite remember the details, but I remember her
sitting angrily on the hot roadside stones. One up for the human race; a guy -
middle aged - drove his motorbike over from his house 500 yards away + asked
if we wanted help or at least shade in his house. Mormons!

'We take the dud wheel off + I hitch into town with it. Find a garage, while tyre gets done I have some cold milk from a supermarket - feel guilty about Lins guarding the car + bags back on the hillside. Lug the tyre back to the outskirts of town - hot work in hot weather is more than just hot work.

'Tyre on, lunch inside us we snake through a mountain motorway that follows the course of the Colorado River. Suddenly we're in Nevada, + suddenly it's 105 when we stop for gas. Lins proceeds to put legs out of the windows and we search for a swimming site en route for Vegas.

End up at a campsite on the northern tip of Lake Mead. Stony beach but O.K. water + a nice little holiday cafe with a verandah + juke box. Lins is getting on well with the lilo - it's getting to be part of the family.

'About six o'clock - Las Vegas, past the suburban rows of cheap food chain cafes, past a commercial district of garages + 1 storey factories, past the rows of wedding /massage parlours - "d'you want it quick or slow - it's the same in the end", the catchphrase of both - and into the hotel land. A six lane city street lined with block after block of big sky scraper, blunt, unappealing hotels. They are made bearable - almost 'right' - by the desert backdrop + coloured neon light monstrosities which by day and by night - somehow make them work. We go straight to the Circus Circus for a room - spend, spend, spend - but they're full full full and we save save save by going to the Golden Key, a quite acceptable alternative motel - well not exactly alternative - they didn't have dope in the rooms - but we did and I got ill - went + bought some Eno's.

'Lins watched T.V. a bit and re-examined her suntan. "Tomorrow I want sun" - to hell with America - this trip is about flesh.'

Thursday June 2nd
'Spend the morning driving round Southern Las Vegas looking for a branch of our car hire firm - looking to put right the spare wheel situation. Find nothing - except lots of mid morning heat.'

CHAPTER 3
Bitten by Rabid (and Punk)

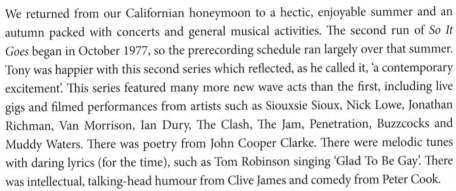

We returned from our Californian honeymoon to a hectic, enjoyable summer and an autumn packed with concerts and general musical activities. The second run of *So It Goes* began in October 1977, so the prerecording schedule ran largely over that summer. Tony was happier with this second series which reflected, as he called it, 'a contemporary excitement'. This series featured many more new wave acts than the first, including live gigs and filmed performances from artists such as Siouxsie Sioux, Nick Lowe, Jonathan Richman, Van Morrison, Ian Dury, The Clash, The Jam, Penetration, Buzzcocks and Muddy Waters. There was poetry from John Cooper Clarke. There were melodic tunes with daring lyrics (for the time), such as Tom Robinson singing 'Glad To Be Gay'. There was intellectual, talking-head humour from Clive James and comedy from Peter Cook.

I accompanied Tony to most of the prerecorded live shows – including Buzzcocks and Penetration at the Electric Circus in August, and we also went to an obscure venue in Wolverhampton where the Sex Pistols appeared on their SPOTS tour ('Sex Pistols On Tour Secretly'). This was a six-night tour and the Pistols used a different name for each night, one being 'Acne Rabble'. Given their media reputation as hellraisers, this necessary secrecy gave them a chance to play without the police or local councils shutting them down. When we went backstage I boldly asked Sid Vicious how he'd got cuts all over his chest. He rather shamefacedly mumbled something about his razor blade slipping, which was clearly bullshit. He either did it deliberately to himself or it may have been his girlfriend, Nancy Spungen, as domestic and heroin abuse was a constant in their relationship. Sid would later be charged with Nancy's murder, but he died in February 1979 of a heroin overdose before the trial.

We saw Iggy Pop on compelling form at Manchester's Apollo, and it was interesting sitting in Iggy's dressing room while Tony interviewed him. Iggy was then young and vibrant and oozing with confidence – the kind of confidence to admit, 'I'm a nerd, a dork…', which seemed the complete opposite of what Tony was trying to be. Still, the two shared a similar vision and ambition. Unfortunately, Iggy's live act, swearing and parading around with a horse's tail protruding from his backside – which in this day and age no one would bat an eye at – prompted Tony's bosses to cancel plans for a third series. Bob Dickinson, a producer at Granada, remembered: 'Yes, the tale of Iggy's tail was still infamous when I was working at Granada. It's crazy how unimaginative and conservative Granada could be about a pop show when they were so adventurous and risk taking in the field of documentaries and news'. The cancellation was a blow to Tony, even if he was secretly proud to have outraged Granada. It was odd that it hadn't been the Sex Pistols who'd curtailed the show's series; the ethos of punk was to offend – and they excelled at it. Exuding anarchy on *SIG*, Johnny Rotten's leer announced he was an 'Antichrist', and then to 'get pissed' and 'destroy'. Almost the first words he screamed were, 'Get off your arse'.

Although enjoying the spectacle, I wasn't a particular fan of punk and certainly not obsessed with it like Tony. I liked Buzzcocks (and Peter Shelley became a great friend) but, despite their early origins in punk, they were really a pop group. I could see value in youthful rebellion and loved that women such as Siouxsie Sioux were taking over the front of the stage with angry expression, but the general atmosphere of it didn't appeal, let alone the behaviour. When The Electric Circus closed in October 1977, Tony went up on stage to speak: within minutes he was soaked from head to foot with beer, gob, wine – anything the youths in the mosh pit had to hand. He came back to me as exulted as if he'd been baptised by the Holy Spirit, but I was revolted. I was all for the *avant-garde* but couldn't raise interest in people jumping up and down and gobbing on one other.

Warsaw (who later became known as Joy Division) played the Circus – that night possibly – but, again, the loud and aggressive nature of their expression hid their budding talent, which was something producer Martin Hannett would later bring to the fore. Ian Curtis wearing a leather jacket with the word 'HATE' across the back springs to mind, yet this punk period was no doubt an important part of their development and expression.

With *SIG* discontinued, Tony remained determined to carry on in the field of music. He still had his TV career at Granada, which was just as important to him, but he needed this other outlet. The roster of rock and pop acts he put on TV during the seventies and eighties was seriously impressive but, lacking a music show of his own, it wasn't enough for him. This scenario continued until the end of his life – he wanted and needed both careers. He had plenty of energy, intelligence and enthusiasm for both, and like a puppy dog he could bound from one thing to another with aplomb.

Several acts he'd featured on *SIG* and the 'What's On' element of *Granada Reports* went on to find fame: Elvis Costello was virtually unknown when he gave his first ever performance of 'Alison' on 'What's On' in 1977. Blondie appeared the same year performing 'Rip Her To Shreds'. It nearly ripped *me* to shreds when I saw this, as she was the most beautiful creature, super talented and Tony clearly worshipped her, throwing a rose at her feet. All of this was prior to the abundant showcase of *SIG*. Back in 1977, many stars of the music world were on first name terms with Tony and there was no way he could get by with just presenting Granada Reports and 'What's On', especially in this fertile phase for music. The joke was that, as someone ironically pointed out, an anagram of Anthony Wilson is 'Only in What's On'.

Thus, Tony was determined to continue his foray into the music business, desperately wanting to remain socially within the culture; a man with a plan. Another man with a plan was Alan Erasmus, Tony's friend from Didsbury who took to hanging around a lot at Cotton Lane in Withington, Manchester, where Rabid Records was based. Tony was also watching with keen interest to see what they were up to. Rob Gretton, who had been a northern soul DJ, hung out there more than either of them.

Rabid had emerged from a musicians cooperative called Music Force, which was created in 1972 to help safeguard the livelihood of musicians and support them in performing live. Pubs were increasingly opting for DJs as a cheaper option than live bands and there were very few other live venues in Manchester, so bands from the late sixties onwards were finding themselves out of work. Tosh Ryan said that Music Force 'had political motives, musicians working for themselves, but musicians, especially pop musicians – their politics are up the shoot, they're nearly all egotistical capitalists so it collapsed, there wasn't the same kind of political interest that the founders of it had'. But for four or five years Music Force helped to keep the live music scene alive in Manchester. They built an infrastructure to do this and also published a fanzine called *Hot Flash,* which Martin Hannett often contributed to with his cryptic wit. The Music Force founders were the aforementioned directors of Rabid, as well as Victor Brox, whose band was the Victor Brox Blues Train, and Bruce Mitchell, the then drummer with comedy rock band Alberto Y Lost Trio Paranoias, who runs a stage and lighting company to this day.

Music Force Flyer

In 1976, when Devoto and Shelley brought the Sex Pistols to Manchester, it was Music Force they went to, who rented a PA to them and directed them to the Lesser Free Trade Hall. They'd first thought of holding it at their college in Bolton, a request that the college rejected, which actually turned out to be fortuitous. When Howard told Malcolm he suggested they 'find somewhere else.' Far better that it was in Manchester than Bolton. Tony would have missed it, for a start.

The original motivation behind Rabid's creation was because of Martin Hannett's ambition to start a record label. He found and saw potential in Slaughter & the Dogs and would go on to produce theirs and Rabid's first release 'Cranked Up Really High', which sold well and earned them a deal with Decca. Rob Gretton got involved with Slaughter & the Dogs, and also released a record by The Panik called 'It Won't Sell' on Rainy City Records – the name reflecting the wet weather in Manchester. Rabid Records had the contacts and bought and distributed the EP through their own cartel. Director Lawrence Beedle would send packages to Rough Trade and Lightning Records in London and also had distribution through Wynd Up Records in Prestwich. Rough Trade later became the main distributor for Factory. Lawrence's letter confirms Rabid's deal with Rob. Lawrence also snapped the pictures taken at Rabid.

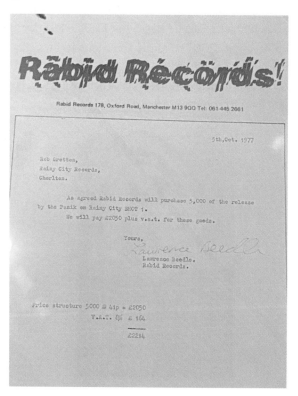

Rabid Records letter to Rob Gretton

Rob Gretton, Tosh Ryan and Graham Fellows (Jilted John) at Rabid

John Cooper Clarke and Martin Hannett at Rabid

Images on this spread courtesy of Lawrence Beedle

Slaughter played support to the Sex Pistols at their second Manchester gig on 20 July 1976 along with Buzzcocks. Eddie Garrity (now Edweena), lead singer of Ed Banger & the Nosebleeds, worked as Slaughter's roadie on this occasion and his (now her) band got their name after a riot broke out and he and a friend got injured. Someone remarked, 'You're a right bloody mob, aren't you? Headbanger here, and him with a nosebleed…' and so the band changed their name from Wild Ram to Ed Banger & the Nosebleeds. After the band's recording of the single 'Ain't Been To No Music School', released by Rabid, Tony put them on his 'What's On' slot at Granada. Despite the success of this record, which featured the vibrant and powerful guitar-playing of one Vini Reilly, the band broke up shortly afterwards. Causes mentioned were arguments between Ed Banger and their manager Vini Faal.

In many ways Rabid Records set the template for Factory. They had similar personnel, director Martin Hannett produced the in-house bands, Rob Gretton was involved and Vini Reilly played guitar with Ed Banger. Lawrence recalled, 'I remember showing Tony what 5,000 singles looked like – a stack of boxes at Tosh's house. You could see on his

The picture shows Ed Banger & the Nosebleeds on 'What's On' with a beaming Vini Reilly. The backdrop displays American singer Jonathan Richman and his band the Modern Lovers.

face he was thinking he could make records, put sleeves on and sell them from one room. That room was Alan's flat.'

The money to launch Rabid had come from Tosh Ryan's postering business. Heading south from town in the seventies, down Oxford Road or Princess Parkway through Moss Side, their posters were visibly plastered everywhere. Music Force and Rabid weren't just about music but were affiliated with the Socialist Labour League and organised many anti-racist and anti-war gigs and campaigns.

There was, however, another significant independent label in Manchester. Richard Boon, mentioned in one of the next letters, was now managing Buzzcocks after having arranged gigs for them earlier on. He and Howard Devoto, old school friends from Leeds Grammar school, formed the independent record label New Hormones, releasing the Hannett-produced *Spiral Scratch* EP by Buzzcocks in January 1977. It was one of the earliest punk records ever to be released in the UK. Martin had met Howard Devoto in the Music Force building, and was the only person Howard knew who called himself a record producer. This *Spiral Scratch* release, with tracks 'Boredom', 'Time's Up', 'Breakdown' and 'Friends of Mine', marked the beginning of independent recording in Manchester and inspired Tony, who imitated it to a degree later on: Factory's first release was also an EP but, instead of four tracks, it featured four separate acts.

As well as these two independent pioneers, Tony and I also often went to London to see what Geoff Travis's company Rough Trade were up to. It had started out as a record shop, but the label was launched in 1978.

All three labels – Rabid, Rough Trade and New Hormones – were a big influence on Tony. That said, he always firmly believed in the idiom: 'Don't give up your day job'. He still loved being on TV and was addicted to what he called 'the red light syndrome'. When the TV camera's red light went on, he would get a surge of adrenaline.

To start a label you need a group; Martin had found Slaughter & the Dogs, Rob had got The Panik, so Tony and Alan put together their own band of musicians, almost in the style of a boy-band from *X Factor*. This development followed a phone call Tony received from Alan on the 24 January 1978. Alan had been managing a band called Fast Breeder, and he had just been ousted as had the drummer Chris Joyce and guitarist Dave Rowbotham. Upon hearing this news on that particular day, Tony decided to venture into music management with Alan himself, pick up the pieces and build a new band out of the remnants of the old. In the style of what later became the Factory catalogue, Tony christened the birth of this venture, and the resultant publishing company, with a title: 'The Movement of the 24th January'. Later, using a bank account under this name, the first cheque, written in the summer of 1978, was £250 for a bass guitar for this band. Incidentally, Fast Breeder had previously been known as Flashback in 1977 – Tony went to see them with CP Lee (then frontman of Alberto Y Lost Trio Paranoias) on Tony's stag night, fuelled by Dutch speed and LSD.

CP Lee with the Albertos on Granada Reports

In addition to Chris and Dave, the two ex-members of Fast Breeder, guitarist Vini Reilly was brought in. Tony Bowers, bass player from the Albertos, happened to be living in the ground floor flat of the same house as Alan at the time, and he was also added. Finally, Phil Rainford was brought in on vocals. Tony named the band The Durutti Column, appropriated from a chapter in a Situationist anthology entitled *Leaving The 20th Century* – the chapter was called 'The Return of The Durutti Column'. This was itself an homage to the anarchist column under Buenaventura Durutti that marched to save Madrid from fascists during the Spanish Civil War. Tony had been aware of the student uprisings in Europe who were, in his words: 'fired with the cult brand that goes by the name Situationism' and he'd become involved with it while studying at Cambridge. Tony was very fond of the term 'praxis' which he personally defined as explaining the reason for one's actions after the event, perhaps giving *carte blanche* to doing whatever you want and inventing the reason for it later. He told CP Lee: 'I have to say that I think Factory's concept from day one has always been, do what you want, and Factory's overriding characteristic is wilfulness, and wilfulness seems to me to be a simplified version of Situationism.'[1] In Marxism, however, praxis has more to do with changing the world in line with Marxist theory – i.e. to bring about a more equal and fair society.

One night in April 1978, Tony and I went to an event at Rafters called The Stiff Chiswick Challenge. Organised by two London independent labels, this travelling showcase aimed to give local bands a chance of being heard by their A&R men. I say men, because they usually were. The night and the bands left no impression until Joy Division came on. To their annoyance they went on last at 2 p.m., but they gave a great performance and Rob Gretton, who rightly recognised the potential in this group, duly became their manager. Tony met Ian Curtis for the first time that night and, although I wasn't a witness to this and only ever saw Ian as polite and reserved (except on stage), Tony told me in an interview for the book *Torn Apart*, 'I saw the belligerent side of Ian that night – he said: "You're a fucking cunt, you haven't put us on television," to which I didn't reply but I said to myself, "You're next on the list, you stupid twat".'

Tony would often go round to Alan's flat in Didsbury, planning how to make The Durutti Column a success via gigs and/or recording tracks (all while consuming lots of hashish). This was how the Friday Factory night at the Russell Club came into being – basically as somewhere for The Durutti Column to perform. Alan knew Don Tonay, a Mancunian underworld character and the owner of the Russell Club in Hulme, along with an off licence on Claremount Road and certain suspect venues such as The Baby Doll Sauna. A friend of ours, promoter Alan Wise, was already working with Don Tonay running nights at the Russell. This club was nestled beside, and overshadowed by, 'The Crescents'. The crescents, built in the sixties, housed myriad flats that ended up being demolished in 1993. It began as an urban dream but became an urban ghetto. Despite that, I found something poetic about them and suggested later to Section 25 (a band on the Factory label) that we film a video there to their track 'Looking From a Hilltop'. This we did, featuring me arriving there in my slightly battered but stylish Karmann Ghia, then strolling around the crescent walkways and leaving with a young male band member, all intercut with footage of the two lead singers.

In the picture on the next page you can just see one of the curved crescents behind the Factory Club. The Friday Factory nights became hugely popular and, despite the location, took over from Rafters as the premiere rock venue of the city. Manchester was alive in the late seventies with a revived and vibrant music scene, and the vibe of these club nights drew in the crowds.

---

1 Lee, CP, *Shake Rattle and Rain: Popular Music Making in Manchester 1955-1995*, Hardinge Simpole, 2002, p.171.

Courtesy of Stuart Murray

The Factory/Russell Club on the edge of the Hulme crescents

During the summer of 1978, while Tony was working, I took a short holiday in Wales with my mum, sister, brother-in-law and their first baby boy, Ross. The following letters he sent refer to that time in 1978. Our relationship seems as loving and strong as it ever was. His closing line in the first letter quotes a line from Joni Mitchell's 'My Old Man'.

Sunday night

Charlesworth. '78

Love you. It is, as thought, a good idea. You don't know what water's like until you get thirsty. The house feels like a cold cave. You feel like a warm dream; *magistratu volente* (dat's latin). I'll be with you at the weekend; the gala can go fuck itself. Send me map of a) your locale b) an exact street diagram c) a plan of the bungalow with your room clearly marked ; ; ; ; and then leave your window open on Friday night ; ; ; ; tell your momma you want to catch the nightingale.

Nice to see the house so lovely, you are GOOD. Oh and you are bad, but what was it the guy said about Anthony and Cleo this afternoon; ah yes, this afternoon. Cricket lot's of fun. out for 13; of course. Shared a monster opening partnership against Peter Lever; of course it means nothing nothing to you; it's just background detail. Opened as I said with 38 Steve Coppel (And who the fuck's he ;;; well I was always into Spartan athleticism and heroes.) Wicketkeeper I was; the inside of my thighs feel like sensitive punch

Sunday night,
Charlesworth. '7

Love you. It is, as thought, a good idea. You don't know what
water's like until you get thirsty. The house feels like a cold cave.
You feel like a warm dream; magistratu volente)(dat's Latin) I'll
be with you at the weekend; the gala can go fuck itself. Send me
map of a) your locale)(b) an exact street diagram, c) a plan of the
bungalow with your room clearly marked;;;;and then leave your window
open on Friday night;;;;;tell your momma you wante to catch the
nightingale.
Nice to see the house so lovely, you are GOOD. Oh and you are bad, bu
what was it the guy said about Anthony and Cleo this afternoon; ah
yes, this afternoon. Cricket lot's of fun. out for 13; of course.
Shared a monster opening partnership against Peter Lever; of course i
means nothing nothing to you; it's just background detail. Opened as
I said with 38 with Steve Coppel (And who the fuck's he;;well I was
always into Spartan athleticism nd heroes.) Wicketkeeper I was; the
inside of my thighs feel like sensitive punch bags; everybody's
sensitive;; lits of fun at cricket; ritual, crouching by the wickets;
triple imagery of life; mystical arrangment, maybe not, went to Nev's
and you'll never believe it but (bet he had his tea there) Right, a
Nev nosebag; pork, luscious, so are you, then Wordsworth which was
good and left you wanting more;; and then Antony and Cleopatra; Charl
ton Heston (does he play football for somebody?) in a well acted
Hollywood version of Sharkespeare;;;great lyrics; oh yes, good and
bad;;hold on while I grab the Bible;.....''For vilest things / Become
themselves in her, that the holy priests/ Bless her when she is riggish'' Riggish being Shakespeare's way of describing, well let's say,
female behaviour.
Right I'm off to bed; though having got the quotation marks out I'm
loathe to leave them so underused; so lets leave with a little
Rochester to echo the first paragraph;

        Alas 'tis sacred Jealousie
          Love raised to an extream;
        The only proof 'twixt her and me,
          We love and do not dream.

        Fantastick Fancies fondly move;

And in frail joys believe;
Taking false Pleasure for true Love;
But pain can ne're deceive.

Love you, miss you, 'the bed's too big, the frying pan's too large'

SOON

Tony.

bags; everybody's sensitive; ; lots of fun at cricket; ritual, crouching by the wickets; triple imagery of life; mystical arrangement, maybe not, went to Nev's; and you'll never believe it but (bet he had his tea there) Right, a Nev nosebag; pork, luscious, so are you, then Wordsworth which was good and left you wanting more; ; and then Anthony and Cleopatra; Charlton Heston (does he play football for somebody?) in a well acted Hollywood version of Shakespeare; ; great lyrics; oh yes, good and bad; ; hold on while I grab the bible; ..... 'For vilest things / Become themselves in her, that the holy priests / Bless her when she is riggish' Riggish being Shakespeare's way of describing, well let's say, female behaviour.

Right I'm off to bed; though having got the quotation marks out I'm loathe to leave them underused; so let's leave with a little Rochester to echo the first paragraph:

Alas 'tis sacred Jealousie
Love raised to an extreme
The only proof 'twixt her and me
We love and do not dream.
Fantastick Fancies fondly move;
And in frail joys believe;
Taking false Pleasure for true Love;
But pain can ne'er deceive.

Love you, miss you, 'the bed's too big, the frying pan's too large'
SOON
Tony

Tony is showing off with his use of Latin, but he also reveals himself. A rough translation of '*magistratu volente*' is 'willing master'. Even while adoring, he sees himself as the master in this relationship. He refers to Nev, and this is Neville Richardson, a friend who'd grown up in Wythenshawe, was in the same class at school as Alan Erasmus and now lived in Didsbury. Tony and I often visited him and his then wife, Wendy.

Literary references abound as usual. I'm not sure why Tony had to grab a bible since the quote is directly taken from *Anthony & Cleopatra*, not the bible: 'Other women cloy the appetites they feed, but she makes hungry where most she satisfies; for vilest things become themselves in her, that the holy priests bless her when she is riggish.' Here perhaps we have some evidence of Tony's sexism, since he's tacitly referring either to me or all womankind. The word 'riggish' describes wanton and lustful behaviour in women, a word that rightly now has become obsolete. The word smacks of a time when women were considered 'wanton' if they so much as even enjoyed sex rather than seeing it more as a chore to be endured for their husbands.

Tony often took part in events calling for celebrity appearances. These always took place at the weekends and were quite enjoyable, lucrative too. The gala he mentions in the letter would have been one such event – a swimming gala; he'd probably been asked to present prizes. The cricket match could have been paid or was possibly a charity event. Tony loved sport, especially football and cricket, and he certainly would have enjoyed this particular outing. He never said no to cricket match appearances and that summer I accompanied him to quite a few, usually on Sundays and always in the north-west, where he was a minor celebrity. Regarding the game in this letter, he mentions former Lancashire cricketer Peter Lever, and Steve Coppell, a footballer for Manchester United at that time who also played for England, and who later became known as a football manager. Tony must have been buddies with them both. He's quite right when he observes it means nothing to me despite the fame of the two men, as I've always had zero interest in sport and wouldn't even have recognised them now if it hadn't been pointed out to me. Tony jokes about the Hollywood actor Charlton Heston playing football, knowing that even I would have heard of Bobby Charlton.

His letter ends with a quote from the Earl of Rochester's poem, entitled 'The Mistress'. He was in fact the 2nd Earl of Rochester (aka John Wilmot), a rather debauched English poet from the 17th century. Tony didn't just quote him in letters to me; according to Bob Dickinson, who sometimes worked alongside him at Granada: 'He was always quoting him, he used to do it during camera rehearsals just to be ""daring"".

I sometimes fell short of understanding Tony's literary references, but I gathered the gist of this particular poem to be that love causes suffering and that the suffering is, by itself, proof of that love. Appropriate in both of our cases, as it would turn out.

The next letter appears to have been written the very next day. Tony must have been missing me.

Monday night (presumably the next day)
Charlesworth

You don't ring; are you punishing me? do they have phones in Wales? Did Alexander Bell live in vain? I do. Today? Work; ; late arrival, well, then planning the S: D: special, it's going to be at the Lesser Free Trade which is nice, or rather which isn't particularly nice which is nice. Lunch with Mary and Phil.....
yawn...but also Richard Boone [sic] who is extra lovely (eee bluddy ell, more of your homosexuality)

Only other event of note, played tennis with Nev; ; ; absolutely strawberries and cream (WIMBLEDON) standard; ; well I got excited, and so did Nev. We're very evenly matched though today it was a battle of Nev the net (rusher) and his vile volley against Fat Willy's devastating lob (my bones were too tired to move around the court after the cricket ; ; ; so I just kept lobbing the bastard. First set to F.W. 6-4. Second set to Nev the net 7-5. I was 3-0 up in the third and then blew it. NN won it 7-5; I've just had a Radox bath and I still find it difficult to walk/standup/crawl. I feel too buggered to walk if you'll pardon the crudity.

But then again I have you in my dreams. ('have' as in 'devour')Tabatha's a bit listless; me too; No Lins = No Fun. I've fed him and me Fray Bentos I'm glad to say....fresh meat for the cat. Well you have to have priorities, and before I drag my wretched limbs up the stairs; ; ; we have to have a little Rochester'

'Absent from thee I languish still

Then ask me not, when I return?

The straying fool t'will plainly kill

To wish all day, all night to mourn'

Love you, hope you've sussed how to be a shark; ; ; ; your husband x

---

The 'S:D special' that Tony mentions refers to Shelley (Peter) and Devoto (Howard). Tony devised a special 'What's On' documentary called *B'Dum B'Dum* about the two young men and their respective bands. Howard had been Buzzcocks' singer and lyricist, but he left after their *Spiral Scratch* EP. The title *B'Dum B'Dum* was from the lyrics of 'Boredom', the best-known track on the EP. Howard, already bored, left Buzzcocks and formed the band Magazine. He'd gone off punk, his lyrics described the scene as 'humdrum', that it had got 'aesthetically ugly', and that; 'what was once unhealthily fresh is now a clean old hat'[2]. When advertising for musicians to join his new band Howard wrote on his noticeboard advert that 'a punk mentality is not essential'.

The event Tony is referring to in the letter concerns a gig with Buzzcocks and Magazine that was filmed on 21 July 1978 at the Lesser Free Trade Hall. Tony liked to celebrate anniversaries and this one recognised the second of the two iconic punk concerts of two years earlier, when the Sex Pistols played the same venue along with Buzzcocks. Howard remembered:

'Pete and I tossed for which band would go on first. I lost the toss, so Magazine went on first. I then joined the Buzzers at the end of their set for 'I Can't Control Myself' – see the attached photo.'

---

2 The Guardian, 12th December 2008.

Tony interviewed Howard and Pete for the documentary (which can be viewed on YouTube). Tony was pleased with his choice of venues, thinking them perfectly appropriate for each respectively: Woolworths Cafe for Peter and a box at the Palace Theatre for Howard. Tony thought these locations suited their different personalities – Howard's being the more loftily salubrious and Pete's being more prosaic and down to earth.

The artist Linder Sterling, Howard's girlfriend during 1976, designed a poster for this gig, seen on the next page. I was unaware then of the significance of this performance, something that later events would reveal. I was already good friends with Pete and also his mates, Eric Random and Francis Cookson. These three performed as 'The Tiller Boys' and supported Joy Division on one of the original four Factory nights at the Russell Club. The four of us took magic mushrooms before going to that gig together. Pete wrote 'Ever Fallen in Love' about Francis.

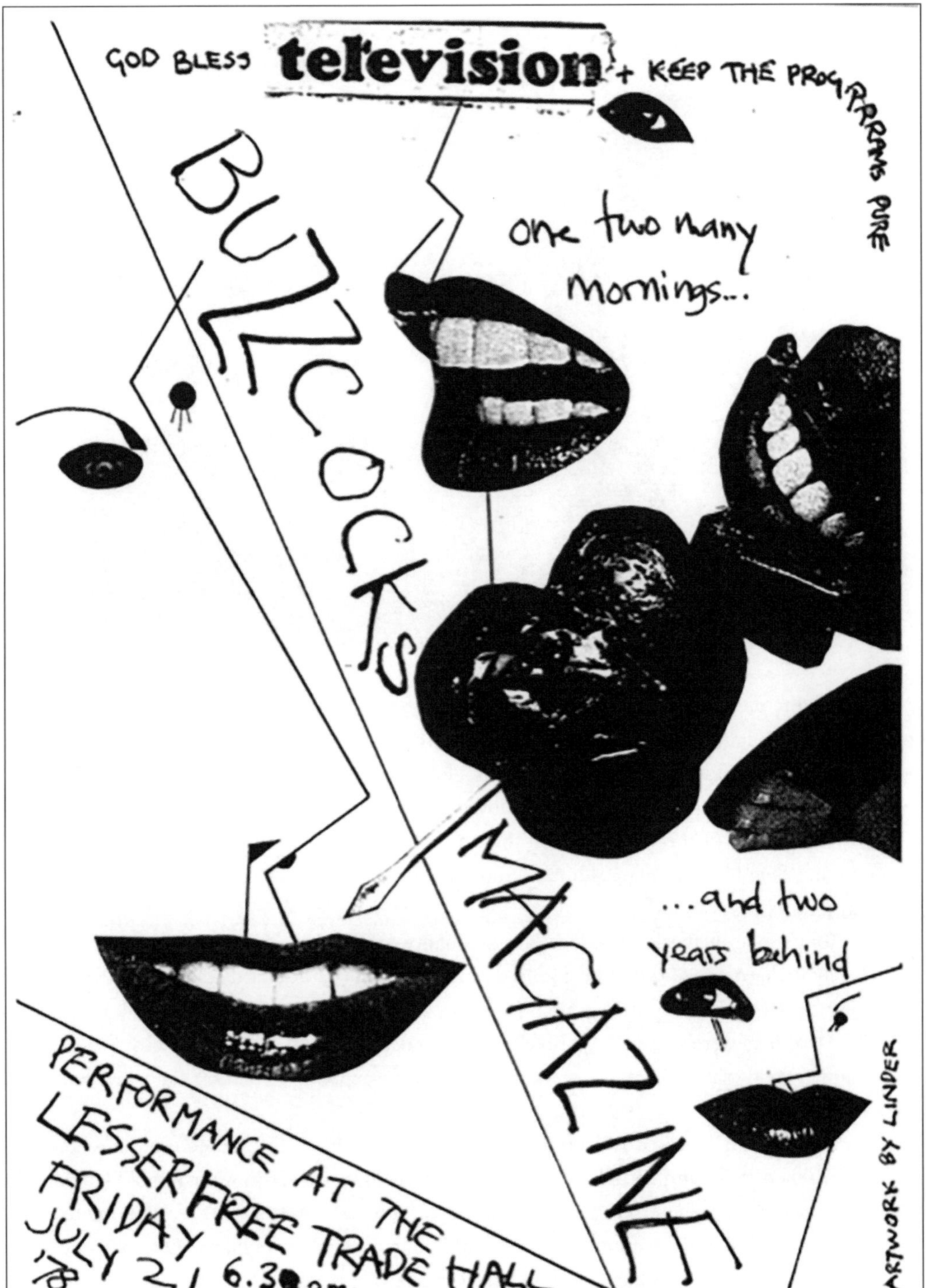

GOD BLESS
television
+ KEEP THE PROGRRAMS PURE
BUZZCOCKS
one two many mornings...
MAGAZINE
...and two years behind
PERFORMANCE AT THE
LESSER FREE TRADE HALL
FRIDAY
JULY 21 6.30 p.m.
'78
ARTWORK BY LINDER

Courtesy of Linder Sterling

I didn't yet know Howard, although this was about to change.

Tony brought home the photograph above, which was taken after the recording of the *B'Dum B'Dum* documentary. In later years, I looked back rather wishing I could go back to this innocent time when Tony and Howard could be photographed together without any suggestion of the recrimination that my future liaison with Howard would bring about. When I left our marital house I took very little, but this photograph was amongst my paltry possessions.

Tony's joke in the letter about homosexuality was perhaps because he'd said how lovely Richard was and that he admired him. Or was it that Richard and Howard were very close friends and had a similar look and intellectual way about them, making us joke that they were a couple. Or maybe it had something to do with Tony's fairly recent confirmation that his own father was gay. I may have expressed a fear of 'like father like son'.

The 'Tabatha' referred to in the letter was a cat that had ventured across the road, where she'd lived with an old lady, and moved in with us (never to return to old lady). Tabatha was very old herself. Tony calls her 'him' for some reason. I don't recall the game we played involving learning to be a shark although remember we had a phase of being addicted to it. We also liked playing backgammon. Tony had a Mahjong table in the lounge, but we rarely used it.

As for the Fray Bentos reference, Tony's favourite dish was the steak and kidney pie I made, and I'd left him the Fray Bentos equivalent in my absence.

Tony ends with a quote from Rochester again, this time taken from a poem entitled 'Return'. It quite touched me since the lines indicate the author is useless without his lover, and is weak with longing. Tony didn't quote the full poem obviously but, somewhat prophetically perhaps, Rochester goes on to talk about the torments of infidelity as being the only way to test the relationship and to prove love for one another.

Another letter swiftly followed.

Charlesworth,
 Wednesday night

What Wednesday and we're still apart;; this feels like a farce.
'We can't go on meeting like this'. Granada feels like a real limbo situation.
When you've gotta go you feel like you've gone already; ; ; nicest bit of the day was getting my hair cut. Tom, despite his father dying of cancer, was in lovely form. I think he's very warm.
Which the rest of life isn't ; ; ; without you ; ; ; 'the sun ain't gonna shine anymore etc........ feel zero   temptation to wander ; ; your strange emasculating power over those who have dared to venture between your legs and who ever after are under your thrall, be they in Hale or the North Western territories.
Must go and water the plants...get to bed... have nightmares about being banned from driving tomorrow morn; ; ; oh the torturous process of justice ....
so in aid of a good nights sleep or five and a half hours of it ; ; ; a brief farewell and a long piece of John Wilmot tonight, well I reckon if you're still in taffy land you need a bit of entertainment ..... this is the story of Strephon, a sussed young shepherd......tight pants, you know the scene, and Daphne ..... innocent and beautiful country girl... you in the white dress. Strephon has been giving Daphne the ' listen let's mess about, I really need a bit on the side.... this is the last bit of the conversation.

    DAPHNE Cruel shepherd I submit;
    Do what love and you think fit
    Change is fate and not design,
    Say you would have still been mine.
    STREPHON Nymph I cannot; 'tis too true
    Change has greater charms than you
    Be by my example wise

Charlesworth,

Wednesday night.

What Wednesday and we're still part;;this feels like a farce.
'We can't go on not meeting like this'. Granada feels like a
real limbo situation. When you've gotta go you feel like you've
gone already;;;nicest bit of the day was getting mi hair cut.
Tom despite his father dying of cancer was in lovely form. I think
he's very warm.
Which the rest of life isn't;;;without you;;; 'the sun ain't gonna
shine anymore' etc........feel zero temptation to wander;;;your
strange emasculating power over those who have dared to venture
between your legs and who ever after are under your thrall,be they
in Hale or the North western territories.
Must go and water the plants..get to bed..have nightmares about m
being banned from driving tomorrow morn;;;;oh the torturous
process of justice...so in aid of a good nights sleep or five and
half hours of it;;;; a brief farewell and a long piece of John
Wilmot tonight, well I reckon if you're still in taffy land you
need a bit of entertainment.....this is the story of Strephon,
a sussed young shepherd....tight pants, you know the scene, and
Daphne....innocent and beautiful countrygirl..you in the white
dress.   Strephon has being giving Daphne the 'listen let's mess
about, I really nee a bit on the side....this is the last bit of
the cinversation.

DAPHNE   Cruel shepherd I submit;
              Do what Love and you think fit
              Change is fate and not design,
              Say you would have still been mine.
STREPHON: Nymph I cannot; tis too true

Change has greater charms than you
Be by my example wise.
Faith to Pleasure sacrifice

DAPHNE   Silly swain, I'll have you know
Twas my practice long ago
Whilst you thought me vainly true
I was false in scorn of you
By my tears my hearts disguise
I thy love and thee despise,
Woman kind more Joy discovers
Making fools then keeping lovers.

Uuuuummmmmmmmmmmmmmmmmmmmm

Miss yer something Johnny rotten.

T.

Faith to pleasure sacrifice.
DAPHNE Silly swain, I'll have you know
Twas my practice long ago
Whilst you thought me vainly true
I was false in scorn of you
By my tears my hearts disguise
I thy love and thee despise
Womankind more joy discovers
Making fools than keeping lovers.

Uuuuummmmmmmmmmmmmmmmm

miss yer something Johnny rotten.

T.

It's likely that Tony was referring to Granada feeling like 'a real limbo situation' due to discussions centring around the cancelling of a third series of *So It Goes*. Ambitious for a better career in TV, it wouldn't be that long before he'd be offered a job presenting *World in Action*. The future of his ventures into music management and running a club night were, at this point, less than assured. Tony loved current affairs and, if Granada wouldn't let him present the current music scene, he could always turn toward the political scene. He'd initially seen himself as a serious journalist and believed that his main career would follow in the footsteps of political journalist and presenter Robin Day. Day was the clever chap who always wore a bow tie and presented *Panorama* and *Question Time* from 1979–1989. Day had also begun his career at ITN and had the courage to talk to politicians in a way that wasn't deferential. This was something Tony admired and aspired to; in fact, he replicated it while interviewing politicians himself, and also in talk shows such as *Upfront*. In later years, at his panel for the New York Music Seminar in 1990 entitled *Wake Up America, You're Dead!,* he was extremely forthright, not to say rude. Basking in the success of The Haçienda and Factory act Happy Mondays, who were also in New York at that time, Tony would begin his speech to the sedate audience with the words: 'You used to know how to dance here. God knows how you fucking forgot.' Eruptions soon followed.

When Tony got the job presenting *World in Action* in 1980, it looked, very briefly, as if he was on track to follow in Day's footsteps. Believe it or not, he thought then of betraying his beloved Manchester and moving to London. He stopped the car once to show me the kind of place he'd like us to move to in Ladbroke Grove. Perhaps it was fate that put an end to that career move. Tony was appointed to interview Thatcher minister and Secretary of State Keith Joseph in London, but he got stranded in snow soon after leaving our Charlesworth house in Derbyshire. Joseph, a baron, wasn't the sort of man you keep waiting and, to make matters worse, Tony was far from deferential to him when he arrived, even bordering on insulting him. But then Tony was never going to have much respect for someone who'd been described as the 'architect of Thatcherism'.

Tony had refused to take the advice of his superiors to take the train the day previously, mainly because he wanted his car in London so he could deliver some master tapes for pressing, possibly tapes by The Durutti Column. Presenter Richard Madeley would comment that Tony was 'the original deconstructor of television, in fact he deconstructed *World in Action* so conclusively that he was taken off it because *World in Action* wasn't built to be deconstructed. He didn't care what his colleagues or his viewers thought about him because he had total belief in himself.'[3]

Tony did hang on for a short while longer, making one or two other programmes for *World in Action* but his card was marked. One evening he came home and told me he'd been caught flicking a roach out of his car window near Granada. I thought he must have been watched because it could just as easily have been a cigarette butt. The police picked it up and caught him. It seemed a strange thing to happen, but this put an end to his network political career. He was quite upset over this.

Yet Tony's intuition wasn't that far off the mark in terms of a political career, even if it was only regional. The very last thing Tony ever presented – right up almost to his last breath – was *The Politics Show,* which went out live on the BBC every Sunday lunchtime. I was at his apartment on the day of his last presentation about a month before his death in August 2007. When the car came for him he could barely walk or talk. His voice was very raspy and his weight loss severe, as was his weakness. I couldn't believe he was going ahead with it. But he did – his spirit for the job far stronger than his failing body. It would be his last appearance; he was politely told to take sick leave after it aired on the basis that he needed to rest and get well. But it was obvious to us all that he was inches from death.

Tony yet again ends his letter with John Wilmot, aka Rochester. Despite Rochester's literary obscenities, witnessed in such lines as, 'I send for my whore, when for fear of a clap, I spend in her hand, and I spew in her lap...' he nonetheless credits Daphne in this dialogue – quoted by Tony – with, if you'll excuse the pun, having more of the upper hand.

---

3 BBC Newsnight Obituary interview, 10 August 2007.

CHAPTER 4
The Darkening of the Light

Our marriage would deteriorate between the letters of 1978 and those of the following year. We were both headstrong and volatile, but at the same time avoided revealing our insecurities to one another – or even to ourselves. Strangely enough, even in the first throes of love we'd consulted the *I Ching* oracle to question our future together. The trigram we got back was called 'The Darkening of The Light' which Tony had mentioned in our honeymoon diary. It was certainly prophetic.

The Durutti Column singer, Phil Rainford, and his girlfriend, Glynis, had become good friends of ours, and things were going along quite nicely in the first months of 1978; the band was recording, and would perform at the first Friday Factory night at the Russell Club that May. Also on the bill were Jilted John, who were soon to release their eponymous Hannett-produced single on Rabid: it would reach number four in the singles chart in August 1978. Nathan, Thelma's son, remembers I was DJ that night at the Russell Club, and played a record at the wrong speed; this was something that often happened to the BBC DJ John Peel, so I was in good company.

Below are pictures of Phil Rainford and Dave Rowbotham that were taken on that May 1978 opening night.

Phil Rainford   Dave Rowbotham

The plan for the Factory nights was to initially present four shows at the Russell Club and, in the manner of a showcase, The Durutti Column would play at two of them. Tony imagined big things to come out of this unveiling of his band to the public. Cabaret Voltaire appeared with them on the second occasion and Joy Division performed on the fourth show. I happened to be standing very near to the stage when Joy Division came on and remember being mesmerised, if also quite shocked, by Ian's strange, hypnotic dancing. It left a strong impression that lasts to this day.

These four gigs provided the prototype for the forthcoming *A Factory Sample* EP. Along with Tony and Alan, I was involved with the idea of putting out this record. Tony asked my permission to spend his inheritance; Tony's mum had left him £15,000 which, in 2024 would equate to £135,000. I think he was planning to spend half of this as he'd used the rest for a deposit on the house. The idea was to make an EP featuring tracks by Durutti and also Joy Division, whom we'd now seen give more than one compelling live performance. Tony wanted four acts on the EP, so included Cabaret Voltaire from Sheffield and the humourist John Dowie. I gave full support to this; I didn't seriously expect we'd get the money back, but, in the name of creativity, that was also fine. I was against keeping money in a dead stone vault, and we were able to live without dipping into savings. Although it had been his idea to use these savings, Tony still had some misgivings about using it in this way, and wondered if his mother, who'd died the year before, would approve. Actually, from what I later learned about her, she probably wouldn't have.

I was upset when, only two months after that Factory opening night and after Phil's considerable contribution to the recordings intended for the 'Sample', Tony decided to sack Phil from the band. Tony had huge ambitions for this group and felt that they wouldn't get anywhere without a 'star' as a frontman. He tried to justify it with one of his theories, such as 'he's not weird enough' or that he was better suited to a pop band. It felt wrong, Phil being thrown out, especially as it seemed unnecessarily controlling on Tony's part. I didn't have the right to object though, as they weren't my band. Alan Erasmus usually supported Tony no matter what, and perhaps abnegated responsibility except for giving Tony his full support. Vini Reilly told me later that he himself had demanded Phil had to go because he was 'too nice and ineffectual'. I don't know to what extent Vini influenced Tony's decision, but Tony wasn't keen on 'nice' at the time (except when I wasn't being nice to him, that is).

I asked Phil for his recollections: he said the day in question was etched in his memory. Tony had gone round with a gift of a Bruce Springsteen album (*Born to Run*, he thinks). After presenting Phil with this, Tony apparently started cutting up lines of coke. Then, out of the blue, he told Phil he was out of the band.

The new singer duly arrived, dressed as a punk rocker, which had already gone out of style by then. Tony still had a residue of fascination with punk and felt that a unique strangeness, the like of which he saw in Ian Curtis, was essential in a lead singer. The man in question, Colin Sharp, was actually an actor so perhaps this was the part he'd been given. Tony thought Colin was weirder than Phil – and he probably was: he would later go on to form a glam rock band. Phil's vocals were mercilessly stripped from the two *Factory Sample* tracks and Colin's added instead. It seemed unnecessary – ruthless, even – and no improvement. It even sounded pretty similar. It can't have been that vital, as when, in 2007, I told Tony about a book Colin had written entitled *Who Killed Martin Hannett?*, he didn't even recall that Colin had been in the band.

Needless to say, the remaining members of the band also weren't happy with Tony's domineering actions and had a major row with him after they refused to give agreement to the release. Tony told me it was because they were unhappy with Martin's production of the record. He used the tracks for *A Factory Sample* anyway and it seemed appropriate that the title of The Durutti Column's contribution was 'No Communication': there wasn't any – it was merely orders from on high. The rest of the band thought Tony was an impossible twat who was dictating to them, and I was honestly somewhat relieved that I wasn't alone in thinking so myself. Before this I'd thought it was just me that had a problem with Tony's behaviour, and that our difficulties were all my fault. The three musicians – Joyce, Bowers and Rowbotham – quit to form post-punk band The Mothmen, and later still Bowers and Joyce would join Mick Hucknall and Simply Red.

Tony had found a like-minded soul in Peter Saville, who had already designed a poster for the four Factory nights. Between the two of them, they came up with a design for the packaging of the EP. It had to be assembled by hand: sheets of silver paper folded up, inserted into a plastic bag with two 7-inch singles inside along with five stickers. I made loads of them myself so it's ironic that I don't own a copy. The planned release date for *A Factory Sample* was Christmas Eve 1978. Christmas always had a special significance to Tony but, as it turned out, the EP wasn't ready in time and so came out in January 1979.

Guitarist Dave Rowbotham would have been a better choice as frontman than Colin Sharp, but he also rebelled against the way Tony was running things. Dave was a friendly guy and a great guitarist – I liked him, and I was sorry when he left The Durutti Column as we ended up losing touch. His own story would later inspire the BAFTA-winning Colin O'Toole film *Cowboy Dave* – named after a Happy Mondays song that alludes to the suspicious circumstances of Dave's tragic murder in 1991. Dave's girlfriend found him dead in his Burnage flat on 2 November 1991, having been killed with a plasterer's hammer. No one has yet been convicted of his murder.

But back to 1979. Tony was happy to let the insubordinate band members go, and base The Durutti Column solely around Vini Reilly. From that point on he had a huge investment in Vini's future. It was a typical case of his oft-used maxim – 'praxis'. Find the

Courtesy of Ged Murray's family

Dave Rowbotham

reasons for doing what you did after you've done it. His reason was that Vini was a genius but, despite his skill with the guitar, recognition of that still remained in question. Not to Tony, of course. If he pronounced someone a genius, then they were and that was that.

Since The Durutti Column was now, in Tony's own words, a 'concept not a band' – particularly since there was only Vini left – Tony really wanted a proper group of his own. It was inevitable, therefore, that he'd get excited about some boyish lads in a group called A Certain Ratio (ACR) that Rob Gretton had told him about. He thought ACR were the bee's knees and instantly became their manager. They looked great (very young and handsome) but when he took me to hear them play in a rehearsal room in Stockport, I thought they were terrible, and told him so. They sounded post-punk, not quite having reached their funk sound but, basically, they could hardly play a note. There was no arguing with Tony though, and besides, weren't we just emerging from an era when not being able to play was no hindrance? If anything, my objections only geared him up even more and he put his heart and soul into giving them the best chance a group of young boys could have. He became increasingly absent from our home, giving his all to something that seemed suspect to me. He started dressing in military garb like they did, which I found off-putting. It was as if they were Privates and he was the Sergeant Major. It didn't look quite so ridiculous on them – youthful, skinny things – but on a somewhat portly older man, I thought it did.

I was left many days and nights in deepest Derbyshire, cooking dinner for a man who would wander in very late, if at all. Tony took to going round to Alan's flat after his live stint on the 6 p.m. show of Granada Reports. My secondment as a schoolteacher had lapsed by then, and I was helping my mum with her market research interviews. The main role I'd taken up was that of housewife, thinking that we'd eventually have children. Both raised in the fifties, Tony and I imagined a traditional family life as it still was then (i.e. the husband bringing home the metaphorical bacon, and the wife and mother of children cooking it for him). We both admired our mothers and that was what they had done. It was a very different world in the seventies than the one we inhabit now, and successful female role models were few and far between: author Caitlin Moran once jokingly observed that, even as late as 1985, we had to make do by choosing between Margaret Thatcher or Miss Piggy[1]. Although invidious to the rights of women, Thatcher probably did inspire a lot of women to compete with men on equal terms (although not this one).

Back in the seventies, men were rarely even seen out shopping or cooking at home. Yet, out in the music world, away from the kitchen sink, a cultural shift was subtly taking place. Coming to the fore there were a number of punk bands featuring women: suddenly there were artists like Patti Smith, The Slits, Siouxsie Sioux, Debbie Harry, Poly Styrene and Linder Sterling[2]. This change was also important for many female-led post-punk bands that emerged too, such as the Raincoats, the Au Pairs, Cocteau Twins, even pop groups like Bananarama. Change was afoot. Women were beginning to revolt.

I wish I'd been amongst them. But, programmed from an early age to be a housewife, my early experiences of living with a boyfriend also tended to convert me into a household robot who shopped, cooked and cleaned. He probably expected me to take over where his mother had left off. Then, with Tony, I continued to be a household slave which was utterly unappreciated by him. He gradually took less and less notice of me

1 'Every few years, I reread How To Be A Woman and marvel at what I got wrong', Caitlin Moran, *Guardian*, 29 August 2020.
2 Linder, best known as a visual artist, was also the founder of the avant-garde punk group Ludus.

except when I screamed and then his concern was to get me off his back. I found the role of housewife boring, unfulfilling and quite isolating too, being out in the sticks. The big event of the day, the evening meal, was not of great interest to Tony. When he finally arrived home he wasn't inclined to engage in conversation, preferring just to watch television. I felt invisible until we were in bed.

I also washed and ironed his shirts for his daily TV appearances and realised, close to the end of his life, when he asked me to pick up his ironed shirts at the dry cleaners – being too poorly to go himself – that I should have outsourced the ironing and housework and got on with a career rather than waste my time over something he didn't even notice. The days were long, and I needed an involvement in music even more than he did, because he had his TV life as well as that. I was interested in the Factory nights at the Russell Club, but by 1979 I felt shut out of Tony's music world. This was partly my own doing, not being a fan of combat trousers or either of his bands particularly. Tony seemed to hold an unhealthy obsession with these young ACR boys and eulogised them at every opportunity, sometimes with ridiculous notions – proclaiming them 'the new Sex Pistols', for example. The episodes with The Durutti Column had left a sour taste in my mouth as well. Lacking an outlet for my own youth and unspent energy, it was perhaps unsurprising that I developed an interest and musical passion elsewhere.

I'd been appreciative of Magazine and their singer Howard Devoto having seen them play at Rafters in 1977 and was impressed by this musical development, evolving from his earlier efforts with Buzzcocks. His performance had a compelling, theatrical quality about it but, equally captivating, was the musical accompaniment behind him, the distinctive bass and guitar sound, and especially the keyboards of Dave Formula. After so many punk bands it was refreshing to hear a melodious and lyrical sound that soothed and inspired rather than jarred.

That said, I'd forgotten about Howard until I got talking privately to him for the first time at a Factory night at the Russell Club in 1978. I'd become convinced Tony was having an affair: I'd witnessed him staring at a beautiful girl entering the club, after which he shared a knowing look with Alan Erasmus who gave a nod to him. My insecurity and paranoia immediately flared up, and I jumped to a conclusion that he'd either been unfaithful or was about to be. I opted to shoot from the hip rather than drown in jealousy; I surveyed the floor and saw Howard as the most interesting and appealing person present. He'd promoted the Sex Pistols, brought punk to Manchester, headed up Buzzcocks and shown even more guts by moving away from punk to form Magazine. Plus, I liked his face. Maybe there was further revenge to be had by consorting with someone who'd been a real punk, because however much Tony had worshipped the cult, he'd never been one himself and neither had anyone in his entourage, unless you counted Vini playing guitar with Ed Banger. I downed a double brandy while sitting near the gents toilets. To my surprise, Howard asked me to mind his beer while he went in there and when he returned, he sat at my table. As we were talking, I became quite brazen in coming on to him. Being an original proponent of punk rock, I didn't think he'd be shocked by my saying I didn't want us to chat, but rather to fuck. I must say, he remained as cool as a cucumber. The act itself came months later but, in words, I'd opened the door to it that night.

Tony eventually squeezed every last detail of this affair out of me, including my conversation with Howard near the gents. Many years later, during discussions with scriptwriter Frank Cottrell-Boyce for the 2002 Michael Winterbottom film *24 Hour Party People*, which chronicled Factory and The Haçienda, Tony suggested they ought to depict Howard and me having sex in the toilets of the Russell Club. This was after I'd objected to an earlier script depicting me having serial sex with seven men in tandem, including Vini Reilly, none of whom I'd ever had sexual congress with. Doubtless the reason was that otherwise, in the first half of the movie, there'd be drugs and rock 'n' roll but no sex, as there were virtually no other women in it. Tony responded to my objection by saying, 'We'll just have to have you having sex with someone you *did* have sex with then,' and he got his way with the toilet scene. I was further piqued when the real Howard played the part of a toilet cleaner and said to camera, 'this never happened', which of course it did, just not in a toilet. Needless to say, I was outraged, but liked the film, nonetheless.

As it turned out Tony *was* having an affair, but not with the beautiful woman. It was likely rather with his home-made group[s], his new ventures with Alan and the hordes of people that were coming into the club. The Factory Club nights were proving surprisingly popular for a little-known venue in a run-down area of Hulme. In fact, more people attended the nights at the tiny Russell/Factory Club than they did during the first few years at the cavernous Haçienda. The Russell Club, unlike The Haçienda, worked as a live venue. Plus, the bands that came along in the early years represented a huge new wave of talent coming out of the north of England. Joy Division, The Fall, Buzzcocks, Ultravox, John Cooper Clarke, Orchestral Manoeuvres in the Dark (OMD), Magazine, Cabaret Voltaire and Scritti Politti all played there within the first year.

Magazine's album *Real Life* was released in June 1978, and I kept listening to it throughout that summer while Tony was largely absent. I thought the lyrics showed wisdom and clever insight, lines such as: 'we stay one step ahead of relief'. How appropriate – so difficult to stay present while worrying about the future. Not that Howard necessarily meant it that way. Or, 'time flies, time crawls, like an insect up and down the wall'. The result of it all was that I went on a far-fetched romantic tangent and became totally infatuated, as if Howard was the fount of all wisdom. I became enamoured seeing him perform (while standing as near as possible to the front – something I'd never done with punk acts). He felt like my familiar. He was thin, he was clever, and he had the same sharp, high cheek bone structure as me. I adored the music of Magazine, the swirling keyboards and this enigmatic frontman. The whole spectacle swept me away, something that neither Durutti Column nor ACR had ever done. When Tony and I went backstage at Rafters after a Magazine gig in October 1978, my heart was racing so much on seeing Howard that I thought I might faint. It was a kind of insanity that swept me away. Tony had his love affair(s) with his groups, and I developed my own, believing in Magazine and Howard more than any of Tony's protégés.

And then I made some errors. The absences and neglect from Tony amounted to cruelty in my mind. This perhaps *was* just in my mind, a paranoia that he didn't care about me, rather than that he was just hugely ambitious and very busy. I needed a focus of my own that wasn't another man, but, as I've said elsewhere, relationships were always my major interest. Also, I had no need to make money which rather curtailed my ambitions in the career department. I had severe misgivings but eventually felt driven, that November '78, to ring Howard, imagining him to be my great love, rather than Tony. Sleeping with him was doubtless a mistake since Howard shared none of my feelings. He wasn't in love with me at all, and if I'd been wiser I would have known that before I ventured into his flat, carrying a bottle of Blue Nun.

My fantasy would inevitably crumble. It took some weeks – until the end of that year, in fact – for it to dawn on me that Howard not only didn't see us as a couple but didn't even especially intend seeing me again. I was as upset as anyone can be when a romantic notion is shattered. And then, on New Year's Eve, shortly before the stroke of midnight (and impending doom) I made an even bigger mistake by confessing to Tony what had happened, assuring him it was now over. I'd wanted to be honest and start the year afresh, holding some misconceived notion that we couldn't build our future on a foundation of dishonesty. The bigger reason, probably, was my fear that he'd find out from another source. A girlfriend of Howard's called Laura, whom I didn't even know about – all I knew was that he'd broken up with Linder – rang me with threatening, nasty words, wishing me dead.

I now think telling Tony was one of the more stupid things I've ever done in my life. I agree with the Austrian novelist Vicki Baum's popular quote, commenting on her relationships, that marriage demands the greatest understanding of the art of insincerity possible. It was beyond naive of me to imagine Tony would behave as my friend and even sympathise over my mistake; if I'd thought my own jealousy that night at the Factory Club had been severe, Tony's, although hidden, went much deeper and was more far reaching. He suddenly showed a covert interest in reading my diaries and notebooks, picking at his wound; I didn't know, or I would have hidden them. Thinking he had little interest in my scribbles, I unwisely hadn't destroyed my vain attempts to soothe my aching heart.

Thus, it was that 1979 opened with the slow decline of our marriage, a constant series of, to quote Tony, 'revenge fucking' and much heartache. I hadn't expected Tony to immediately become infatuated with someone, but he did, and his choice was weirdly apt, in fact it felt like a deliberate target. It was Howard's ex-girlfriend, the artist Linder Sterling, the woman who had designed the artwork for Magazine's *Real Life* and the striking Dada-esque cover of Buzzcocks' 'Orgasm Addict', depicting a naked woman with an iron for her head and mouths instead of nipples. Tony wanted her as his new girlfriend, and I never knew then whether or not he and Linder were lovers. I did know, though, that if it had been up to him they *would* have been, which is just as bad when you think about it. I only read her statement after Tony's death that she had 'firmly but politely refused him.'

There are two letters of interest that Tony sent in January 1979: one to me, asking me to move out, and one to Howard. I only got to see Howard's letter forty-four years after it was sent. I'd got in touch with him, after so many years, regarding this narrative, initially with a query about the *B'Dum B'Dum* documentary. Subsequently he came across this letter amidst his archives. Its content surprised me. Both appear below.

Tony had posted the photocopied note through Howard's letterbox in Chorlton in January '79 while Howard was away in London recording *Secondhand Daylight*. Why a photocopy, neither Howard or I know, but one guess is that it's Tony's own hand holding the note, and that he kept the original. It had been written presumably on some sort of a flyer, possibly to promote a joint Factory/Eric's event at Eric's in Liverpool on 22 October 1978. Read vertically it says: 'Records, Eric's, Factory, Tomorrow, So What?'. As mentioned previously, Eric's, run by Roger Eagle, was a club Tony and I frequented often. Joy Division played Eric's almost as many times as they played at the Russell, helped by an alliance struck between Roger and Tony.

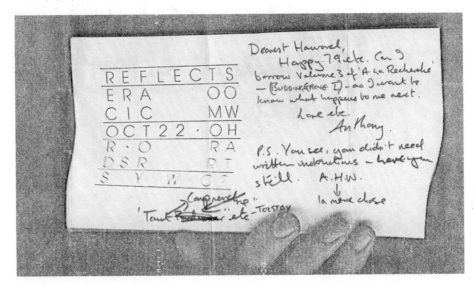

Courtesy of Howard Devoto

Dearest Howard,
        Happy 79 etc. Can I
borrow Volume 3 of 'A La Recherche'
– (BUDDING GROVE 1) – as I want to
know what happens to me next.
Love etc.   Anthony
P.S. You see, you didn't need
written instructions – Love you
‑ Comprendre "—still.   A.H.W.
'Tout ~~Pardonner~~ "etc – TOLSTOY   la meme chose

Then on the back of the envelope:

P.P.S, Happy New
    Year to Laura

F.P.P.S. Your
pipes have burst.
Flooded on both
sides.

I asked Howard why he might have needed written instructions? His reply: 'I think this is Tony quoting me back at myself. Back then I think I had a smart-ass line in interviews: when I was asked something like, "Does Magazine plan everything carefully ahead of time?" I'd reply with something like, "Yes, I just follow written instructions."' I also queried why Tony was talking to him about Proust. Howard: 'He knew I was interested in Proust. And I guess 'Within A Budding Grove' could be seen to be contain some relevant themes.'

Tony was convinced his life was running parallel to that of Marcel, the narrator in Proust's *À La Recherche* or *In Search of Lost Time,* and this theme again appears in future letters he would send me.

Tony wrote *tout pardonner* but scribbled out *pardonner* and replaced it with *comprendre.* In other words, he hadn't forgiven Howard, but he did understand. But, then again, the full quote is: *tout comprendre, c'est tout pardonner* – if you understand all, you will forgive all – so perhaps Tony is taking issue with that. The phrase is in *War & Peace,* explaining why Tony has written 'Tolstoy' by it. Tony read *War & Peace* at university.

While on the French tack, Tony writes *la meme chose* with a line reaching down from the H in A.H.W. This is because Tony's middle name was Howard. On the back of the envelope, I wondered if Tony was rubbing it in wishing a 'happy new year' to Laura? Howard's response: 'Not sure what you mean. Rubbing what in? I'd be more inclined to view it as a veiled threat. That he was reminding me he'd met Laura, and that maybe he could stir things up between me and her in some way.'

The envelope also informed Howard his pipes had burst – flooded on both sides. Perhaps Tony was making some clever allusion to Magazine's first release 'Shot By Both Sides', which reached forty-one in the singles chart. My initial reaction on reading this note, more than four decades later, was surprise that Tony was being so nice to Howard. Literally less than two or three weeks after he'd found out about the affair, he is writing, 'Love you still' to him. I thought it strange that Tony's punishment seemed directed only at me. Howard didn't agree: 'Oh, I wouldn't say that. I would say things definitely got frostier between us, not that we ever talked about it directly. But I moved to London in March 1979 so was very much out of the Manchester orbit after that, so it's hard to tell. As I told you, he did his best to try and exclude me from playing at the Festival of the Tenth Summer.'

This festival, organised by Factory in July 1986, was to celebrate ten years of punk's effect on Manchester. It was almost a forerunner to the Manchester music festival 'In The City', run by Tony and Yvette in the nineties, which ceased soon after his death. From the 12 to 20 July 1986 there were ten different events taking place all over the city including 'the new, new music seminar' in The Gay Traitor bar at The Haçienda. The festival culminated with an all-day music concert at G-Mex, with bands such as

New Order, ACR and Orchestral Manoeuvres in the Dark, and it was held on the tenth anniversary[3] of the legendary Sex Pistols and Buzzcocks gig (the second of the two 1976 Pistols gigs in Manchester). Pete Shelley performed at the Tenth Summer, but it was incongruous that Howard hadn't been invited: it was famously because of Howard and Pete that the Sex Pistols event had come about in the first place. Howard told me he only managed to get around Tony's hostility due to his friendship with Morrissey, as his band The Smiths were on the line up. Howard and multi-instrumentalist and composer Noko, aka Norman Fisher-Jones, had been writing together and managed to play their set, despite not being listed to do so, by jumping on after The Smiths and using their backline. They played, ironically, under the name of 'Adultery'. I asked Howard, why this name? He replied: 'We're an adult thing. We play adult rock 'n' roll. Rock 'n' roll for adults'.

A year later Howard and Noko would sign to the Beggars Banquet label under the new name of Luxuria. Their debut album was entitled *Unanswerable Lust*. Indeed.

Tony also wrote to me in January 1979:

Charlesworth, January 27th, 1979

Lindsay

This seems to be the best way to communicate with you at present, in particular when what I have to say seems to make both you angry and me sad, together making explanation/declaration difficult.

I have attempted to behave in the mature fashion which I once expected from Nathan's dad; hysteria is neither useful, nor attractive in the behaviour of cuckolded husbands; it confirms all those Menelaus stereotypes and further removes the object of desire. However this does not mean I do not feel gain, fear, loss and all the lover's other friends as strong as the next man; the "next man" being also yours. Over the weeks of growing knowledge – the first telling of the story, like the night you never came back, like the conversation on the motorway Thursday night, the look in your eyes at that Italian restaurant, the writing of your poems and my occasional heart-stopping rereading of your proffered love – like incessant drops of water on the tortured man's forehead – that increasing knowledge gnaws away at my reserves and strength. The increasing knowledge that you love someone more than me; or you would say love less, but merely 'in love' more. Isn't that everything. Love is all very well; but it is only happiness. 'In love' is joy. The active emotion is in a realm above

---

3 20 July 1976.

Charlesworth, January 27th, '79

Lindsay,

This seems to be the best way tom communicate with you at present, in
particular when what I have to say seems to make both you angry and me sad,
together making explanation/declaration difficult.

I have attempted to behave in the mature fashion which I once expected from
Nathan's dad; hysteria is neither useful, nor attractive in the behaviour
of cuckolded husbands; it confirms all those Menelaus stereotypes and further
removes the obscure object of desire. However this does not mean I donot feel
pain, fear, loss and all the lovers other fiiends, as strong as the next man;
the"next man" being also yours. Over the weeks of growing knowledge - the
first telling if the story, hike the night you never came back, like the
conversation on the Motorway Thursday night, the look in your eyes in that
Italian restaurant, the writing of your poems and my occasional heartstopping
rereading of your proffered love- like incessant drops of water on the
tprtured man's forehead - that ijcreasing knowledge gnaws away at my reserves
and strength. The increasing knowldge that you love someone more than me; or
you would say love less, but merely 'in love' more. Isn't that everything.
Love is all very well; but it is only happiness. 'In love' is joy. The active
emotion is in a realm above mere contentment/fulfillment/happiness. That that
is shared with another is the lover's pain, it says so in all the books, and
now it says so in all my mind. The images of pain and paranoia build up;
your imagined anguished plea to our mutual friemd , your much cinjectured
spoken denial of the man you have been married to less than two years,
tear me more than the two people who first heard them.

And I know only one solution. I hing in with Eithne when my hearts was being
ripped apart, Spring '71. I swere never to do it again but to turn off the
heat, turn off the intensity of feeling which turns its hands back on
myslef.

So, pain now and fear of the laceration to come (no we still haven't had all
the 'nitty gritty' - 'insatiable' and 'of course I mad a choice, what do you
expect I did, you always want what you can't have';have been the nearest
approaches so far and quite make me lose my breath still but since there is so

mere contentment/fulfilment/happiness. That that is shared with another is the lover's pain, it says so in all the books and now it says so in all my mind. The images of pain and paranoia build up; your imagined anguished plea to our mutual friend, your much conjectured spoken denial of the man you have been married to less than two years, tear me more more than the two people who first heard them.

And I know only one solution. I hung in with Eithne when my heart was being ripped apart, Spring '71. I swore never to do it again but to turn off the heat, turn off the intensity of feeling which turns its hands back on myself.

So, pain now and fear of the laceration to come (no we still haven't had all the 'nitty gritty' - 'insatiable' and 'of course I made a choice, what do you expect I did, you always want what you can't have'; have been the nearest approaches so far and quite make me lose my breath still but since there is so much more to come, I'm afraid my learned paranoia will make it impossible for me to behave like a mature husband and all that.....crap. My only solution, as yours I believe, is a form of separation.

In a year when I feel my life is about to change considerably, and by the end of the year I feel I shall be living in Didsbury/London/New York; I am not prepared to spend time and money on buying anywhere else, in any of those places. I therefore insist on my right to remain in this/our house until the real time comes to leave. You can have £250 a month for as long as you want if you wish to move to London or anywhere else, though I wouldn't expect to go on supporting you after some other lucky gentleman had replaced my financial protector etc. role, nor I suspect would he....or you.

If you don't want to be hassled moving out, or can't face a flat in Chorlton..... with burst pipes..... oh and if you do move out it should be agreed that you would cease to use this house as the pain of being subject to occasional visits from another man's lover who looked like you would be quite unbearable.....then we will have to remain living in the same house. In that case I will move properly into the spare room.....I feel very spare. ...weak.....anyway....we will live separate lives like people who share flats. Alan doesn't ask what time Charlie gets in, Charlie doesn't phone Alan to see if he's coming home from town for tea. We would meet and hopefully be pleasant in the manner of flat mates.

I find it quite unbearable to be subject to your romances and your unfounded jealousies, and utterly unjust.

Though I dearly enjoy the company of Lind/say/er, and though I enjoy what is I suppose flirting with them, it seems to me little different from my relationships with Jon Savage or Richard Boon. If I could fall in love with either of them I would welcome the experience with open arms as some treatment

much more to come, I'm afarid my learned paranoia will make it impossible for
me to behave like a mature husband and all that.....crap. My only solution, as
yoursI believe,is a form of separation.

In a year when I feel my life is about to change considerably, and by the
end of the year I feel i shall be living in Didsbury/London/New York; I am
not prepared to spend time and money on buying anywhere else, in any of those
places. I therefore insist on my right to remian in this/our house until
the real time comes to leave. You can have £250 a month for as long as you
want if you wish to move to London or anywhere else, though I wouldn't expect
to go on supporting you wfter some other lucky gentleman had replaced my
financial protector etc role, nor I suspect would he...or you.

If you don't want to be hassled moveing out, or can't face a flat in Chorlton
..with burst pipes ...oh and if you do move out it should be ggreed that
you would cesae to use this house as the pain of being subject to occasional
visits from another man's lover who looked like you but would be
quite unbearable....then we will have to remain living in the same house.
In that case I will move properly into the spare room....I feel very spare.
..weak..anyway...we will live separate lives like people who share flats. Alan
doesn't ask what time Charlie gets in, Charlie doesn't phone Alan to see if
he's coming home from town for tea. We would meet and hopefully be pleasant i
the manner of flat mates.

I find it quite unbearable to be subject to your romances and your unfounded
jealousies, and utterly unjust.

Though I dearly enjoy the company of Lind/say/er, and though I enjoywhat is
I suppose flirting with them it seems to me little different from myrelationsh
With Jon Savage or Richard Boon. If I could fall in love with eithert them I
would welcome the experience with open arms as some treatment for the pain in
my gut from your insatiable Christmas. I can't. I assume you are right in your
interpretation of the beauty trap, that with your vision cut into me, a woman
without your kind of real beauty can never approach my senses once refined by
waking up to you. Unable then to take anything but passing comfort from Lin2
I exoect I will push myself into work, like I did last night. Itseems then

for the pain in my gut from your insatiable Christmas. I can't. I assume you are right in your interpretation of the beauty trap, that with your vision cut into me, a woman without your kind of real beauty can never approach my senses once refined by waking up to you. Unable then to take anything but passing comfort from Lin2, I expect I will push myself into work, like I did last night. It seems then quite ridiculous for you to pile more agony in my head by screaming and making my life double troubled. I understand that you cannot control your hypocrisy, in fact it is one of the few sections of this affair which is in any way flattering to me, but I do think you should control your stupidity, and your refusal to live as separate people which is the only way I can hope to survive your love for another man. However sorry you feel for yourself, and watching you go through agonies of self pity over losing Howard is just another of those wincing delights I am now forced to watch, and which I feel you should try to control. You have just had eight months of delightful/painful/invigorating infatuation/'in love'. You're lucky. Luckier than me. And now you have to pay.......a little....it's always the way, but the pain as I recall is quite sweet, in fact it rather encourages the feelings just as the sight of Howard filled you again with all those bittersweet emotions. For me, the sugar has already run out and I can't say I blame the road haulage dispute. For the man whose woman loves another, there is no redeeming feature in his life. 'But I love you too' always sound so hollow, and the phrase 'too' cuts as it soothes. You couldn't stop yourself falling in love again, therefore I don't blame you for that, the most intense part of pain, but you can stop yourself making the rest of life hell for some stupid imaginings of your own.

So separate lives, I am begging you for at least that cold water comfort. I feel like that sick man Proust talks about, the one with wounds all over his body who feels he just has to move in the bed even though he knows he will reopen the gashes. Each time he moves he screams, but he keeps moving. This afternoon I reread your poems to Howard. If I am to stop gauging myself so readily, I need help, I need to be able to feel apart, to feel disentangled from the brambles and barbed wire. I would expect you to have patience with that process.

Yours well I probably will be in the end,

Anthony

Tony mentions a girl called Eithne in this letter; she was his first really serious girlfriend, his first love and obviously a very clever girl, as the two had met at Cambridge University. Subsequently they'd shared a flat in London when Tony worked at ITN. I met her only once and she seemed a bit angry with him, sarcastically

quite ridiculous for you to pile more agaony on my head by screaming and
making my life doubly troubled. In understand that you cannot control your
hypocrisy, in fact it is one of the few sections of this affair whichis in
any way flattering to me, but I do think you should control your stupidity,
and your refusal to live as separate people which is the only way I can hope
to survive your love for another man. However sorry you feel for yourself, and
watching you go through agonoies of self pity over losing Howard is just anothe
of those wincing delights I am now forced to watch, and which I feel you should
try to control. You have just had eight months of delightful/painful/invigorati
g infatutaion/'in love' . You're very lucky. Luckier than me. And nowyou have
tp pay....a little..it's always the way, but the pain as I recall is quite
sweet, in fact it rather encourages the feelings just as the sight of Howard
filled you again with all those bittersweet emotions. For me, the sugar has
already sun out and I can't say I blame the road haulage dispute. For the
man whose woman loves another, there is no redeeming feature in his life. 'But
I love you too' always sounds so hollow, and the phrase 'too' cuts as it soothe
s. You couldn't stop yourself falling in love again, therefore I don't blame
you for that, the most intense part of the pain, but you can stop yourself maki
the rest of life hell for some stupidg imaginings of your own.
So spparate lives, I am begging you for at least that cold water comőort.
I feel like that sick man Proust talks about, the one with wounds all over his
body who feels he just has to move in the bed even though he knows hewill
reopen the gashes. Each time he moves he screams, but he keeps moving. This
afternoon I re-read your peems to Howard. If I am to stop gouging myself so rea
dily, I need help, I need to be able to feel apart, to feel disentabgled from
the brambles and barbed wire. I would expect you to have patience with that
process.

          Yours
                well I probably will be in the end,
                        Anthony

emphasising the hippy use of the word 'man' when addressing him. I didn't know why she seemed resentful although it becomes clear after reading Thelma's explanation of events below. But Eithne struck me as lovely really, and I sensed that she and Tony had shared a rare closeness.

Eithne with Nathan McGough

Courtesy of Thelma McGough

Although, in the letter, Tony writes about Eithne's own earlier love affair, Thelma told me: 'The tragedy for Eithne was that she'd given up her job as a teacher (in London) to move to Charlesworth where she was to begin a new September school year in (Stockport?). Our [Thelma and Tony's] relationship began in August before she moved in – too late and too difficult for 'A' to be truthful and stop her. To be fair, neither of us knew if our love would last. But the outcome for her was a disastrous four months of deceit – which to my regret I was a party – and a further two months of living in Town Lane with the knowledge before she could leave her job.' (Eithne had to give notice and leave at half term in the following year.)

Tony probably had it coming to him, based on the above, but what is shocking to me about Tony's letter is recognition of the pain I'd put him through, something that only maturity has made me realise. At the time I read it just as further rejection of me. He, of course, hadn't recognised how lonely and rejected *I'd* already felt in our marriage, and how silently painful that can also be. Isn't it the case that we humans can never quite resonate with one another's pain? Tony tortured himself by dragging out of me every possible piece of information about the affair, and I must have unwisely used the word 'insatiable'. I meant it not in terms of the act itself but more in terms of my desire for the act. Most of this love affair took place not by action but entirely in my imagination.

Not only pained by the rejection from Howard, it felt far worse now my husband was rejecting me as well. This letter is fair given the situation, although lines such as 'your insatiable Christmas' were annoying as the brief fling had ended in November. Plus, his daily punishment bordered on cruelty. He writes that he's unable to take anything from passing comfort from 'Lin2', but I lived with the threat of another woman hanging over my head like the sword of Damocles, along with a callous coldness from him that I'd never experienced before. It would probably have been better if I'd moved out, but I don't remember that I did for long; I didn't really see why I should. Nor did he move into the spare room.

Tony was enamoured by the Trojan War, particularly as depicted in Homer's *Iliad* and *Odyssey,* and he often referred to the characters from Greek legend. He mentions 'Menelaus stereotypes' in the first line of this letter: Menelaus was the husband of Helen of Troy. A nobleman named Paris ran off with Helen and Menelaus and his brother, Agamemnon, raised a thousand ships to bring her back, which so began a ten-year war.

This was the first letter with no quotations from his favourite poets but, instead, a mention of my own poems to Howard. Of course, I never sent these poems to Howard, and it's a pity that Tony read them. I found something I'd written on hotel notepaper when Tony and I were on a half-term holiday in Madeira – before I'd told Tony, but after it had happened. Predictably the holiday didn't go too well. I'm horrified to think Tony may have read it because it's obvious who it was referring to. I was obsessed with Howard, you can tell by the slanted references to his lyrics (e.g. *'Sometimes I forget that we're supposed to be in love,'* a lyric from my favourite Magazine track 'Parade' which has a slight fairground feel.

How was it? you asked.

You tell me, I replied, momentarily lost for words.

It was....(stumbling) fine, you said.

A memory of same, all we can do is glimpse at past and future, let me tell you how it seemed before I forget to erase the same memory.

I was so excited I felt nauseous.

Sometimes I pretended I was in love, sometimes I pretended I was not.

Now I pretend I am still in love with you.

On the same letterhead I quoted the lines below as they resonated with how I felt:

'These foolish and always short affairs were threadbare rags against a cold wind, but they were better than no rags at all. The terrible knowledge that if you accept the unworthiness of the object of your love, then your love itself is discredited and all the good in its past becomes poisoned retroactively.'[4]

---

4 Athill, Diana, *Instead of A Letter,* Chatto & Windus, 1963.

Tony always equated sex, passion and being 'in love' with the highest love but I disagree. The trouble is, of course, that 'in love' can so easily be confused with 'in lust'. It can certainly feel stronger and in my deluded mind I'd imagined, therefore, a higher love for Howard. But afterwards, when the sex act was over, those were the telling moments: what came across from Howard felt like indifference. Politeness, yes, but not love or even affection. I'd stayed the night with Howard, but he took me to the door next morning as he was preparing to leave for London, busily holding the offending sheets he'd already stripped from the bed. With him that was the first time, but not the last, that I saw with absolute clarity that sex, and its friend passion, can be in quite another orbit from loving, caring and commitment. Years later, when I was out in the wilderness looking for a partner to love, I saw it more than once. Men will fuck you, but it doesn't necessarily mean they give a damn about you. Women ought to have that same freedom if they want it, and perhaps in this more modern day they do. I never equated the two things as separate back then, being programmed or duped into believing sex and love were supposed to be on the same page. The trouble always was, and probably always will be, that the nice guys, the men that do care, seem less interesting, less exciting, and therefore less attractive, especially to the young and to those with low self-esteem.

Another factor in this is the mass scale manufacturing of desire by the film, TV and music industries. Desire everywhere and, naturally, a partner you've seen every day for three years, often at their worst, someone you've stopped believing in, doesn't generate the desire you think should be happening. So when a new, exciting, more attractive proposition comes along, it's hardly surprising that desire rears its head and, perhaps women – certainly this woman, anyway – can more easily fool themselves that lust is really love. Many of the female artists who came to the fore during the punk era were politically angry and sexually provocative at the same time, however 'alternative' and somehow 'above all that' this branch of the music industry thought itself. The notion of desire applies to male artists too – Tony's attraction to ACR, for example, and, much later, the mass adoration of Joy Division. Then there was the way the TV audience 'desired' Tony. Tosh Ryan remembers Tony waving like royalty to the crowds while sitting on the bonnet of a car as it was slowly driven down Deansgate, the historic thoroughfare in Manchester's city centre. This was during a festival in the early seventies, organised by Granada and Music Force (the aforementioned musicians' cooperative) to celebrate the opening of Crown Square in Manchester.

I don't agree with Tony that 'in love' is joy, unless it is a mutual thing. Yet in 2004, he rather contradicted this. He and Yvette appeared on *The Keith Barret Show*, a spoof chat show hosted by comedian Rob Brydon, a friend of Steve Coogan. (Coogan had played Tony in the film *24 Hour Party People* two years earlier.) During the interview Tony remarked that he and Yvette had tried to escape each other and the reason they couldn't, 'It's not love, that's something that's wonderful,' he said, 'It's *in* love, which isn't wonderful.' Perhaps by 2004 Tony had learned the hard way. Yvette is undeniably beautiful and stunning on this appearance while he looks older, overweight and somewhat out of his league.

My unreciprocated feelings for Howard brought me mostly pain. And even if 'in love' is a mutual thing, there's usually an element of wanting something from the other, be it sex, or some other demand. Unconditional love is rare and, in my case and also I suspect, in Tony's, it was mainly only truly experienced via our respective mothers.

Tony (amongst others) showed me how much I fell short of love. I constantly had an expectation from him, a picture postcard idea of how it should be, and how he wasn't living up to that. If only I could just have seen him as a separate, clever and driven individual, flawed but someone who still deserved to be loved. Instead, I made demands, wanting attention, feeling that he wasn't seeing, or interested in, the real me. I felt like an object of beauty to him (or worse, just an object); he wanted my body more than he wanted me as his real-life partner. This was probably part of the reason I rejected him in the bedroom: it was the only power I had left. It was the only place where I had a voice that could be heard. I probably loved him most when we were illicit lovers in 1998, and in 2007 during the months he was poorly with cancer and sex was no longer relevant. Then and only then did we place no demands on each other. I only wanted to give and to be there for him whenever possible.

Back in 1979, I was in denial and completely unaware that I still loved Tony, being so focused on his imperfections. Tony writes that he's 'in love' with me, but this never came across in the daily tedium of our lives. The days were long without him as a life partner, it was lonelier than living alone. And he never brought me flowers.

Love is blind, they say, and it sure is. My imagination ran riot where Howard was concerned when I didn't even know him. I thought his indifference to me might be feigned and blindly imagined he shared the same passion as myself underneath. It really came home to me at the last that he'd never felt even one jot of it.

Months after the affair had ended, in May 1979, I took a tab of acid by myself, looking for an insight into my unhappy situation. Tony was absent as usual. On this night in question, under the influence of LSD, I imagined I'd been mistaken, and that Howard was *the* significant love after all. It was, in fact, significant, but mainly because of the devastating effect it had on my marriage. I didn't know when, or even if, Tony would come home that night. As midnight approached, I read in *NME* that, as part of their tour, Magazine were performing in Leeds and so I impulsively set off in search of Howard's hotel. I put a vinyl record that I smashed into pieces (my copy of *A Factory Sample* I think) on Tony's coffee table and added a note that read, 'My heart, you wanted it,' (indicating that my heart was broken like the record). Since Howard had shown me lyrics to 'I Want Your Heart' the previous year and subsequently changed them to 'I

Wanted Your Heart' for the release, the message was perhaps more appropriate for him. Or probably relevant to both of them. After a long search, I did find absolute closure with Howard though: I finally found his hotel in the early morning and spent the next day driving to Liverpool with him where his next gig was.

In the cold light of day – and, as Tony wrote: 'like the day after good acid when things look bleak, no colour in anything, cut yourself and the colour would be grey not red' – the stark reality of my infatuation hit me. It was a pure, one-sided, fantasy. Howard was interested in sex but nothing much else. I felt so depressed and ashamed on my return to Charlesworth that I took an overdose of Valium. It wasn't a true suicide attempt, merely a wish to be unconscious for as long as physically possible. I felt I didn't belong in Tony's bed any more than Howard's. Alan Erasmus happened to ring and, realising all was not well with me, told me I'd be all right if I just 'put some sounds on'. He contacted Tony who came home soon afterwards. I was grateful for the concern on Tony's face when he came into our bedroom and I knew it was then forever over with Howard in my head, whether Tony was seeing another girl or not.

My 'in love-ness' was shattered. This is why I have always believed the state of being 'in love' to be a lesser thing than 'love' in its purest form. To the end of his days Tony seemed to be caught by 'in love' far more than love itself. He even tried to come back to me around the time of the Brydon interview in 2004. He'd been taking me out for meals quite often but one night, at his behest, we made love again. I imagined we were back together, but he appeared not to want to repeat the event, so I moved on (darling). He told me he loved me, but wasn't in love with me, as if to imply that love was an inferior thing. I can well understand, how 'in love' can be so much more compelling than love, but the latter lasts – the former can melt like candy floss. In 2005, a few weeks after I began seeing Tosh Ryan, Tony asked me to go on holiday to Vietnam with him. I couldn't accept under the circumstances and thought his timing strange since he'd heard about my new relationship.

If I'd moved out of the house in 1979, following receipt of the above letter, I might have been spared some of the agony to come. It seemed pointless though given I then wanted only to be faithful to him. Also, *A Factory Sample* had just been released and I was involved with the project, believing that it belonged to both of us, and not just because our money had paid for it. Perhaps Tony's real reason in wanting me out of the house was so that he could more easily get his own back. I clearly remember the upset that Tony's behaviour caused me while I stayed and hoped for a better outcome. He taunted me over his fantasy relationship with Linder and/or another. Doubtless I deserved it, but he seemed to want to punish and hurt me with it. Admittedly I'd hurt him terribly, but I hadn't deliberately wanted to, though I underestimated the hurt it did cause him.

Linder's group Ludus had played at the Russell Club that January (shortly before he wrote the above letter). She had obviously made a big impression on Tony. She was fearless and had shown talent with her radical cover designs and he probably foresaw her promising future as a visual artist. Linder's appearance fronting Ludus was similarly dramatic, but none more so than when performing at The Haçienda in 1982, when she wore a bodice covered in raw meat. She was protesting against the porn then being projected against the walls, something that Tony probably considered to be artistic and suitably outlandish. Linder then revealed a dildo under her skirt, while meat wrapped in pornographic literature was handed out to the audience alongside bloodied Tampax visibly on display. How admirable and ahead of her time. If I hadn't been jealous I would have adored her. All of it reflected right rebellion.

I wondered if Tony was referring to Linder when he wrote: 'Though I dearly enjoy the company of Lind/say/er, and though I enjoy what is I suppose flirting with them, it seems to me little different from my relationships with Jon Savage or Richard Boon.' He seems to be implying that he and Linder were just friends but, knowing him well, it was obvious to me he wanted more than that from her. It was possible that Tony had decided, when he saw Linder at that January '79 gig at the Russell Club, that he wanted her: ironic if so, since I'd made the same decision about Howard in the exact same place.

Tony subsequently used Factory as a way of seeing more of Linder. Rightly fascinated with her artwork, he planned to bring her menstrual egg timer into production on Factory for release in spring 1979, and it was given FAC number 8. It wasn't always actual products that were given catalogue numbers but plans such as this that never came into being, and assorted oddments such as a trip Alan Erasmus made to Russia. I vaguely recall seeing a possible prototype of Linder's egg timer, a small abacus or counting frame, but below is the drawing that Tony made of it. I'd thought the menstrual egg timer a good idea as Tony favoured the rhythm method of contraception, as did I, not being a fan of the pill. I hadn't realised this was the only contraception then accepted by the Catholic church.

Despite everything and all of the hurt we gave each other, I still cared for Tony and, at that point, wanted our marriage to work. Clearly it wasn't going to be easy.

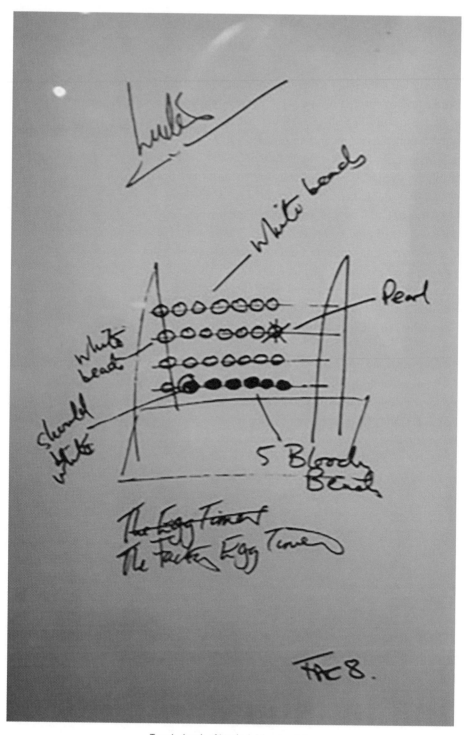

Tony's sketch of Linder's Menstrual A

CHAPTER 5
Acts of Creation and Destruction

Nineteen seventy-nine was a prolific year musically for Factory. Tony had put Joy Division on 'What's On' towards the end of 1978, during which they performed 'Shadowplay'. Opening with Hooky's distinctive bass chords and Stephen's cymbals, the song quickly gained momentum as Bernard's guitar and Ian's voice took over the lead. It was obvious that this group had a more promising future than The Durutti Column.

Graphic designer Peter Saville had become the third partner of Factory, after designing the yellow and black club poster and *A Factory Sample* sleeve, and then, when it transpired that the '*Sample*' EP had actually gone into a small profit, Tony invited Joy Division manager Rob Gretton in as a fourth partner. Rob, aware of the profit that the '*Sample*' had made, suggested that Tony should record Joy Division's album on Factory so, as he told Tony, 'he wouldn't have to go to London and talk to cunts'. There was naturally an advantage in having more control and this way he'd be both manager and label director. Tony's discussions with Rob didn't involve me, despite marital monies being used for the band's first album.

Joy Division had self-released their debut EP, titled *An Ideal For Living*, in 1978, and Tosh Ryan remembers Rabid HQ on Cotton Lane being stacked full of copies. Martin Hannett had been championing the band and wanted to put them out on Rabid. He told Tosh they were 'the dance music of the 80s' but Tosh refused, objecting to their name, as well as the sleeve of *An Ideal For Living*[1], which he associated with fascism. If you were in the know – which I wasn't – the phrase 'Joy Division' was originally linked with Nazi concentration camp brothels in which Jewish women were used as sex slaves by German soldiers[2]. The compromise was that Lawrence arranged distribution of the EP.

---

1 *An Ideal For Living* featured a black and white drawing of a Hitler Youth member beating a drum, drawn by guitarist Bernard Sumner.
2 As described in the 1953 Ka-Tzetnik novella *House of Dolls*. *An Ideal For Living* also features a song, 'No Love Lost', which includes references to *House of Dolls*.

After Rabid's rental of Cotton Lane ended, Tosh moved boxes of these EPs into his own basement but eventually became so fed up with them – particularly taking exception to the Hitler Youth drummer boy on the cover – that he threw around 5000 copies in a skip. When the skip man came, the skip was so heavy that the front wheels of his truck lifted off the ground. Nowadays a single original copy can fetch nearly £2000. Tosh contributed to its rarity.

Soon after Rob became a director of Factory, Tony made Martin Hannett one as well. I wonder if it was significant, or merely coincidence, that four out of five of these men had a Catholic upbringing like Tony? Tosh said he had a feeling Factory was a 'fairly Catholic closed shop' and that Martin used to joke that 'you don't get on that label unless you're a Catholic'. Tony liked Christian liberation theology – i.e. liberation for the poor and oppressed. His interview with Cardinal Arns, the Archbishop of Sao Paulo, made a big impression on him. After intense discussion, Tony leant forward and said, 'But Cardinal, are you saying that just to be rich, of itself, is a sin?' The Cardinal replied, 'Yes, at last you've understood.' The impact this interview had on Tony helped him be philosophical when Factory went into receivership in 1992 and Factory could have made £5,000,000 from the deal offered by London Records but instead ended up with nothing. The reason? The contract, if any, with his bands was that 'the musicians own everything, the company owns nothing.' Perhaps Cardinal Arns had an influence on both the birth and the death of Factory.

To return to the birth, however, certainly it was significant that all the partners were male. I saw it as unnecessary male domination (rather than Catholic) and thought this gender imbalance was getting a bit much. Where would it end? That said, although it was the addition of Martin that annoyed me, with him being the fifth, he was doubtless the most vital to the future success of Factory. In fact, without him, I even doubt if Factory, and/or Joy Division, would have ever made quite the same mark. I vaguely wondered why *I* didn't qualify as a director, particularly given my involvement and the contributions I'd freely made. I never voiced that to Tony though, and wasn't especially conscious of it at the time, since I saw the two of us principally as a partnership. I think it's only in later years that women – and me – have more easily found their own voice; the music industry back then was very misogynistic, and given Tony's penchant for punishment, it was perhaps hardly surprising that he didn't include me.

The recording of Joy Division's album *Unknown Pleasures* took place around April 1979. Tony and I spent several late nights in Strawberry Studios with Martin, usually for the mixing when the band either weren't there or were downstairs playing pool or relaxing. Martin preferred them out of the way. It was enjoyable watching Martin at work, smoking joints and listening to the sounds. He made me really sit up and take particular notice of this band, much more so than when I'd seen them live, however compelling Ian Curtis had been to watch on stage. The music was less aggressive and more sophisticated now, with Martin's ingenious use of gizmos, one of which was a digital delay AMS machine giving a unique drum sound echo. This gadget, incidentally, had been paid for by Rabid at a cost of around £2,000. Martin would go to great lengths with all sorts of other unusual sound effects to add depth, such as a lift shaft opening and closing, or milk bottles smashing.

While Martin worked on the mixes for Joy Division, Factory released the single 'All Night Party' by A Certain Ratio, which had earlier been produced by Martin in the more economical Cargo Studios. As with Joy Division, Martin added something to their sound and the group learned much by working with him. I'd warmed to ACR by this point and now supported them – they'd developed talent in writing and performance, and would be further transformed soon after this release once funk drummer Donald Johnson joined the band. Funk or no funk, similarities were drawn, much to ACR's annoyance, between them and Joy Division, or more particularly between their singer Simon Topping and Ian Curtis. I'd become friends with the band members, especially Jez Kerr and Pete Terrell, but that didn't stop me feeling perturbed by Tony's obsessive management of them and the hours of time he spent with them. Then there was his purchase of an ugly estate car specifically for driving them and their instruments around in, and his further neglect of me and our marriage.

Around the same time Factory also released another single – 'Electricity' by Orchestral Manoeuvres in the Dark. They were actually *my* band; in that I'd found their demo and highly rated it. I picked it out while playing a huge pile of cassettes that Tony had been sent at Granada, which he was ignoring. Tony wasn't particularly enamoured of the track because he saw it as 'pop', but he must have been feeling generous the day I played 'Electricity' to him in his car. After I enthused about them being a surefire hit, he rather patronisingly patted me on the knee and said, 'Well then, darling, I'll put it out especially for you,' and the track became OMD's debut single. Tony saw this as indulging me, but that was as far as my voice was heard because, on the strength of the success of this single, Tony sold the track and the band to Virgin/DinDisc, again without discussing it with me until the contract had been signed. I felt cheated, but this was probably something he wanted me to feel since I'd cheated on him. He was unmoved by my protestations and justified his actions by insisting that that's what Rabid did, indeed that's what all independent labels do with their bands if they can: sign them to a major. I felt he was merely sidelining me, or else why were we paying for Joy Division to record their album with a planned release on Factory only one month after the OMD single release? And who else on Factory signed to a major? It would have been nice if Tony had at least talked it over with me first and involved me in negotiations, if any were agreed on.

Peter Saville designed a great sleeve for 'Electricity', with raised Braille-type lettering, indicative of 'manoeuvres in the dark'. The creation of this design prompted a chain of events whereby Peter moved from resident to occasional designer for Factory. Following the deal Tony made with Virgin/DinDisc, Saville became busy designing further sleeves for OMD and, becoming more and more in demand in London, he ended up moving there.

I didn't take Tony's dismissal of my input lying down, and he didn't like that. I took the following picture one evening as he was so pissed off with me. Studio recording tapes are visible on top of LPs behind him. On this occasion he wasn't annoyed because we'd rowed (for once) but rather because I'd moved the furniture round in the lounge while he was at work. He liked to sit on a cane rocking chair directly in front of the TV, but I'd moved the sofa there instead. My thinking was we could sit there together but no such luck, he sat on a cushion on the floor to watch TV, covered the sofa with the bag he used every day along with other stuff and sulked. He soon moved it all back the way it had been before.

The big event of the year for Factory was the release of *Unknown Pleasures* in June. Some of the band members hadn't been all that happy with Martin's production. Guitarist Bernard Sumner said: 'I remember hearing the album after it had been mixed and being absolutely shocked at the sound of it 'cos it wasn't the way the band envisioned it sounding. We just wanted a quite hard rocking sound and Martin used all these ethereal sound effects[3].'

3 Granada TV, *Close to Absolute Zero*, 1996.

Personally, I thought Martin's production brought out a musical quality that had previously been missing. The songs had nuance now, and much more depth. It sounded less jarring and aggressive. Martin made the most out of every instrument, including the voice. He was one of the earliest users of the AMS digital delay amongst other contraptions and was always ahead of his time in the field of technology. His vivid imagination produced wonders with echoes, reverb and ARP synthesisers.

The deal that Rob had worked out with Tony gave Rob and the band a severe advantage over Factory, quite apart from the fact that they had the freedom to, as Tony would phrase it, 'fuck off' – and take the master tapes with them as well. As noted earlier, making money from Factory was never as important to Tony as it was to others – he had his day job and was greedy for product rather than money. Rob took advantage of this, as well as Tony's lack of business acumen, and sketched a deal whereby Factory would pay mechanical royalties to the band out of their own 50/50 share. This made the scales very uneven. Mechanicals represent the fee the record company pays to the publisher on behalf of the songwriter whenever a copy of their material is made (i.e. manufactured, not necessarily sold). This would apply to all Factory product, not just Joy Division. Tony referred to Rob during my aforementioned interview:

TW: 'He's my mate and he repeatedly fucked me over.'

LR: 'In what way did he fuck you over?'

TW: 'Having invented what I call the modern independent record movement, exactly about 20 seconds later he said, "Here's the deal we will do," and then this kid from Wythenshawe proceeded to sketch out a deal, which I agreed to on the spot – because why not? This turns out to be the most generous record deal ever done for musicians – in history. His other thought was, "Tony's a fucking idiot and I'll get a fantastic deal out of him," which he did that very day.'

LR: 'Maybe the working class ones were more motivated to make money.'

TW: 'Very true. I was your typical middle-class wanker who didn't need to make money. I always think that the real idealist in the whole thing was Erasmus. Erasmus did things like … we'd get an enquiry, "Can The Durutti Column play a gig in Tel Aviv?" and Alan would say, "Yes, we'd love to, when you withdraw from Palestine."'

However, I got the impression that Factory could be somewhat hit and miss when it came to accounting. Tony would just write out the odd cheque when pressing demands were made on him, but I did wonder if there was any serious reckoning of actual royalties owed, especially to the less well-known bands. Still the ethos of independence and a supposed 50/50 share appealed to band members – but only so far. I watched with dismay over coming years the anger many of them felt over never receiving any money.

Charlesworth

b'nvot sd sdtsed gnimsl1 ruc tsl   While in that sacred fire; Tuesday night, very late

Nice to talk to you; you sounded very down. I think I understand.
So many people are strangers, even people you love. Vohnegut calls
it your 'karass', all those people you are tied to by family,
job, situation even tenderness, BUT not your people; maybe you don't
meet your people except very occasionally. To me, this silly
absence is the lack of one of the few non-strangers I've ever met;
I knew you weren't a stranger that first afternoon on the hillside
in Disley. Funny how clear you can see from 200 miles.
Funny also; you on the phone, and not at home and then me with
Howard, ...didn't feel I could really get to know him, or rather didn
t feel any desire to get to know, got those "oh he's just from another
planet like all the rest shrugs" on me. My infatuation waned somewhat
He's still lovely but he takes himself very seriously and seems,
at least he did tonight to lack wisdom. We didn't talk much of my
'wife' except to say that you didn't like the cap; he was a little
offended but it was one of the more pleasant interludes. I like him,
just don't feel any strong desire for knowledge of him. Come back and
rekindle my appetite with yours, perhaps.
And then there was tennis, and GTV and Greaves ina good mood, and the
car sounding awful and my law case coming up and Tabatha eating lots
of tinned rubbish and me missing yourotten...missing your otten, did
n't know you had one)   etc.......goodnight darling,

"I took this time to think what nature meant,
          When this mixt thing into the world it sent,
              So very wise yet so impertinent."
Have you met Rockester....... on the other side he says
             cpme back quickly,and I love you,

Chenlasworth

Then let our flaming hearts be joyn'd
While in that sacred fire;
E'er thou prove false, or I unkind
Together both expire."

Love , of husband, lover, boy, besotted
wretch close, close friend.

Along with Factory, Tony continued with his weekly 'What's On' show on *Granada Reports*, and he was able to feature chosen bands on air. Magazine released their second album *Secondhand Daylight* in late March 1979, and on Monday 19 March, according to Howard's pocket diary, they performed 'Rhythm Of Cruelty', and 'Permafrost' on Tony's Granada show. It felt as if there was a message to me in some of his words, such as those referring to loving someone 'when the devil is blind', and telling someone they've 'got it coming all the way' to them.

This letter from Tony wasn't dated, and I struggled to place it but decided it may have been sent in 1979 after Tony had met with Howard for this 'What's On' show in March. At that point my affair with Howard was definitely over; it was only a mad night under the influence of LSD in May that made me briefly imagine otherwise. The warmth in the letter suggests it could instead have been sent before the affair and after the *B'Dum B'Dum* gig, but I'm inclined to think not.

Charlesworth

Tuesday night, very late

Nice to talk to you; you sounded very down. I think I understand. So many people are strangers, even people you love. Vonnegut calls it your 'karass', all those people you are tied to by family, job, situation, even tenderness, BUT not your people; maybe you don't meet your people except very occasionally. To me, this silly absence is the lack of one of the few non-strangers I've ever met; I knew you weren't a stranger that first night on the hillside in Disley. Funny how clear you can see from 200 miles. Funny also; you on the phone, and not at home and then me with Howard, ...didn't feel I could really get to know him, or rather didn't feel any desire to get to know, got those "oh he's just from another planet like all the rest shrugs" on me. My infatuation waned somewhat. He's still lovely but he takes himself very seriously and seems, at least he did tonight, to lack wisdom. We didn't talk much of my 'wife' except to say you didn't like the cap; he was a little offended but it was one of the more pleasant interludes. I like him, just don't feel any strong desire for knowledge of him. Come back and rekindle my appetite with yours, perhaps. And then there was tennis, and GTV and Greaves in a good mood, and the car sounding awful and my law case coming up and Tabitha eating lots of tinned rubbish and me missing you rotten....missing your otten, didn't know you had one) etc.......goodnight darling,

"I took this time to think what nature meant,
When this mix thing into the world it sent,
So very wise yet so impertinent."

Have you met Rochester.......on the other side he says

come back quickly, and I love you,

Then let our flaming hearts be join'd

While in that sacred fire;

E'er thou prove false, or I unkind

Together both expire."

Love, of a husband, lover, boy, a besotted wretch a close, close friend.

So, all was not lost. Yet.

The letter suggests Tony had come to terms with the affair (assuming it was sent after my confession to him), and that perhaps he felt we were now even. Odd that Tony describes his own infatuation with Howard. It's almost as if he'd empathised with mine.

I don't remember it, but I must have gone away for a short while. Tony describes it as a 'silly absence'. I was probably staying with my parents, or was away with them, and likely having difficulties with my dad. I'd already judged my father, found him guilty and rejected him because of the awful way he treated my mother. I rarely spoke to him but occasionally told him what I thought, which would always cause ructions. This might explain Tony's observations in the letter about 'karass' – Kurt Vonnegut's word for people you are tied to, such as by family, 'But not your people'.

'Karass' is taken from Vonnegut's novel *Cat's Cradle*. Tony suggests it refers to people you feel related to because of some kind of contemporary association rather than the unmistakeable closeness felt with one of your own. I'm not entirely sure this is the exact way that Vonnegut meant it, as I understand that 'karass' is a genuine spiritual linkage, whereas a false 'karass', or 'granfalloon' as Vonnegut calls it, is more of an association that, despite a shared purpose, is actually much more meaningless. Tony thought that he and I belonged, that we were never strangers, even on our very first meeting. There is truth to this. To this day I feel the loss of him; I felt it even while he was alive, never mind dead, and know with certainty he was one of MY people, even if we couldn't hack it and I sometimes hated him. In which case, perhaps my dad was one of MY people too.

The phrase 'So It Goes', the name for Tony's TV show, was also lifted from Kurt Vonnegut, his book *Slaughterhouse-Five*. There the quote is used every time someone dies; it suggests that life goes on and that's just the way the cookie crumbles. Perhaps it helps us to face death (although the phrase is not as flippant as it sounds, since there is still a sadness that cannot be spoken of). Tony was always more matter of fact about death than I ever was, more accepting of it. He showed huge dignity in his own death. Before he ever became ill he was often fond of quoting *Hamlet*, Shakespeare's most important work in his view, speaking about destiny and letting things be, placing particular emphasis on the words: 'the readiness is all'. Tony waxed lyrical before his cancer diagnosis, saying he'd be ready to die because he'd had such a wonderful life. When the cancer diagnosis came he realised he'd been presumptuous thinking that way, because he didn't feel in the least bit ready after all. Hamlet's quote comes in the final act when Horatio fails to persuade him not to duel with Laertes. Hamlet believes in an immutable plan and is accepting of his fate. He dies in the duel.

'There's a special providence in the fall of a sparrow. If it be now, 'tis not to come. If it be not to come, it will be now. If it be not now, yet it will come—the readiness is all. Since no man of aught he leaves knows, what is 't to leave betimes? Let be.'[4]

Tony mentions GTV (Granada) in the letter and refers to being with 'Greaves'. Bob Greaves was Tony's usual co-presenter on *Granada Reports*. The show went out every evening and the two shared a lovely camaraderie. For instance, when Tony put Joy Division on 'What's On', Greaves, obviously unaware of the dubious significance of the group's name, remarked: 'They were called Warsaw once, but Joy Division, I think, has a nicer ring to it and we hope that we're launching them on a real joyride as we have before with many others, haven't we, Tony? Yes'.

Howard had worn a flat cap for his live reunion appearance with Buzzcocks at the Lesser Free Trade Hall in 1978, two years after their original show there. This was featured in the *B'Dum B'Dum* documentary, aired on Granada later on and watched by Tony and me at home subsequently. Despite my earlier devotion to Howard, Tony had given him the one negative criticism I'd made of his appearance – and yet this was one of the more 'pleasant interludes'. Perhaps it diffused some of the tension. Howard wore a flat cap on other occasions, and he sent me evidence of him wearing one in May 1979.

Tony asks in this letter if I've met Rochester, aka the Earl of Rochester, John Wilmot, forgetting that Rochester has been quoted in three consecutive letters prior to the last one. The first quote is taken from 'A Letter from Artemesia in the Town to Chloe in the Country', and it appears the correct reading is 'she' sent, not 'it'.

Tony had the kind of brain that remembered whole poems, but he surely couldn't have remembered this extremely long one. He doubtless knew what it was about, which is more than I can admit to. The second quote comes from 'Song', a dialogue between a nymph and a shepherd. The last line speaks volumes. Although the letter suggests a reprieve, a hope of reconciliation, sadly we were, both of us, false and unkind.

'E'er thou prove false, or I unkind, Together both expire.'

In the autumn of 1979, there were two 7-inch single releases on Factory: The

---

4 *Hamlet,* William Shakespeare, Act 5, Scene 2.

Howard in a flat cap May 1979

Distractions' 'Time Goes By So Slow' and Joy Division's 'Transmission'. The Distractions had previously released the EP *You're Not Going Out Dressed Like That* on TJM Records, run by Tony Davidson. Davidson owned TJM Studios on Little Peter Street, almost opposite where Tony lived in a loft apartment. TJM held both recording and rehearsal spaces but was better known to me as the place where Joy Division rehearsed, and where the video for 'Love Will Tear Us Apart' was filmed. Tony felt sure that 'Transmission' was a hit and had 10,000 copies of it pressed, many of which were piled up in the Factory office (aka Alan's flat) for years to come. His instinct was correct but off the mark. He even drove to London and arranged a plugger for the track, but Martin Hannett objected to the treatment of music as a commodity (Factory did use pluggers later on). Although it was a kind of catchy song, with its 'dance, dance to the radio' refrain, Joy Division weren't exactly a pop band to be marketed as such. Their appeal, like a fine whisky, was destined to take longer to mature.

As the year drew to a close, Joy Division recorded the song that many, including me, think was their finest: 'Atmosphere'. In the name of economy, the session took place at a sixteen-track studio, Cargo in Rochdale. I believe this was *the* song – not 'Love Will Tear Us Apart' – that characterised the best that the guys between them could produce. It had meaning, it had feeling. The sound effects were subtly beautiful especially given Hannett's genius in using the bells (or chimes). Due to some sort of argument between Tony and the studio owner, there were only a few hours for mixing but guitarist Bernard

Sumner thought Martin did some of his best stuff when he had to work quickly. Ian's lyrics were melancholic and deep, particularly with hindsight, 'don't walk away in silence,' something that he did himself. The record came out on a French independent label called Sordide Sentimental and copies of the record were very limited (unlike 'Transmission'). After Ian's death, the track was released as a 12-inch.

Nineteen eighty opened with the release of ACR's debut album *The Graveyard and the Ballroom* (FAC 16). It was called this because one side had tracks recorded at Graveyard Studios in Prestwich (on a four-track, believe it or not) and a live session at London's Electric Ballroom on the other. There was prescience in the title, given the themes swirling around and what was to come. The album, unusually, was on cassette, housed in different coloured plastic pouches (orange, blue, red etc,) and with slightly different designs. The idea was that the pouch resembled a clutch bag that one might take to a ballroom. It was as if Tony was envisioning the collectability of Factory product. Certainly, the packaging was a novelty and I remember we were all pleased with the result.

The contents were a huge improvement from those early days in the rehearsal room. Produced by Martin Hannett, here were some of ACR's best tracks, such as 'Flight'.

That January also saw a release from Tony's other management project – the debut album by The Durutti Column entitled *The Return of The Durutti Column,* named after a four-page Situationist comic by André Bertrand. One of the comic strips was a sticker that had been given away with *A Factory Sample* featuring two cowboys. Tony chose to put the record in a sandpaper sleeve. The inspiration came from a book from 1959 called *Memoires* that was published with a sandpaper sleeve designed to destroy the books around it. This record sleeve was, of course, designed to ruin the record covers next to it.

Joy Division agreed to spend a day in Alan's living room for a glueing session. As well as a small financial incentive (£5) they were provided with a porn video to keep them

ACR's debut album (on cassette and in pouch), *The Graveyard and the Ballroom.*

entertained. Tony called round and saw Ian glueing away at the desk, while the others were sitting on the sofa watching the porn. He thought it would make an amusing scene in a film as there was white glue all over their hands and the desk.

The Return of The Durutti Column consists mainly of Vini's guitar and some clever sound effects from Martin. It wasn't exactly revolutionary (other than the sleeve), but Vini's guitar sounds lyrical; if you ever hear his guitar-playing, you immediately know it's him, it's such a distinctive sound. 'Sketch for Summer' was the main track on there and it opens with bird sounds that Martin found quite by accident while experimenting with some gadget or other. Initial copies of the album came with a free flexi disc – a clever marketing spin if ever there was one. People love getting things for 'free'. However, I should think both sides of the Flexi necessitated taking as many drugs as Martin did to fully appreciate the weird sound effects.

Vini appeared to be a sweet soul then, and he seemed to fall in love every five minutes: there are three tracks on there dedicated to different girls. He worshipped Tony and so by default, to a degree, me as well (back then). His uncertain health was a constant issue and would deteriorate further with age. Tosh remembered that Vini would send in sick notes for rehearsals with The Nosebleeds in advance – 'Sorry I can't make it on Thursday, as I think I'm going to be ill.'

In March, Tony and I went down to Britannia Row studios in Islington, North London, to check out the recording of Joy Division's second album, *Closer*. The dynamic between the band and Martin had altered and it wasn't just Tony, me and Martin sitting cosily in studio anymore. The band were now being taken more seriously – Martin was still completely in his element but was giving the group more sway in the studio. Ian Curtis had fallen in love with Annik Honoré, a cultured and dignified girl from Belgium, and they were together during the recording in London. Annik was a music enthusiast and the only one amongst us all to raise concern over and recognise the impending doom within Ian's lyrics. She'd met Ian while interviewing the band for a Belgian music fanzine and, as a promoter of bands, she later arranged for Joy Division to play a gig at La Raffinerie du Plan K on 16 October, 1979 in Brussels. After his death she was co-founder of record labels Les Disques Du Crepuscule and Factory Benelux and also promoted the band Front 242.

Ian really loved Annik, yet she has often been vilified and wrongly depicted as a marriage-wrecking lover. Annik was Ian's comforter, supporter and muse in terms of his music. All would have been well except that Ian had married very young at 19 and fathered a daughter not that long afterwards. Ian's letters to Annik, copies of which she gave to me when I was researching Ian's life for the book *Torn Apart*, reveal his insistence that his marriage was over or Annik would certainly have walked away. However, not long before his death, Annik received a phone call from Ian's wife, Debbie. Annik: 'She was screaming insults in my ear. Never had anyone spoken to me like that in my whole life. I felt so bad.'

Annik told me she hadn't realised someone was getting hurt from her relationship with Ian and, when she'd asked him about his wife, he'd say it was something from his previous life as a youngster and now he was a different person, and it was no longer what he wanted. She tried to walk away, but a typical example of the words in Ian's letters to Annik followed this phone call: 'Please do not think you are a pressure on me. I would die if I didn't speak or hear from you. Everyone seems to have everything wrong and they've been told so many times before. I have no choice to make, everything was coming to an end at home and the only thing was when it would actually end and whether I should go before. As it is, things have now finished.'

Unfortunately, it wasn't so simple; Ian had become an epileptic (his first seizure followed a gig with Joy Division in December 1978), he was struggling to cope with the demands of being on the road, he had a baby daughter, and he loved someone other than her mother. Tragically, what was actually about to 'finish' was not his marriage, but his life.

Ian made a suicide attempt in April 1980. We listened to the finished album on cassette in the car on the way to visit him in hospital in Macclesfield. I thought how powerful it sounded. I couldn't imagine anyone who'd been involved in such a creation could possibly want to die. At my suggestion, thinking he might need time away from everything, Ian came to stay with us and spent a week alone with me while Tony was largely absent. Ian was terribly depressed, and it was difficult for me, particularly as the powers that be – Tony and Rob – made it a rule that Ian was to have no visitors at all. I did my best, making meals, playing records, but he never moved from sitting on the floor with his feet under our low table, chain smoking. By the end of the week, I felt acutely depressed myself. Ian realised this on his last day with us; it was Saturday, and he must have overheard me telling Tony how I felt and complaining that no one was doing anything. I was out of my depth. Ian left our house immediately and went to stay with Bernard Sumner, and then, towards the end, he was at his mother's house. The day he died he'd received divorce papers from Debbie and had gone to their house in Macclesfield to speak with her.

The death of Ian in May 1980, six weeks after the week I spent with him, was a tragedy beyond our imagining. I suspect all of us in Ian's orbit were profoundly affected by his suicide in ways that we weren't necessarily conscious of. Annik's suffering however, was on a totally different level; she was utterly lost in grief. She also stayed with us, coincidentally for the same number of days as Ian, immediately following his death. I took this photograph of Tony and her during that time. Her sorrowful face, with tears in her eyes, isn't visible but Tony's expression speaks volumes. He looks shocked, sad and older than his thirty years. Although forever changed by her love for Ian, Annik would eventually pick up the pieces of her life and her vital enthusiasm for music which, like

her grief, continued to know no bounds.

Tony, indomitably, carried on with his usual enthusiasm and any grief he felt, he didn't actively show. I thought Factory had let Ian down and had, therefore, failed miserably, and I felt a deep disappointment that Tony, unlike me, appeared to carry no guilt over Ian's death. I was wrong to judge him perhaps, he'd only helped Ian to achieve the very thing he was driven to do. I was, however, upset that Tony and Rob had left Ian and me alone that week, and angry that the machinery of the record company had put the promotion of Joy Division, with endless gigs, before Ian's health when he was clearly not well. My own guilt went deeper than any of that though. Tony cheerfully continued to champion Ian's group and product which almost felt sacrilegious to me – I wanted the record to be put away for a lengthy period of mourning.

And yet, reading Tony's words in the house-for-sale letter on p.134, having a more sensitive appreciation of his words than I was capable of then, I can decipher that he may have been immersed in a hidden grief. There are lines in this letter in which it can be detected, especially in phrases like, 'it's too soon to talk of futures … the future and the past don't really exist'. Men do generally tend to shut down emotionally more than women, and it's likely that Tony either wasn't consciously aware of the depth of his grief or chose not to show it. It took me several years to process my own, and I'm affected by it to this day. I had to walk out of a performance of a play about Joy Division called *New Dawn Fades* quite recently because I couldn't bear the audience laughing and seeing the Joy Division story as entertainment.

Tony told me he had a 'delayed reaction' to his grief over Ian. It was about a year or

Courtesy of Annik Honoré

two later when what had happened truly hit him, and he suddenly cracked and began crying. He said the same thing occurred to Martin Hannett: that he came round to Tony's house one night almost five years later, and openly wept. I suspect Martin had, at least subconsciously, been immediately affected as he became much more self-destructive following Ian's death. Bernard thought that Martin was never the same again.

Closer was one of the most important albums Factory ever produced. I never imagined then that it would continue to be listened to over forty years later. Yet, although I loved both of Joy Division's albums while Ian was alive, I discovered it was too painful to listen to them after his death. This was a pity because I stopped believing in and supporting Factory in the same way.

Tony, meanwhile, was positively gung-ho with his usual enthusiasm. Annik had taken the above photo of Tony working away, sitting on the floor of the living room in Alan Erasmus's flat, and it accurately reflects how he was. She gave me the original photograph before her own death in 2014.

Sadly, yet unsurprisingly, our marriage deteriorated further in 1980, with both of our respective escapades and my newfound antagonism to Factory. He continued to demand his right to another lover, and I had a continual unease with no real idea of what he was up to or who he was seeing. As a result, my imagination ran riot when his behaviour might have been entirely innocent. But his hours at home were few, and I do remember him talking about a woman he'd slept with, he even went into some detail about the Sellotape she had wrapped around her breasts. The fact that it had been a bizarre one-night stand didn't console me – in some ways it felt worse than if he'd had some feeling for her. In truth, I was relieved: she wasn't a threat. But he'd laid out his stall – he was free to sleep with whomever he wanted.

Because of his attitude I didn't see why I should continue to remain faithful to him, and besides, I was lonely. During a trip Tony took abroad in 1980, and following yet more absences from one another, I'd started working with a small group of friends in forming the Beach Club. The idea was to create a space showing films as well as bands and somewhere people could go now that the Factory Friday nights had ceased. Richard Boon headed up meetings at the New Hormones office on Newton Street, Manchester, where decisions were made before

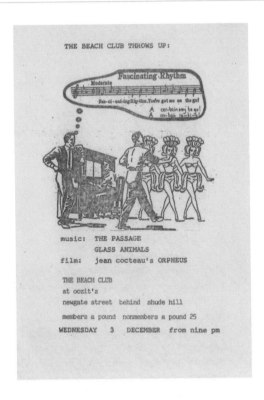

we launched the weekly nights in April. The venue was seedy but worked well, being on different floors for the different activities.

The slogan was another Situationist reference: 'under the pavement, the beach'.

The remaining Joy Division boys had evolved into a new group – New Order – and they played their first gig without Ian at the Beach Club on 29th July 1980. It was disappointing as they didn't sound great and they were taking turns at being the lead singer, which was painful to watch without Ian. I thought perhaps it was therapeutic for them, and it probably was. They had to either pick up the pieces and find a way forward or give up entirely. Ian had told me he'd foreseen, while standing in the wings at the Bury gig after his earlier suicide attempt, that the band would carry on and prosper without him. I thought it would all fizzle out. Ian knew. That Bury gig, held in April 1980 on the very day Ian left hospital, ended in a riot as belligerent members of the audience were annoyed that, due to his delicate health, he'd been replaced on vocals for most of it. I ended up taking one of the roadies to A&E.

Tony didn't seem all that interested in the Beach Club and was rarely present. It was there that I met John Scott, as mentioned in Tony's next letter, and Tony did give me daggers when he once happened to walk in and saw me with John. John was a good companion and friend during those days of isolation from Tony (the Cold War, you could call it). In hindsight, while it felt justified to me, I made the mistake of not hiding

FACTORY RECORDS
86 Palatine Road, Manchester 20.
Telephone 061-434 3876

August 5 '80

Lindsay,

Such appropriate notepaper....since for so many reasons, I need to sell 45, Town lane, and since that means being present to show Sutton's guests round, we need to make a few plans for the next few weeks. I feel strongly that a separation, of at least two weeks is vital, for you to find what you want, for me to also find out but more just to keep sane. I don't think you have really understood the nature of my pain, but at least understand that to lie night after night beside a woman who wants another and not you, to lie there waiting for that day when she no longer wants him but wants you....night after awful night, that (and I went through it once before in 1971) is no fun...in fact I find it completely unsupportable...so if you don't mind we won't do it. Instead let's sort out this minimum two week caesura. I'M fine here but will need to spend next week at the house of Suttons. For all I know you may have already moved out, found a flat, or whatever; if you have, fine. If not then could you arrange to move to your Mum's for a week beginning this Sunday morning. I'll stay for the week and move back here on Sunday 17th August, though by that time two weeks will have elapsed and it may or not be time for us to talk to each other in person. Since the arrangements above are simple and necessary, we really need no more communication as long as everything goes as planned. If you have problems moving out on Sunday then you'll have to let me know; as I in turn will let Sutton's know by the end of the week that I'm available for appts.

Since we're ¼ down the page let us remove any unneccessary suffering (you see how I still refuse to accept Karma -) concerning your feelings about my trip to les Belgiques. I did not, surprise-surprise, have any form of physical contact with Kate, save a final quikkiss at the airport. The reasons are three-fold. a) She has so many boyfriends; and you know how I hate to be one of the crowd. b) She is one of those women who know they can have any man they want... .....like someone else we know...and that makes her very very dangerous...like someone else........so she is best observed from behind bolted gates of non-desire. c) Most specifically, our New York relationship was entirely non-carnal above all out of FEAR, SHYNESS, AND ROMANTICISM most of all. To have suddenly changed at this weekend would obviously have been nothing to do with me or Kate, but almost entirely due to John S. and Lindsay R. To have fallen from the heights of pure and distant emotion to a sordid revenge act would really have been what northerners used to call a "poor do".

VAT. No. 305 630196 Reg. No. 2340540
A.Erasmus, R.Gretton, M.Hannett, P.Savile, A.Wilson

I don't really know why I went through all that...I don'tv really feel all
that much pity for you, in fact for all I know you may be having a fine time
and already 'turned to your next set of lives'.
Anyway we can talk on the 16th or 17th. Even that ssems almost too soon to
to talk of futures...in such a landscape I seem only able to relate to today..
when the other two dimensions seem so stocked full of potential pain. Anyway,
as we all know the future and the past don't really exist...etc etc....
so if you could make the necessary arrangements for next week, and if possible
for the sake of the present emptiness refrain from any contact or communication,
etc etc....I'd be very grateful.
Yours,
Tony.

VAT No. 305 6301 96   Reg No. 2340540
A.Erasmus, R.Gretton, M.Hannett, P.Savile, A.Wilson

our relationship. We met mainly in pubs, as John liked to drink. John hung out at Rabid headquarters in Withington, being their resident guitarist – playing with Jilted John and John Cooper Clarke, for example. Tosh Ryan told me he remembered John regularly and mysteriously running off. They all got curious one day when John didn't even stay for the sandwiches they'd just ordered. Bernard Kelly, aka Gordon (the Moron), who appeared on the single 'Jilted John' (Gordon being the 'moron' who Julie ditches John for), then announced to the assembled that he'd seen John Scott sitting in The Red Lion pub down the road. He said, 'He's with Wilson's Mrs,' to which they all exclaimed, 'Oooooh….' I didn't see why I should hide seeing John: Tony had been very open about his right to see another woman. But, to this day, I feel somewhat ashamed that I wasn't, at the least, more discreet. I misguidedly still saw honour in playing the 'honesty' card but perhaps there was revenge in it too – if Tony was flaunting his right to another then why shouldn't I do the same?

Things had really hit a low point, as shown by the next letter from Tony. Objectively, when he wrote it, he was trying to address the state of our marriage, but there is a sense of further monumental loss hanging over everything. Loss of Ian, loss of our fidelity, loss of our home, and the loss of a foreseeable future together.

86 Palatine Road

August 5, '80

Lindsay,

Such appropriate notepaper….since for so many reasons, I need to sell 45, Town Lane, and since that means being present to show Sutton's guests round, we need to make a few plans for the next few weeks. I feel strongly that a separation of at least two weeks is vital, for you to find what you want, for me to also find out but more just to keep sane. I don't think you have really understood the nature of my pain, but at least understand that to lie night after night beside a woman who wants another and not you, to lie there waiting for that day when she no longer wants him but wants you….night after awful night, that (and I went through it once before in 1971) is no fun…. in fact I find it completely unsupportable….so if you don't mind we won't do it. Instead let's sort out this minimum two week caesura. I'm fine here but will need to spend next week at the house of Suttons. For all I know you may have already moved out, found a flat, or whatever; if you have, fine. If not then could you arrange to move to your mum's for a week beginning this Sunday morning. I'll stay for the week and move back here on Sunday 17thAugust, though by that time two weeks will have elapsed and it may or not be time for us to talk to each other in person. Since the arrangements above are simple and necessary, we really need no more communication as long as everything goes as planned. If you have problems moving out on Sunday then you'll have to let me know; as I in turn will let Sutton's know by the end of the week that I'm available for appts.

Since we're 3/4 down the page let us remove any unnecessary suffering (you see how I still refuse to accept Karma -) concerning your feelings about my trip to les Belgiques. I did not, surprise-surprise, have any form of physical contact with Kate, save a final quick kiss at the airport. The reasons are threefold. a) She has so many boyfriends; and you know how I hate to be one of the crowd. b) She is one of those women who know they can have any man they want.......like someone else we know.....and that makes her very dangerous......like someone else......so she is best observed from behind bolted gates of non-desire. c) Most specifically, our New York relationship was entirely non-carnal, above all out of FEAR, SHYNESS, AND ROMANTICISM most of all. To have suddenly changed at this weekend would obviously have been nothing to do with me or Kate but almost entirely due to John S. and Lindsay R. To have fallen from the heights of pure and distant emotion to a sordid revenge act would really have been what northerners used to call a "poor do".

I don't really know why I went through all that....I don't really feel all that much pity for you, in fact for all I know you may be having a fine time and already 'turned to your next set of lives'. Anyway we can talk on the 16th or 17th. Even that seems almost too soon to talk of futures.....in such a landscape I seem only able to relate to today...when the other two dimensions seem so stocked full of potential pain. Anyway, as we all know the future and the past don't really exist....etc.....etc.....so if you could make the necessary arrangements for next week, and if possible for the sake of the present emptiness refrain from any contact or communication, etc..etc.....I'd be very grateful.

Yours,

Tony.

Harsh words from Tony. I don't recall him sleeping at Alan's flat for very long, even though he wrote this while staying there. He'd been spending a big portion of his free time there whether he slept there or not. I can understand in some ways – Alan would have been supporting him, whereas I was critical and resentful. Rather than sympathise with the pain he says he was enduring, I thought Tony was deliberately driving a wedge between us.

The letter carried something of a threat and zero affection. It wasn't, 'WE need to sell the house,' it was Tony stating his own wish to sell it and asking me to move out while he did it, probably because he didn't trust me to handle the sale of 'his' house. I'd been deeply hurt when Tony came home and told me he'd bought a house in Didsbury that he'd seen with Alan. He even had the gall to call it a 'great family house'. I swore I'd never live in it and never did, even if it is worth a million now. Then, he mentions another potential lover (Kate) whom I knew he was quite seriously interested in, but the crime, as ever, was all my own. Tony didn't think I'd be bothered when he visited her in Belgium and imagines he is exonerated because nothing physical took place (then). It was wrong of me though to see John in public places, yet I'd wanted to demonstrate that freedom goes both ways. But what really drove Tony to the point of revenge, even if he did consider revenge a 'poor do', was my rejection of him in the bedroom.

Although Tony is asking for a separation, deep down it wasn't really what either of us wanted. I was living at Town Lane, certainly hadn't moved out as he suggested, nor was I having fun. His long absences from our house – days and nights – made me feel worse than lonely. There was no peace because it carried with it a rejection, and a judgement to the point of condemnation. He wanted sex but did he even want my company? And then, admittedly, there was my own jealousy. Who was he with that he liked better than me? Be they female or male now made no difference – I wasn't comforted if it was with Alan or Rob or anyone – it still felt like a rejection of me. I'd willingly accepted the long and antisocial hours of his day/evening job working at Granada, but his other activities, running around with musicians, were not only entirely voluntary, but they frequently covered the night shift. This left very little over.

Tony refers in the letter to his 'refusal to accept karma' and 'the next set of lives.' Years later he told me that my disappointments with men were the karmic result of the disappointments I'd given out to them. Bearing in mind his treatment of many women, I wonder now why he didn't apply this to himself. Perhaps, silently, he did.

I do remember one night, when he had cancer but was optimistic about beating it, he said something concerning God. He said it is easier to explain the miracle of this amazing world, and the life sustained upon it, with a belief in God than without one. On another occasion at his apartment, when his illness was more advanced, he wanted me to find just the one package, amongst many, that contained a book about Jesus. I said, 'What do you want that for? You're not religious'. 'I fucking am now', he replied.

I also caught him reading *The Tibetan Book of Living and Dying* around a similar time. Tony was friendly with Patrick Gaffney when they were both at Cambridge University and Patrick was the co-editor of this book, written by Sogyal Rinpoche and published in 1992. Tony's reactions surprised me, as he'd always struck me as disinterested in this kind of thing. He'd given me the impression Buddhism was my area, not his. In fact, I was so astonished that I took a photo of him reading this. However it was 2007, before iPhones, and the photo is unfortunately very poor quality.

The last time I ever saw Tony alive, just hours before his death, I told him I felt sure that we'd known each other before this lifetime and felt equally sure that we'd meet again. He rolled his eyes and shook his head in disbelief. At that point, understandably, perhaps he believed in nothing.

CHAPTER 6
To Broadway (Or Not)

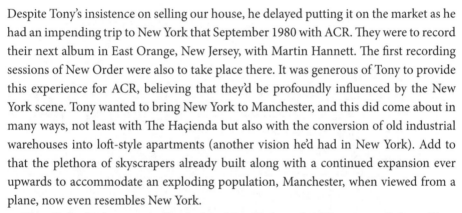

Despite Tony's insistence on selling our house, he delayed putting it on the market as he had an impending trip to New York that September 1980 with ACR. They were to record their next album in East Orange, New Jersey, with Martin Hannett. The first recording sessions of New Order were also to take place there. It was generous of Tony to provide this experience for ACR, believing that they'd be profoundly influenced by the New York scene. Tony wanted to bring New York to Manchester, and this did come about in many ways, not least with The Haçienda but also with the conversion of old industrial warehouses into loft-style apartments (another vision he'd had in New York). Add to that the plethora of skyscrapers already built along with a continued expansion ever upwards to accommodate an exploding population, Manchester, when viewed from a plane, now even resembles New York.

New Order had some gigs booked in New York, and ACR supported them. Tony mentions one at Tier 3 in the next letter, which was in the Tribeca neighbourhood of lower Manhattan. As well as Tier 3, the two bands played at the famous Hurrah nightclub at 62nd and Broadway.

Music promoter Ruth Polsky was the booking agent for Hurrah, as well as several other well-known venues, including Danceteria. Ruth had arranged Joy Division's North American tour for May 1980, which sadly never took place as Ian died the day before the group were due to fly there. However, Ruth's connections with booking Factory bands, especially New Order, continued. Her life was tragically cut short in 1986; she was standing outside the Limelight Club in New York when a car hit a yellow cab which spun out of control, pinning her against a wall. She was killed instantly, aged just 32. New Order played a benefit for her that year – it was the first time they'd performed 'Atmosphere' since Joy Division.

Danceteria was less of a punk club than Hurrah: true to its name, it was more about dancing. The New York experience, which would be repeated two years later, proved extremely influential to both bands but particularly New Order. The inspiration for

FACTORY RECORDS
86 Palatine Road, Manchester 20.
Telephone 061-434 3876

Sep 19/20
5.00 am
112, Hudson St
NYC 10013

To my wife,
Well - you didn't come - as I waited in the car for
Martin to come out of the terminal - this blue sunny
afternoon - of course I was hoping. Funny how love
disturbs even my immaculate sense of reason. It
should have been obvious - it is/was, but for the
frail heart reason never beats down the dreams. I
hate the way I can't shake my obsession with you.
If my leg hurt as much as my heart (or pride or desire)
it would be reasonable to cut it off. And I
could do that - anything seems within my power
except you - or rather my thralldom to all those
stupid, infantile, overpowering things like desire,
jealousy, loss - of a woman.
If I push myself - crawl across the glasses broken
on the floor - I can see what my life is - the boys
arrive - they ask if I'm writing a script - "your
bloody life is a script" - and the plot. Great
achievements in the public eye at a price - you are
the price - I pay in every moment of loving care you
give to your other men.
In Tier 3 tonight - our local neighbourhood club - a
lovely-small, lively little place - sitting round the
table upstairs - Hannett, Gretton, O'Hara and Wilson
we went thru the truth agains - 20 minutes bitching
about Saville - oh it was like being at home - and then

VAT. No. 305 6301 96 Reg. No. 2340540
A. Erasmus, R. Gretton, M. Hannett, P. Saville, A. Wilson

FACTORY RECORDS
86 Palatine Road, Manchester 20.
Telephone 061-434 3876

Gretton, in that "cruel honesty" style so beloved of my mother, made a fine jest which thankfully I can't remember about my wife and another man, the conversation switched to the subject of John Scott and for ten minutes I laughed with gay ease and inside just held back the bile. A funny old night.

If I push myself — and it gets harder, I know that the reason you couldn't come was that adultery has not gone out of style and you were doing me the kindness of sparing me those horrendous question and answer sessions here in my beloved Manhattan. For that small mercy, my love, I am most grateful.

And me — well not for want of hoping — praying (apart from the fumbling encounter with Julie's flannelette night shirt 3 months ago — in fact including that — I really can't remember what proper sexuality is. You know I can't even remember what it feels like. And the jealousy. But looking back I seem fated to be a monk I think — particularly N. York. On my first night here in June 73 I slept with Hilary — it was a disaster — I don't remember why — after that we didn't touch — and my 2nd + 3rd times here — no sex — and my 4th time — Katy and that platonic emptiness — and this time — just emptiness. Heigh Ho.

Still — now I can write to you — which I like — away from the visuals — easier to express — think through — news — well, all O.K. I suppose — Rates area all hit

VAT. No. 305 6301 96   Reg No. 2340540
A. Erasmus, R. Gretton, M. Hannett, P. Saville, A. Wilson

FACTORY RECORDS
86 Palatine Road, Manchester 20.
Telephone 061-434 3876

in town — the loft is minimal and absolutely perfect — we have a super 9 seater Station Wagon, and with all the team now here - except your good self — it seems like some bizarre idea of an L-S.D. crazed Billy Butlin. For me it's fairly constant work. Meetings — arrangements — driving — electrician (Pink Floyd's transformer — incredibly big — immovable - a story in itself) daddy + non-daddy (when I get pissed off with them) to the boys. Funny — I have no idea what they think of it. Perhaps neither do they. Like in a dream you don't stop to think — you hang in to the story with all its twists and weird changes — until you wake — maybe their reactions can be analysed after return.

And after my return — oh, well, the thorn bedecked merry go round of my life with you will have one or two more painful turns to go — even if we fall off before Christmas. But I can't bear to think of it. Much more of my "life with a woman prone to illicit affairs" could truly finish off my habitual 'joie de vivre'.

I must preserve my panache/nobility though all else may/will crumble.

Yours faithfully

Tony

VAT. No. 305 6301 96   Reg. No. 2340540
A. Erasmus, R. Gretton, M. Hannett, P. Saville, A. Wilson

The Haçienda would also spring from there; I remember Tony telling me at the time that Danceteria was the kind of club that Manchester needed. The concept of Danceteria and Hurrah was almost a blueprint for The Haçienda design, although it would only be after five years of failing as a live venue that The Haçienda would find its niche as a DJ and dance nightclub.

And so, Tony went off to New York in 1980, leaving me very unsure as to the status of our marriage. He packed his bags and was somewhat cold and aloof. Then I received the following letter (admittedly rather warmer than the last). Some women may like being addressed or referred to as 'my wife' but I disliked it; I felt it implied a kind of ownership or possession rather than affection.

Sep 19/20 (1980)

5.00 am

112, Hudson St

NYC 10013

To my wife, Well – you didn't come – as I waited in the car for Martin to come out of the terminal – this blue sunny afternoon – of course I was hoping. Funny how love disturbs even my immaculate sense of reason. It should have been obvious – it is/was, but for the frail heart reason never beats down the dreams. I hate the way I can't shake my obsession with you. If my leg hurt as much as my heart (or pride or desire) it would be reasonable to cut if off. And I could do that – anything seems within my power except you – or rather my thraldom to all those stupid, infantile, overpowering things like desire, jealousy, loss – of a woman.

If I push myself – crawl across the glasses broken on the floor – I can see what life is – the boys arrive – they ask if I am writing a script – "your bloody life is a script" – and the plot. Great achievements in the public eye at a price – you are the price – I pay in every moment of loving care you give to your other man.

In Tier 3 tonight – our local neighbourhood club – a lovely, small, lively little place – sitting round the table upstairs – Hannett, Gretton, O'Hara and Wilson, we went through the twin agonies – 20 minutes bitching about Saville – oh it was like being at home – and then Gretton in that "cruel honesty" style so beloved of my mother, made a fine jest which thankfully I can't remember about my wife and another man, the conversation switched to the subject of John Scott and for ten minutes I laughed with gay remorse and inside just held back the bile. A funny old night. If I push myself – and it gets harder, I know that the reason you couldn't come across was that adultery has not gone out of style and you were doing me the kindness of sparing me those horrendous question and answer sessions here in my beloved Manhattan. For that small mercy, my love, I am most grateful.

And me – well, not for want of hoping – praying (apart from the fumbling encounter with Julie's flannelette night shirt 3 months ago – in fact including that – I really can't remember what proper sexuality is.) You know I can't even remember what it feels like. And the jealousy. But looking back I am fated to be a monk I think – particularly in N.York. On my first night here in June '73 I slept with Hilary – it was a disaster – I don't remember why – after that we didn't touch – and my 2nd and 3rd times here – no sex – and my 4th time – Katy and that platonic emptiness – and this time – just emptiness. Heigh Ho.

Still, now I can write to you – which I like – away from the visuals – easier to express – think through – news – well, all O.K. I suppose – Ratio overall hit in town – the loft is minimal and absolutely perfect – we have a super 9 seater Station Wagon, and with all the team now here – except your good self – it seems like some bizarre idea of an L.S.D. crazed Billy Butlin. For me it is fairly constant work. Meetings – arrangements – driving – electrician (Pink Floyd's transformer – incredibly big – immovable – a story in itself) daddy and non-daddy (when I get pissed off with them) to the boys. Funny – I have no idea what they think of it. Perhaps neither do they. Like in a dream you don't stop to think – you hang in to the story with all its twists and weird changes – until you wake – maybe their reactions can be analysed after return. And after my return – oh, well, the thorn bedecked merry go round of my life with you will have one or two more painful turns to go – even if we fall off before Christmas. But I can't bear to think of it. Much more of my "life with a woman prone to illicit affairs" could truly finish off my habitual *'joi* [sic] *de vivre'*.

I must preserve my panache/nobility though all else may/will crumble.

Yours faithfully

Tony

This letter confused me with its mixed messages (it still does, to be honest). On the one hand he was hoping I'd have been on the plane with Martin and on the other he is thanking me that I wasn't and signing the letter 'Yours faithfully'. He must have been confused himself. His reference to 'a woman prone to illicit affairs' was taken from a personal astrological chart that had been drawn up for me when I was just 17. I dismissed it at the time, thinking I would never behave like that, but I have to now admit to the truth in it. Incidentally the same horoscope predicted that I would have a 'marriage above status'. Although we came from a similar socio-economic background there can no doubt that this was correct (despite the fact I ended up more impoverished than if I'd married someone of equal status).

Tony returns in places to using romanticised and Victorian-sounding words, such as in the sentence where he talks about 'my thraldom to all those stupid, infantile, overpowering things like desire, jealousy and loss – of a woman.' Why 'thraldom'? Why not 'servitude'? It sounds almost masochistic, as if he got pleasure from such things. Here too Tony associates feelings like desire, jealousy and loss with being infantile (and being overpowered), as if to be adult you're not supposed to feel any of these emotions. Loss is the ultimate emotion on the list and he, doubtless, because of the hyphen ('loss – of a woman') wasn't just thinking about loss of me, but also of the loss of Ian.

Then there's the description of the meeting of 'Gretton, Hannett, O'Hara and Wilson' (alphabetically ordered like the name of some legal practice), in which Gretton is noted for his 'fine jest' in the 'cruel honesty style so beloved of my mother'. It was no surprise to me that Rob seized the opportunity to stick the knife in, however humorously. There was no pathos here, no concern for the problems in our marriage, it was just a laughing matter. He'd already taken the moral high ground with regard to Annik, and now he was doing so with me. When Annik accompanied Joy Division on tour and objected to sleeping in a brothel, she apparently accused Rob of being a pig for bringing them there. Rob's response to this was: 'I'm immoral? I'm not the one fucking a married man with a kid.' Actually, she wasn't – Annik and Ian had never actually had sex, partly because the epilepsy medication that Ian was on made it impossible. But it was none of Rob's business anyway. As ever, the double standard played out: what can be acceptable for a man to get away with can be taboo for a woman. Rob had a love of bawdy humour but often, as in the case of Annik, and myself at the Tier 3 venue, it was at someone else's expense.

It's significant that Tony's mother enters the story again, and also Tony talks about his relationship to the bands as 'daddy and non-daddy to the boys'. The parent-child relations floating about in this letter may well reflect Tony's inner feelings of responsibility about Ian along, perhaps, with his desire for a child of his own (which was also never directly stated but was soon to become very apparent).

In the letter it's almost as if Tony was asking me to feel sorry for him that his sexual desires hadn't been fulfilled – that he'd been fumbling with Julie's nightie (whoever she was) and only got as far as a kiss with Kate (thus far – although this was likely to change). And the one-night stand didn't count because he hadn't been in love with her, nor had he enjoyed it. I don't think he understood that I hadn't seen John because of sex, it was primarily for his company. It was also good to be with someone who didn't judge me as guilty and who didn't see themselves as superior to, and dominating of, me. Perhaps I deliberately chose someone who was talented yet without a huge ego, someone who simply had time for me. It may just have boiled down to my loneliness. Tony mentions 'the loving care you give to your other man' but actually the relationship with John had ended before this. It had been a mutual decision; we'd said goodbye on an amicable note. The relationship had no future and was analogous to a playtime hour in the school day.

It's not surprising I hadn't gone out to New York, given that Tony had asked for a separation only the month earlier. The letter did intimate that Tony might want me there and he subsequently rang to ask me to go. He said it was an experience I shouldn't miss. For that reason, I did fly there not long after receiving this letter, but this was a mistake and if I'd had more sense I would never have gone; it certainly would have been better for our marriage if I hadn't. I'd never been to New York, and I suspect Tony felt slightly guilty that I was missing it while extortionate sums were being spent on musicians. He loved New York so much, even to the point of being carried downstairs from his bed shortly before his death in 2007 so that he could visit it one last time.

The circumstances in 1980, however, were dire. I at least arrived to a warm greeting from Martin Hannett – 'Welcome to New York, Lins,' he said from the back of the car as I climbed in – but it was hardly the romantic reunion between Tony and me that I'd imagined. My first time there was spent sharing the open loft apartment with Tony and the boys from A Certain Ratio. It was on Hudson Street in Tribeca, 'Tribeca' being an abbreviation for 'Triangle below Canal St'. Tony thought it was a happening area of Manhattan and judged the loft 'minimal and absolutely perfect'. I disagreed. There was one large dormitory where the boys slept and a tiny bathroom off it to serve us all. The office/annex that Tony and I were sleeping in was also a hallway to the exit, so all the boys had to come through our room to go in or out. Plus, I had to go through their room to get to the bathroom. There were no curtains or blinds in our east-facing room and the sun streamed in, waking me early after I'd gone to bed ridiculously late. Sleep deprivation added to the difficulties. These are conditions I wouldn't endure now, but I was young and, besides, I wasn't given a choice. The boys were friendly enough but there wasn't a girl in sight. Tony was preoccupied and didn't have much time to take notice of me.

New Order were staying in The Iroquois hotel in New York, as was Martin and his girlfriend, Susanne O'Hara. Why Tony hadn't seen fit to put us two into a hotel I cannot imagine. We needed some privacy and a degree of comfort to have any chance of getting along. After a week we took Martin and Susanne to the airport one evening and they agreed to let us stay in their old room. My relief was palpable until we arrived and saw it had been completely trashed. I spent about an hour cleaning up, removing towels (one was in the loo), emptying ashtrays, only then to discover that both of the king-sized beds were full of pieces of cake. We went back to the loft.

I hadn't realised then how many drugs, other than hash, were being used. Martin Hannett was, unbeknownst to me, experimenting with all manner of drugs. Apparently crystal meth was being taken by some of the group as well as him. This was all hidden from me. I wonder if this was when Tony further developed the taste for class A drugs that would stay with him for the rest of his life? Already addicted to adrenaline, from being on TV, his drug of choice – cocaine – would no doubt give him a similar buzz off camera. Strange that he regularly took cocaine when he once said it was 'the ultimate destroyer of talent'. He imagined it was okay if he wasn't working but I'm not convinced.

ACR were at or near the end of their recording by the time I arrived. Jez Kerr of ACR recalled: 'We'd got all the tracks down and had three days left in the studio for the mixing. The sound engineer, Bruce, had zeroed the desk (this is usual practice before a mix) but, when he told Martin what he'd done, Martin screamed out, "YOU WHAT?" Then he kicked a table over sending biscuits flying all over the place. We think he wanted to mix the album in Strawberry where all his usual toys were and with Chris Nagle instead of Bruce. But then ESG came in and used the three days with Martin so maybe that was it. We think it was an excuse anyway. ESG recorded 'You're No Good' and 'Moody'.

Tony and the gang had seen ESG perform when they'd opened for ACR at Hurrah and only three days later they were in the studio with Martin. ESG were sisters from the South Bronx who were apparently given instruments by their dad to keep them off the streets. They sounded great, with a good beat and use of percussion, and the tracks with Martin were released on Factory in 1981 (FAC 34). Tony would describe their sound as 'PiL meets Motown on the wrong side of the Triborough Bridge'. The following year ESG would perform at the opening night of The Haçienda in May 1982. They looked and sounded cool despite the fact that the acoustics never quite worked for live bands. They fitted in with the surroundings better than most of the audience, who looked as if they were on a night out in their local pub. Tony, though, was handsomely dressed and this was before he hired Richard Creme to restyle him in designerwear. Then it was all Yohji Yamamoto suits and Comme Des Garcons clothing amongst other expensive outfits, but I thought they sometimes looked rather baggy, as if they didn't fit him. Creme, who was over seven feet tall, owned L'Homme boutique store in St. Ann's Square, Manchester.

The album ACR recorded in New Jersey, now with added funk grooves, was subsequently mixed at Strawberry Studios and released in May 1981 as *To Each...* The single 'Flight' was also recorded in New Jersey, but Factory had a policy of not putting singles on albums, so this had been released earlier, towards the end of 1980. Jez told me that he thought 'Flight' was the best track they'd ever recorded with Martin, and among the best tunes they'd made over the course of their long career.

I sent Jez the section of Tony's letter where Tony wrote that; 'it seems like some bizarre idea of an LSD-crazed Billy Butlin', and that he was 'daddy and non-daddy (when I get pissed off with them) to the boys'. Jez read it out to Martin and Don of ACR and they all said that they 'loved it, we miss him real bad, we miss him dearly. He was responsible for the band's early success and, by allowing us the freedom to do our own thing – and of course taking us to NYC – he put down a template that we still adhere to today'. I asked Jez what this template was, and he replied, 'I guess the template is: there are no rules and that everything should be done with passion.' That said, there were ructions between the band and Tony as they were leaving, and I witnessed one of them even spitting in his face. Best if we can only remember the good times, though.

Near the end of my stay, I saw ACR being filmed in the loft by a guy named Michael Shamberg. This short film was given the name *TriBeCa*. I wasn't introduced to Michael, but he would later run Factory New York, and this ended up have dramatic consequences for me.

New Order were understandably still finding their feet back in 1980. Footage taken from Hurrah on 27 September even showed drummer Stephen Morris singing the lead vocal. Their first release on Factory in January 1981 was a single consisting of two Joy Division songs: 'Ceremony' and 'In A Lonely Place', both recorded in New Jersey. Rob meanwhile was the master of bonhomie, laughter and male bravado. He told the band they'd be huge in ten years' time. One day Tony and I were in one of the band member's rooms at their Iroquois hotel and one of the band member's dirty socks were soaking in the washbasin. Someone bet Rob a ridiculously small amount – $5 or $10 – that he couldn't drink the water. I was gobsmacked when he actually did this. Talk about male bravado.

Although I was enjoying the musical endeavours, things inevitably weren't going well between Tony and me. There was an awful night when, at around 2 a.m., Tony and I were driving along in a van in some derelict meat warehouse area near the river, having collected equipment belonging to one of the groups.

Tony: 'You've gone off sex anyway.'

Lindsay: 'Correction: I've gone off sex with you.'

At which he screeched to a halt and dragged me out of the van on the passenger side. He looked as if he wanted to beat me up but instead drove off, leaving me near the river. I had no idea where I was but knew the loft apartment was near the river and south of where I was, so I managed to navigate my way back. I was wearing unsuitable footwear (as ever a slave to heels) and, to make matters worse, the strap on one shoe snapped so I had to hobble along the road. I attracted one or two kerb-crawlers, men on the look-out for a prostitute. Apparently the Meatpacking District was a well-known cruising area. I should have known better than to hurt Tony that way, but he shouldn't have left me in such a dangerous place at that time of night. In later years, Tony laughed at this incident, he thought my line back at him was hilarious.

The day after this incident, feeling unforgiving and very hurt over Tony's abandonment, I went on a bar crawl with some American guy who got drunk with me. Nothing happened, fortunately he turned out to be a gentleman, but I was as sick as a dog the next morning. Dignity was lost as I was reduced to using a bowl – the tiny single bathroom was too far and often in use, not that there was any privacy as the boys would have to pass through our bedroom on their way out anyway.

Unsurprisingly this whole experience rather ruined any plans for our reconciliation; the New York experience more than likely damned them.

As anticipated after this disaster, once Tony returned to the UK he put our house up for sale. We spent a cold Christmas together and, on the day itself, I was hurt and insulted when he refused to go with me to my parents' house for dinner and I left him in his dressing gown, on his rocking chair, with a porn video. By January 1981, the property – 45 Town Lane, Charlesworth – had sold, immediately, to the very first viewer. We were both present when he looked round the house and declared his avowed intention to buy it. I was mortified: I'd hoped Tony's plan to buy the big house in Didsbury would be thwarted so that he and I could choose another one together. The very next day Tony left for London in an icy mood, stating he wanted us to take a break. I could see there wasn't much point in delaying further, took the cat to her original home across the road and moved out to my parents' house. Pride comes before a fall, but I was also adamant I wouldn't go with him to 'our' Didsbury house on principle. I was appalled that he'd bought it without me even seeing it. He'd told me about it as a *fait accompli*. This had been his modus operandi with Factory product – such as selling off my band OMD – but in terms of a future 'family' home it felt like a betrayal of the worst kind. His nerve, telling me it would make a great family house was probably the defining moment when I determined not to go along with his idea of a future family. He spent most of his time around Alan's flat and now chose our 'family' house with him rather than me? What was I, a piece of furniture he was taking along with him? A baby machine? It seemed we were now both at the end of our tethers and a reconciliation unlikely, not to say impossible.

Tony told me this was my punishment for sleeping with John Scott (now history), as if he himself was completely innocent. I told him in no uncertain terms that I'd never live in the house. Tony had been blasé about it, assuming I'd come round, but I tapped into a pride and stubbornness I didn't know I had. Remember the story of Icarus? As Tony, played by Steve Coogan, said in the film *24 Hour Party People*: 'If not, you should read more.' Icarus had made a pair of wings with which to cheat nature and fly, but he was so proud he flew too close to the sun, his wings burned and he plummeted to earth. It was because of my pride that I eventually lost everything with Tony. Perhaps I should have rolled with it to save myself, but I was shouting to be heard.

Tony too was like Icarus: totally overconfident about purchasing the house without my input and assuming I'd meekly go along with it. Time later told that he desperately wanted to keep me as his wife, but this separation put paid to any such plan. With hindsight I can see that Tony was controlling but probably with good intentions, because he believed that he knew best. Maybe he did. It's a pity I couldn't have calmed down and accepted it for my own good. But since Tony had zero intention of backing down on this house purchase, I staged a rebellion which drove a further wedge between us.

I called at Charlesworth one day in February to collect some things while Tony was at work. My diary entry for that day reads:

Yesterday I drove to 'our' house. I had thought he and the cat were away. "What are you doing here?" I said to the cat when I arrived. Other signs of presence – record player and fire switched on, water hot. I walked through the house to make sure no one was there. In the bedroom I paused, went back down and it suddenly hit me that there were two pillows on our bed, not one as on my last visit. Somewhat stunned, I poured a whisky and had a smoke. The final proof I needed was in the bathroom – powdered blusher in the sink under the mirror, still fresh. Yes this was indeed the finest moment of my marriage – the coup-fourré, time to pay up. One cannot be truly free until one has. My escape route lies clear and unfettered ahead.

Incidentally, the phrase *coup fourré* was taken from a card game that Tony and I often played together in which the players are in a road race. It was called *Mille Bornes*, French for 'a thousand milestones'. The term *coup fourré* (pronounced coo-foo-ray) is a fencing term meaning 'counter-thrust', or counterattack. The night I wrote the above I was suffering from severe insomnia and really believed this to be the end, the final nail in the coffin. I had no idea who the woman was but suspected it might be the Belgian woman, Kate.

The next letter was sent from Charlesworth. Tony had closed our joint bank account at this point as we were living apart and I wasn't cooperating with his house purchase. This, a four-bedroomed detached property, with garage and gardens, on the poshest road in Didsbury, was within his means, but he chose to cut me off. All I was offered was the promise of half of the profit our cottage had made – while I'd lived in it. Said profit never materialised either, other than in dribs and drabs. I felt more understanding now for the bands on Factory who were told there was 'no money' and couldn't quite understand why.

Feb 25th 1981

Lindsay

Find enclosed cheque for £200.00. As usual our account is overdrawn – and have just the central heating money in the B.S. – so no spare. I have had to take some interest from Factory Records for the £10,000 I lent it – to pay a £1,700.00 tax final demand etc – so the £200.00 will then have to last a couple of weeks:

Feb 25th 1981

Lindsay,

Find enclosed cheque for £200-00. As usual our
account is overdrawn — and have just the Central
Heating money in the B.S. — so no spare. I have
had to take some interest from Factory Records for
the £10,000 I lent it — to pay a £1,700.00 Tax final
demand etc — so the £200.00 will then have to last
a couple of weeks: by then the house contracts should
have gone through + there'll be £20,000 and we can
sort out shares in that. Please remember — I don't
have a 50,000 pound house. I have 7½ thousand
pounds - ½ what my mum left me. I have a £35,000
mortgage and if I sold the house for what I
bought it — I'd have just 7½ thousand. Please
try + understand. Sorry to sound like a schoolteacher.
I'm back with Tabitha — she'll move with me when the
furniture + the carpets go — so it'll helpler with familiar
smells + butter on her feet.
Tabitha says hello

I'll be in touch when the serious money
arrives — if you have any panic money problems
ring me — but for God's sake stop shouting.
Your best friend.
ALAN

FACTORY RECORDS
86 Palatine Road, Manchester 20.
Telephone 061-434 3876

Wednesday
March 4th 81.

Lins,

Thanks for the card. Much appreciated and I love you too! Very much. Now three things. 1) Alan is doing a job reference thing for you 2) Sean says sorry for not ~~applying~~ replying to your letter but he'd just been hit by potato blight + your response got lost in the ensuing chaos. 3) House sale is moving ahead + by the end of the week I should know the completion date — and when the share out.

Do you want to discuss all that in person or letter. With this process being a rational denial of emotion, letter is really much better and safer; and I'm grateful for your assistance in the non-contact approach. Certainly we shouldn't do it on the phone. I'm tired of all my major life events occuring on the phone.

The top sentence isn't as glib as it sounds. I will always love you very deeply — the fact that that love is destructive of both our personalities is tragic in one sense — but I'm grateful for the 5 years we survived and expect much happiness from our friendship to come. Good luck in London or wherever.

Yours

X

VAT. No. 305 6301 96 Reg. No. 2340540
A. Erasmus, R. Gretton, M. Hannett, P. Savile, A. Wilson

P.S. I will send a bit more money whenever you need it. Up to you.

by then the house contracts should have gone through and there'll be £20,000 and we can sort out shares in that. Please remember – I don't have a 50,000 pound house. I have 7 and half thousand pounds – half what my mum left me. I have a £35,000 mortgage and if I sold the house for what I bought it – I'd have just 7 and half thousand. Please try and understand. Sorry to sound like a schoolteacher. I'm back with Tabitha – she'll move with me when the furniture and carpets go – so it'll help with familiar smells and butter on her feet. Tabitha says hello

—— scribble

I'll be in touch when the serious money arrives – if you have any panic money problems ring me – but for God's sake stop shouting.

Your best friend

AHW

So, is this proof positive that Tony's mum left him £15,000, which was the money used to launch Factory? Or was it actually £7,500, half his mother's bequest, since he mentions having that left over if he sold the house for the price he bought it? I'm inclined to think it was the latter, but he still had managed to lend £10,000 to Factory. I never queried Tony about his inheritance, nor minded what he spent it on. We'd never argued about money before this time, but I was quite hurt that he'd closed our joint bank account without telling me, at the same time as essentially buying himself an expensive detached house by the park. The £20,000 profit he took from the sale of Charlesworth was not shared with me. He decided that the house had gone up in value by half that (£10,000) during the time that I'd lived there and so I was entitled to £5000. This £200 was considered part of it and the rest came in similar small amounts over the following two years. He probably did this partly as a means of control, since it transpired that he didn't ultimately want to lose me, or maybe because he never actually had £5000 in his bank account to give me.

In this next letter Tony seemed to be saying goodbye and farewell. I suspected he was lining up his lover – probably Kate, from earlier on. He was also excited about his move to Old Broadway in Didsbury.

Wednesday

March 4th 81

Lins, Thanks for the card. Much appreciated and I love you too. Very much. Now three things, 1) Alan is doing a job reference thing for you 2) Sean says sorry for not replying to your letter but he'd just been hit by potato blight and your response got lost in the ensuing chaos, 3) House sale is moving ahead and by the end of the week I should know the completion date – and when the share out.

Do you want to discuss that in person or letter. With this process being a rational denial of emotion letter is really much better and safer; and I'm grateful for your assistance in the non- contact approach. Certainly we shouldn't do it on the phone. I'm tired of all my major life events occurring on the phone.

The top sentence isn't as glib as it sounds. I will always love you very deeply – the fact that that love is destructive of both our personalities is tragic in one sense – but I'm grateful for the 5 years we survived and expect much happiness from our friendship to come. Good luck in London or wherever.

Yours,

Tony x

P.S. I will send a bit more money whenever you need it. Up to you.

The sentence beginning, 'with this process being a rational denial of emotion …' suggests he's trying to be sensible but still has feelings for me. I suspect that 'being sensible' meant sleeping with Kate. I disagree that the *love* we shared was destructive of our personalities; it was rather our huge egos, our stubborn pride, bad timing, and all manner of other damaging agencies.

Thinking about what Tony meant by, 'I'm tired of all my major life events occurring on the phone,' he's remembering learning of his mum's sudden death in Manchester by phone when he was in California. Up until this point, her death been the biggest life event he'd experienced.

Since I was now very short of money and refusing, out of pride, to ever ask Tony for any unless he freely gave it, I'd asked for a reference for a job application. I met Tony at Granada one day as I was trying to get in as a researcher, but I'd left it too late. I should have applied earlier when they were looking for people and Thelma had got in. I remember attending an interview to be an air hostess and feeling grateful later that I wasn't accepted. It was a pity I'd abandoned teaching as I now found it hard to get back into.

Tony mentions his childhood Irish friend Sean Boylan, who lives in Dunboyne, near Dublin. Sean ought to have been his best man, as that was really who he was to Tony. They met in 1958, were lifelong friends despite the distance, and Tony asked for him on his death bed – Sean arriving just in time. I don't remember why I wrote to him but suspect it may have been due to some sort of ailment I had, as Sean was, and is, a skilled herbalist. Sean gave Tony medicine when he was poorly with cancer, but he told me he'd struggled to drink it due to the taste.

I was confused. There was a night at the end of March 1981 when I woke with a certainty that, Kate or no Kate, Tony and I belonged together. I got dressed and drove to Charlesworth, arriving there at 3.30 a.m. The house was empty. I slept in our bed and Tony arrived at some point even later in the night. The next day he told me he didn't want us to continue; he was always icy when I wanted us to make up and vice versa.

Although we were now separated, true to type, I helped with the packing up and cleaning of Town Lane prior to the looming house removal. It felt like my duty as it had been my home. Also, I held the cat, Tabatha, on my knee while Tony drove to the house in Old Broadway, Didsbury. He insisted on taking her, but I thought she would have been better left with her original owner, the old lady across the road, in my absence. The move took place in April 1981. I'd already rejected the house without seeing it, but I disliked the atmosphere of it as soon as I walked in. It had great potential but, apart from it being in a really bad state, it felt lonely, I sensed the presence of someone unhappy. So, I let him get on with it by himself. I took the photo of him washing up at Old Broadway as this was a rare event at Town Lane. He doesn't look happy, and as if he's lost weight due to stress. My opposition to this move wouldn't have helped him. His domineering behaviour was perhaps coming back to bite him … a little.

I continued living at my mum's house in Gatley but visited Old Broadway regularly to look after the cat, as Tony was somewhat remiss in his care of this very old and poorly creature. It wasn't deliberate neglect; he was just hardly ever there.

The relationship with John had long since ended, it hadn't felt right. I was seeing no one, living with my mum and dad, and that didn't feel right either. But my fear of returning to Tony outweighed all of it. I was afraid he'd have complete control over me. I wonder if marriage is a constant power struggle? Some people are happy to be dominated but I wasn't – not to the degree he was taking it to at any rate. The fact was that he had the material advantage, but I could have owned what power I did have instead of giving it all away out of pride, and the need for peace.

My overall take from Tony's last letter was that he was saying goodbye to me, and that it was time to move on. So, move on I did.

CHAPTER 7
The Sweet Cheat Gone

—◯—

Tony settled into 36 Old Broadway in April 1981, and I continued living at my parents' house in Gatley, turning up to check on the cat when he was at work. I couldn't embrace my relationship with him, nor could I let go at this stage. Despite his well-quoted and fond phrase, 'move on, darling', Tony was also keeping his options open with me, as evidenced by the fact that he gave me a room in his new house. He offered me a choice and I picked the balcony bedroom. Although small and in quite a decrepit state, it was my favourite room in the house. Much refurbishment was called for throughout the property, but I concentrated on this room and set about painting and decorating it and having curtains made. It was a project, as was the work I did on his typewriter there. I think the latter was a screenplay idea based on the novel by DH Lawrence, *The Rainbow*, which never saw the light of day.

On 11 May I heard from Kuka, a guy I'd met in London back in January. I was staying with a girlfriend (actually the wife of Tony's best man) when she suggested we call in to see Kuka: she said he was an interesting character and an artist. We sat in his studio, and I was able to admire his paintings while he made us tea and biscuits. It was obvious we were attracted to one another upon meeting, but it was still a surprise when he got in touch, out of the blue, asking me to meet him in a country house somewhere near Sheffield to attend an antique auction with him. Buying and selling antiques was his way of making a living. Even though there'd been chemistry when we first met, nothing had materialised at the time as I gathered he was hung up on a previous relationship. Little did he know that I'd be forever hung up on mine. That said, I was ready for a new adventure.

I'm unsure of the date of the next short letter but it was definitely 1981; I suspect it was May. The outing Tony refers to hadn't gone too well, doubtless because I'd had such a nice time with Kuka and probably didn't feel at all conciliatory to Tony. I'd thought Tony seemed a tad cold towards me that night at the pictures, although he remarked that he enjoyed it enormously. It was, as I remember, a good film. I couldn't swear on

FACTORY RECORDS
86 Palatine Road, Manchester 20.
Telephone 061-434 3876

Lins,

Thanks for the ironing.   Where's the charcoal loghter fuel...and
where is the little sponge that was in the sink......very difficult
to trace moved gpods you know...........if you're here today,
please don't put the bolt on the back door as the guy from Adeptus
has the key to get in and cut down the work surfaces......
thanks again for the ironing.............
. Point two. Katy arrives on Sunday I think.. It doesn't mean you
have to forego the typewriter.......I'm sure you'll get on well...but
I understand should you fele differently....she'll be usigg a spare
room...there are so many.....i thought i should check if you have
any objections to her using the balcony room as it has at
least been decorated......anyway....let me know..........
Enjoyed last Friday enormously.....just as Proust describes it...the
sequential return through all the various sttages in perfect reverse order
Lots of luck.

VAT. No. 305 6301 96   Reg. No. 2340540
A.Erasmus, R.Gretton, M.Hannett, P.Saville, A.Wilson

my life what film it was but think it was *The French Lieutenant's Woman*. I vaguely recall identifying with the heroine which would make sense as, in this story, she is a disgraced but independent woman, haunted by an illicit affair, working as a lowly servant, who then meets and falls in love with someone else.

I did feel ready to move on to another proper relationship because with Tony, I remembered the Woody Allen line in *Annie Hall* (a film we watched on our honeymoon) about a relationship being like a shark. It has to constantly move forward or it dies. And what we had was a dead shark. Or at least we had a barely moving shark. The trouble was, it kept twitching.

Note that I was still doing the ironing.

Lins,

Thanks for the ironing. Where's the charcoal lighter fuel....and where is the little sponge that was in the sink....very difficult to trace moved goods you know........if you're here today, please don't put the bolt on the back door as the guy from Adeptus has the key to get in and cut down the work surfaces.......

thanks again for the ironing........... . Point two. Katy arrives on Sunday I think.. It doesn't mean you have to forego the typewriter... ..I'm sure you'll get on well....but I understand should you feel differently.......she'll be using a spare room.......there are so many......I thought I should check if you have any objections to her using the balcony room as it has at least been decorated....... anyway......let me know............. Enjoyed last Friday enormously.......just as Proust describes it.....the sequential return through all the various stages in perfect reverse order.

Lots of luck.

Tony was naive to think that his friend Kate and I could be friendly at this stage of the proceedings. Nothing against her, I believe she was cool, but, although he's saying that they will be sleeping separately, I doubt I believed that was the intention. I felt a bit peeved that he wanted to give my refurbished room to a girlfriend although, if she did sleep in there, she probably used it more than I did.

I'm not clear where exactly Proust describes a 'sequential return through all the various stages in perfect reverse order'. There is Proust's famous description of his immediate return to childhood when tasting a Madeleine cake he'd just dipped in his tea, prompting him to coin the term 'involuntary memory' – reminders of long ago that suddenly arise unbidden. In Tony's mind, taking me to the pictures was perhaps a reminder of earlier happier times. But his statement does imply, or at least it did to me

FACTORY RECORDS
86 Palatine Road, Manchester 20.
Telephone 061-434 3876

Friday afternoon....julytenth

Lindsay,

Just to say that the belgian boiler's gone back,

so feel free to get back on the typewriter

whenever.   Happy Birthday......sorry it was late

but in the regression process I'm back at 77 -76 and

I believe the policy was remembering it but a bit late

which is at least better than total forgetfulness.

I'mm off for a couple of days(Sun night to Wednesday

morning)on business but Alan has full instructions

about the cat...she does like Kattomeat beef....very

peculiar..whatever happened to the Whiskas fascination..

....and maybe Andy or Malcolm will house sit.....

See you around, and if you need more of your money

for the business venture ......just whistle etc.

Yours,

t......

VAT. No. 305 6301 96   Reg. No. 2340540
A. Erasmus, R.Gretton, M.Hannett, P.Saville, A.Wilson

then, that there was no future for our marriage; rather than an attempt to re-invigorate it, the date at the cinema was more of a Proustian 'remembrance of things past'.

The workman may have already started work on the basement using Factory money – which he'd probably lent to them in the first place – for its conversion to an editing suite for Ikon, the video arm of Factory. It also entailed quite major renovation in the cellar before the equipment could be put in place. Initially this was the nicest part of the house. Malcolm (Whitehead) was the lovely filmmaker who ran Ikon. He'd filmed Joy Division amongst many others. Tony was hugely enthusiastic about this video arm and gave every possible encouragement to it.

The relationship with Kuka looked, from our weekend together, as if it could develop into something important, but I stayed in Manchester until the summer. I felt honour bound in some ways toward my husband (hence the ironing) and, notwithstanding his own new relationship, consequently told him about meeting someone. I knew it had the potential to become serious – unlike my previous two affairs – and so I offered to stop things going any further with Kuka if Tony would admit that, underneath it all, he wanted us both to try to save our marriage. Did I really mean that, or was I testing him? I honestly believe that, at this early stage, I would have broken it off if Tony had humbly asked me to. But, on the contrary, he told me he was very glad to hear of it as it would get me off his back at last. Those words seared into my soul.

And so I embarked on a committed and long-term relationship with Kuka. Many years later Tony and I talked about his brutal response back then; he told me that's just what you say to the woman you're in love with when she tells you she's met someone else. Really? Stupid pride, hubris, something Tony and I had in equal measure; we both flew too close to the sun and would equally fall from our different heights. But I'd had no idea then that he was in love with me still. I took what he said at face value.

He was hardly being attentive to me though: in the next note he mentions my birthday in passing which had actually taken place eight days before this.

Friday afternoon....july tenth 1981
Lindsay,
Just to say that the belgian boiler's gone back, so feel free to get back on the typewriter whenever. Happy Birthday.......sorry it was late but in the regression process I'm back at 77-76 and I believe the policy was remembering it but a bit late which is at least better than total forgetfulness.
I'm off for a couple of days (Sun night to Wednesday morning) on business but Alan has full instructions about the cat.....she does like Kattomeat beef...... very peculiar....whatever happened to the Whiskas fascination....and maybe Andy or Malcolm will house sit...... See you around, and if you need more of your

FACTORY RECORDS
86 Palatine Road, Manchester 20.
Telephone 061-434 3876

August 4th '81

Dear Lindsay,

Thanks for the note, and particularly thanks for the
news about the car. I would like to buy it...at a
fair price....and if you can let me know in advance
I'll start selling the "Family" estate.

Tabatha is very well; having made friends with the
lady next door, and taken a liking to her couch, she
has now won over the hearts of the four children who'
ve just moved in next door but one. She goes next door
for lunch and then on to the kids for her tea, before
a quick meaow at No 36 for her supper. She does sleep
here which I suppose is some kind of loyalty....for
a lady.

As for "when the pain goes away", well as you might expect that's exactly what Monsieur Proust is into at
the moment. The last 148 pages have been the slow
painful growing out of the pain of Albertine (disparu).
This volume, the penultimate one is called in english,
"The Sweet Cheat Gone" which you'll be pleased to know
is now the title of that piece of piano which now closes
Vini's new album. (We found a grand piano back stage at
a concert hall in Helsinki last weekend and Vini played
piano - that piece - in public for the first time. Great,
it was.) Anyway Proust and all those strange connections.
Madeira with you and me and Monsieur Swann and Odette.
Italy and the death of his grandmother, and of course

VAT No. 305 6301 96 Reg'd No. 2340440
A.Erasmus, R.Gretton, M.Hannett, P.Saville, A.Wilson

money for the business venture.......just whistle etc.

Yours,

t........

X

I found Tony's term for Kate ('boiler') to be disrespectful and it no doubt had its origins in Rob Gretton's reference to Annik Honoré, whom he also called 'the Belgian boiler'. Annik was highly cultured, and the term 'boiler' was a million miles from the person she actually was. I often heard these kind of put-downs during my years in the music industry. Factory was a bit of a boys' club, as were other labels I was involved with, such as Virgin 10 Records, who signed a group I later managed. It's almost as if these men can't bear to have women around them as equals and so they're impelled to diminish them. I took Tony's use of the term to also tacitly infer that he wasn't that serious about Kate, even if they were lovers.

Tony mentions Alan (Erasmus) as having instructions to feed the cat, but I knew that opening a tin and leaving the contents out all day, or longer, was of no use to her at this stage. She was too ill, was soon to die in fact, and needed titbits every now and then in order to get anything down her. Tony describes her as 'very well' in his next letter – I think he was not paying attention. As for the business venture Tony mentions, I can't clearly remember what my idea was. It was probably inspired by Kuka's business of buying and selling antique rugs and furniture at Camden Lock market. Kuka suggested I check out auctions in the north, and I did begin to do this but lacked funds to buy anything much.

The next letter again illustrates Tony's love of Proust; he read all seven volumes of *In Search of Lost Time* during the years we were together. He refers to the sixth volume, *The Sweet Cheat Gone*, as the name he gave to a Durutti Column piano track appearing at the end of the album *LC*, to be released that November. Tony gave me this album as a gift around then. I naively imagined that *LC* might be some kind of dedication, given that he was once again wooing me by that point, referring to my initials (Lindsay Carole). Actually, it was *Lotta Continua*, meaning 'the struggle continues'. You can say that again.

August 4th '81

Dear Lindsay,

Thanks for the note, and particularly thanks for the news about the car. I would like to buy it......at a fair price.....and if you can let me know in advance I'll start selling the "Family" estate.

the "sweet cheat"."We lie all our life long, especially
indeed, perhaps only, to those people who love us. Such
people in fact alone make us fear for our pleasure and
desire their esteem."
He really is wonderful, even if he had to lie in bed
for four years to write it.
"And since it is the case with grief as with the desire
for women that we increase it by thinking about it, the
fact of having plenty of other things to do should,
like chastity, make oblivion easy."
He goes into lots of theories about time, and memory
and love, but basically is pretty confident. He finds
comfort and fear in the fact that he got over the
death of his grandmother and we all in fact (as we
must both have reflected in past months) survive several
lost loves in one lifetime. Anyway at the end of the bit
I was reading a few weeks back a subchapter ends thus;"As for
the third occasion on which I remember that I was conscious
of approaching an absolute indifference with regard to
Albertine, it was one day, much later, in Venice!"
I felt he was getting a little ahead of me here on our
shared narrative, and since the next chapter began; "My
mother had brought me for a few weeks to venice..." I
immediately stopped reading. If I get to Italy for a week's
break before the end of the Summer, I'll continue and
who knows, no pain, no pain.
Proust regardless, I am sure we will be valuable friends
to each other in later years. Who the hell else is going
to understand all this crap about a guy who lay in bed
for four years.
Yours,

P.S. I'll send you some news of your
money - you must be running low!

Tabatha is very well; having made friends with the lady next door, and taken a liking to her couch, she has now won over the hearts of the four children who've just moved in next door but one. She goes next door for lunch and then on to the kids for her tea, before a quick meaow at No 36 for her supper. She does sleep here which I suppose is some kind of loyalty......for a lady.

As for "when the pain goes away", well as you might expect that's exactly what Monsieur Proust is into at the moment. The last 148 pages have been the slow painful growing out of the pain of Albertine (disparu). This volume, the penultimate one, is called in English, " The Sweet Cheat Gone" which you'll be pleased to know is now the title of that piece of piano which now closes Vini's new album. (We found a grand piano back stage at a concert hall in Helsinki last weekend and Vini played piano – that piece – in public for the first time. Great, it was.) Anyway Proust and all those strange connections. Madeira with you and me and Monsieur Swann and Odette. Italy and the death of his grandmother, and of course the "sweet cheat". "We lie all our life long, especially, indeed perhaps only, to those people who love us. Such people in fact alone make us fear for our pleasure and desire their esteem." He really is wonderful, even if he had to lie in bed for four years to write it.

"And since it is the case with grief as with the desire for women that we increase it by thinking about it, the fact of having plenty of other things to do should, like chastity, make oblivion easy."

He goes into lots of theories about time, and memory and love, but basically is pretty confident. He finds comfort and fear that he got over the death of his grandmother and we all in fact (as we must both have reflected in past months) survive several lost loves in one lifetime. Anyway at the end of the bit I was reading a few weeks back a subchapter ends thus: "As for the third occasion on which I remember that I was conscious of approaching an absolute indifference with regard to Albertine, it was one day, much later, in Venice."

I felt he was getting a little ahead of me here on our shared narrative, and since the next chapter began; "My mother had brought me for a few weeks to Venice......" I immediately stopped reading. If I get to Italy for a week's break before the end of the summer, I'll continue and who knows, no pain, no pain.

Proust regardless, I am sure we will be valuable friends to each other in later years. Who the hell else is going to understand all this crap about a guy who lay in bed for four years.

Yours,

Anthony ?

P.S. I'll send you some more of your money – you must be running low!

The car of mine that Tony wanted to buy was a classic car, a Karmann Ghia, the shape of which he'd always admired. I'd obviously needed the money but, in the event, I never did sell it to Tony as I probably needed the car more. The 'family' estate he mentions was the Peugeot 504 estate that he'd used for ferrying ACR, musical equipment and other musicians around in. I disliked that car the moment I set eyes on it. The rear storage area looked suitable to me for carrying a coffin and so I nicknamed it 'the hearse'. This was before Ian died. It became inadvertently ironic as Tony hadn't had the car all that long before we used it to drive Annik to the morgue to see Ian for the last time. This was to be Annik's only way of saying goodbye, as she wasn't allowed to attend his funeral.

Tony sounds as though he's coming to terms with our separation – or at least is expecting to in the near future. I don't entirely relate to the line 'we lie all our life long'; my mistake had been in baring my truth, telling him about my infidelity when I hadn't even needed to. Perhaps Tony's own mistake was in lying because, at least up until this point, he hadn't made clear any wish for us to continue. Meanwhile I lied to myself, believing he was unworthy of me and that I didn't love him anymore.

The open-air concert at Kaivopuisto Park in Helsinki that Tony refers to was something of a Factory outing. Along with The Durutti Column, also featured were ACR and Kevin Hewick (another of Tony's additions to the Factory roster). Singer-songwriter and guitarist Hewick had recorded two little-known tracks with the three remaining members of Joy Division a month after Ian's death (one, 'Haystack', was released on *From Brussels with Love*). He'd appeared at the aforementioned infamous Bury gig in Ian's place, much to the chagrin of the audience. ACR had American singer Martha 'Tilly' Tilson joining Simon Topping on vocals and Donald on drums, adding an extra special dimension.

The Durutti Column now featured Bruce Mitchell on live drums. I was surprised when Bruce joined Vini; it seemed a strange choice after Bruce's years with Alberto Y Lost Trios Paranoias (who disbanded in 1982). I'd thought Bruce and Vini to be poles apart musically but Bruce did, in fact, add a coolness and a beat to Vini's guitar that actually worked. Tony tried to get Vini to stop singing – his feeling, and mine, was that this particular addition definitely did *not* work. Vini didn't listen and indomitably carried on. Bruce and Tony shared a lifelong friendship, and the picture opposite was taken of them to or from one of this kind of concerts abroad.

As noted years earlier in Tony's letter to Howard Devoto, Tony had a near obsession with the idea that the love life he was reading about in Proust's stories ran parallel to his own. He was Marcel and I was Albertine, Marcel's mistress in the story, of whom he was jealously possessive. She was the 'sweet cheat' who was *disparu*, meaning 'gone'. In fact, just as Marcel is feeling he can't live without her, Albertine dies in an accidental fall from a horse and, subsequent to Marcel's severe grief, he visits Italy, the place that Tony

© Ged Murray's family

indicates he intends to visit next. It's as if his life was a parody of Marcel's and his hope is that he will recover from the loss of Albertine/me there. Towards the end of Tony's life, he thought of me more as Odette, the older woman who'd had an unhappy marriage with Charles Swann in the novels. Albertine would be replaced in Tony's mind in the nineties by his younger girlfriend, Yvette, or so he once told me. Actually, I seem to have changed from Albertine to Odette just in this one letter, when Tony mentions our visit to Madeira, which had taken place a year or so earlier.

By the time this next letter had arrived, in August 1981, I was visiting Kuka quite often in London and even thought about living there. It felt as if Tony and I were finished and, though sad, I accepted that. I was still receiving the dribs and drabs of my £5000 when Tony saw fit, and now often helped my new boyfriend run his antiques stall on Camden Lock at weekends, as well as buying stock at auctions. It was interesting work, although lifting and moving heavy furniture and carpets was difficult and unsuited to my frame – it was work for a strong man rather than a petite and slender woman.

I didn't know if Tony was still seeing Kate at this point as we'd been largely out of touch. Either this letter or the subsequent one was delivered by hand to my parent's house in a Factory envelope, as seen below (he was still addressing me as 'Wilson' at this point).

Tony closed the letter by quoting from 'Ephemera', a beautiful but sad poem by his favourite poet, W.B. Yeats. The last three words seemed an appropriate title for this book.

I didn't take up the offer to star in the erotic video as suggested.

FACTORY RECORDS
86 Palatine Road, Manchester 20.
Telephone 061-434 3876

36,Old Broadway.

August 18th '81

Dear Lindsay   Herewith some more of your money.

I apologise if it's late and you've been going short but

I had thought that if you needed it you'd get in touch.

On further thought, and from what little intuition I can muster

I gather that communication is the last thing you want or need,

so having been remiss in not coming to that conclusion sooner

here it is. It leaves you with 2 and half in the building

society plus whatever interest it all makes while it's there.

It's probably made two hundred already. Oh, usury.

Oh, and I'm giving it you on the drip like this cause

my mum taught me caution with money, don't laugh, and I'm

cautious even with other peoples. If you don't want to

contact me again I'll make sure you get the rest before

Christmas, though I do want very much to purchase the

Karrman Ghia. Perhaps I could do it through your mum.

Donald wants you to star in a piece of video he's doing

for the ACR cassette. It's a visual piece which will have

noises and percussion put on live in a studio after the

piece is edited. It is erotic though not pornographic.

And you are very beautiful. So it's understandable Donald,

who of all the musicians is showing the most initiative in

constructing videos, should want you for his leading lady.

You wouldn't have to see me...I'm quite sure I wouldn't

be able to cope...you'd get paid...and your train fare...

VAT. No. 305 6301 96 Reg. No. 2340540
A. Erasmus, R. Gretton, M. Hannett, P. Saville, A. Wilson

36, Old Broadway.

August 18th '81

Dear Lindsay

Herewith some more of your money. I apologise if it's late and you've been going short but I had thought that if you needed it you'd get in touch. On further thought, and from what little intuition I can muster, I gather that communication is the last thing you want or need, so having been remiss in not coming to that conclusion sooner here it is. It leaves you with 2 and a half in the building society plus whatever interest it makes while it's there. It's probably made two hundred already. Oh, usury. Oh, and I'm giving it you on the drip like this cause my mum taught me caution with money, don't laugh, and I'm cautious with other people's. If you don't want to contact me again I'll make sure you get the rest before Christmas, though I do want very much to purchase the Karmann Ghia. Perhaps I could do it through your mum. Donald wants you to star in a piece of video he's doing for the ACR cassette. It's a visual piece which will have noises and percussion put on live in a studio after the piece is edited. It is erotic though not pornographic. And you are very beautiful. So it's understandable Donald, who of all the musicians is showing the most initiative in constructing videos, should want you for his leading lady. You wouldn't have to see me....I'm quite sure I wouldn't be able to cope....you'd get paid... ...and your train fare....and anyway I'll send you Donald's finalised scenario through your mum. I enclose some stuff in the envelope that came for you.....again apologies for lateness. Everything here is

...and anyway I'll send you Donald's finalised scenario
through your mum.
I enclose some stuff in the envelope that came for you...
again apologies for lateness.
Everything here is fine, Tabitha well, and even the plants
growing. The cellar got flooded, the night of the floods.
But the lightning was wonderful.
I'm sorry we took different paths. Our fate. We still share that.
Let's close with some poetry, a last joint first, and then;

"When the poor tired child, Passion, falls asleep.
How far away the stars seem, and how far
Is our first kiss, and ah, how old my heart.

Before us lies eternity ; our souls
Are love, and a continual farewll."

Good night
Anthony

VAT. No. 305 6301 96   Reg. No. 2340540
A.Erasmus, R.Gretton, M.Hannett, P.Savile, A.Wilson

fine, Tabitha well, and even the plants growing. The cellar got flooded, the night of the floods. But the lightning was wonderful.

I'm sorry we took different paths. Our fate. We still share that.

Let's close with some poetry, a last joint first, and then;

"When the poor tired child, Passion, falls asleep,
How far away the stars seem, and how far
Is our first kiss, and ah, how old my heart.
Before us lies eternity : our souls
Are love, and a continual farewell."

Good night
Anthony

It makes me laugh when Tony writes that he's cautious with money – his own and other people's. It's true that he had a reassuring and reliable monthly income thanks to 'not giving up the day job'. But the large sums of money that went into and out of Factory were staggering, and several expenditures were beyond reckless; The Haçienda and the new Factory office in Manchester for instance. Also, the money belonging to other people – musicians on Factory, for example – was hardly protected, and it annoyed me that he saw fit to manage and oversee the small amount of money that was mine, as if I couldn't be trusted with it. Maybe he was drip-feeding it to me as a way of keeping in touch? A bit like putting me on a private income or buying an option as filmmakers do with books they may want to use. Truth to tell, Tony probably did care about money, in spite of his protestations to the opposite. He never knew what it was to go without it and enjoyed privileges denied to most of us, such as first-class travel and designer suits.

Tony's offer of paying me to feature in a video was a forerunner of a more serious work offer to come from him.

This next letter from September 1981 was written on the backs of sheets of Factory paper while Tony was on a solo holiday to Italy – Sperlonga to be exact. We'd been to Sperlonga ourselves for a week's holiday a year or two earlier, and although the hotel and beach were lovely, it hadn't gone well. I'd felt jealous and annoyed that he'd arranged it in discussion with Thelma and not with me. He hadn't asked me where I'd like to go on holiday but had just gone ahead and booked it on her suggestion. When I demurred, he told me that, unlike her, I was incapable of arranging a decent holiday. The bloody-minded, spiteful part of me therefore felt obliged, to ruin this one as best I could. It's a pity I couldn't have been more mature and simply grateful, as Thelma was right: it was a dream of a place. But we ourselves are heaven or hell.

Tony sounds confused in this letter which, no doubt, he was. I'd thought it was clear that he and I had broken up, but the tone of this letter contradicts his last. The woman called Hilary he mentions isn't the same Hilary with whom he would have a child in 1984. He also mentions Katy and Fran – all three of these women I never met, and I forget his association with them, if I ever knew.

His dream of wife and kids in the house in Didsbury did come true, it just wasn't with me. He did give me several chances to be part of his dream, but I wanted it to be *ours*, and it didn't feel that way – it felt like his, and that I'd just be part of the machinery.

Via Flacca

September 1st 1981

I feel I should write something. The existence of this window, this table, this grey-pink dust over the Mediterranean. It seems to expect some commitment to memory; by writing. I have several possibilities – a long critique of an English T.V. quiz show; I'd be showing interest in my paymasters. But it can wait. 27 pages just to say 'get a <u>real</u> director' can wait for times of less reality – for times of busyness. Or I could write the outline for "How to have a dirty weekend" and show Hilary that I can write a book – even one as trite as that. Though it would be quite stylish, quite witty. I'd like to show myself I can write a book. It can't be difficult – but let's not find out right now. One for *'domani'*. And then I could write a letter – to Lindsay – she has one for me she says. And if she goes to London – letters may be all that remains of our fate.

But I can tell her what I'm thinking. How can I explain the fear I have of her going to London; and yet my continual refusal to end this separation. How can I explain anything. So maybe then just a travel journal for myself. To open and read in ten years time in my diaries. I regretted not writing up my first U.S. trip of '73 but the recollection is there – the young negro in Montgomery, the taxi on Canal Street, the queers in New Orleans, and the cable cars and two years later the tears in Union Square.

So maybe not a travel journal. Do I want to remember the drive from Rome Airport the day before yesterday – the frantic search in a provincial town for a box of matches. The hotels full – 2 nights in the Amide *pensione* before moving down the coast to this white stone serried palace. The bay is beautiful. Screw the other guests. Maybe I resent their bourgeois nature because I see my own reflections.

"This is no country for old men" – nor this for young ones – "*solo*". This is a land of families and couples. There are beautiful women aged either 14 or 44.

Father/Husband nearby. And I who should be a father/husband – still wear my wedding band, but read Proust, eat pasta, drink cappuccino – alone.

I feel perturbed – peeved to be more accurate – that Tony Connolly's Moss Side chic has brought the source of troublesome thought back from an empty space which she seemed to have insistently and successfully created – back to the forefront of my mind just as I didn't need it. This may be my favourite summer spot in Europe but I could do without the memories. Or could I. Probably I need some conclusion – need to arrive. Somewhere. Unlike Proust the wound is as deep and wide as ever. The fact she didn't sue me but believed in the final moments, cool and honourable – the fact that I am unable to angle my heart in any other direction – my appalling performance with Katy, my indifference – physical – to Hilary – my fears and subsequent retreat from Fran – well at least I was right. My mother thought me wise and that afternoon in Disley in the sun, in the seat of my little blue racer – looking through the mirror at the girl getting into the battered MGB – knowing that I had met my destiny. Well I was right. "The only girl for me" – it's gone from the jukebox at the old beach caff but it hasn't gone from me.

But I knew that at Christmas – beneath the anger, the pain – I knew it. But forced by the anger to make a break – by perfect praxis – oh hallowed process – I discovered why it had ended. Without that poor tired child passion, my life in thrall to this beauty who hated my touch – could only be continual agony. She never understood that I loved the beauty of her soul as well. But never saw the value of the aesthetic side of my feelings. To be as beautiful as she – can she not expect a man's sexual adoration, if not as a present given, at least as a bore, a duty, a distraction. And hope: oh yes hope. Her mother said "Perhaps you were punishing him in the war of your marriage". And my heart leapt in the neat little Italian restaurant. And don't I know how Eithne, after her affair with the professor's son, found my slightest touch unbearable, and how, using correct psychoanalytical method, I painstakingly worked on her mind so that after one year she had become obsessed with sex – my sex. Is it the bitter taste of how, having won her body back, I chucked her aside for my pretty wife. Or is it fear. Or lack of time or excess of pain – these times – the black outfit – the "lewd cunt come spewing home" were quite as horrible as those volcanoes of your real pain – but as a youth – confidence in youthful time – now it has all but run out and the world is as it is.

Sept 4th 1981

And now, three days later – Proustian emotion – fears for Saint-Loup – worsening illness exaggerated by massive consumption of L.S.D. and resultant ecstatic hysteria – pink skin and new insights into knots and the art of windsurfing – time to look back and see if my state of mind has altered since Tuesday night. For at least 24 hours following the trip my only desire, more even than for Robert's hacienda-like dream – was to race into Lindsay's arms – tell her I love her and that I now know that she is the love of my life and let's have kids etc. etc. Tempered now on this last but one day by sexual fear – again and again. Even pain – the black body stocking loomed into view like one of these blasted large flying insects escaping the storm in my room – and merging with all those other adoring purchases, worn for them not me, why, why, why? Am I back where I started. Why then did I feel so confident as the acid raged through my brain. If she had been on the phone – at the house when I rang for her – I would have blurted it all out "Let's have our sons and daughters and live in each other's lives – I will love you more" – why was I so confident then – now – so scared – this Sunday – I may even be too perplexed to phone on the pretext of her worries about Tabitha. If I remember rightly there were pieces of acid logic.

What.

1) She knows that when passion really leaves – it is the end. She said as much of Michael. That she is still in love with me – since like me her heart seems unable to open to any other – that she never thought it was really over – well then she must know that passion is not gone.

2) She enjoyed it that time in summer. And that once in N.York. The fact they were the only two pieces of real lovemaking in 12 bitter months does not affect – it – our two bodies - working. It has happened.

3) The idea that refusal of sex with me was 'punishment' – the most painful searing part of her marriage war. My selfishness deserved response perhaps and if she could kick me in the eye then why not the ultimate attack. Nightly castration. In that area of battle it took such little effort – so little planning or thought – to repay me for every wrong I had done – in particular that wrong of saying constantly – 'GO'. And since I know that in that I was unfaithful to my love - did not believe that we were fated – treated our life as an experiment yet to be judged, I was guilty – that refusal to commit in terms of children particularly (and that is what sex is for - providing a pointer for that battleground) may have caused her wrath – wakened that vicious frigidity in our bed. And now that I have seen my destiny. Now after 8 months – know with the shock of a St Paul struck by lightening that – she is the one. Will this not clear matters up.

There are – as I have lain here in my beautifully sited sickbed – eat your heart out Byron – arguments against. Briefly:

1) That she is not living with another is no proof that she is still in love with

you. He may have rejected her. If she is still available it could as easily be by lack of opportunity - indifference to passion – lack of direction. There is no proof that she has any passion left at all.

2) As in those two occasions on which a) she may merely have closed her eyes, shut you out, and treated it as masturbation or b) and particularly in N.York, closed her eyes, imagined John Scott (or others) or even felt slightly titillated by coming straight from an adulterous bed to the marriage bed by way of the Atlantic. When your lewd cunt comes spewing home on a Boeing 747.

3) "Will this not clear matters up", indeed ! ! What if it wasn't punishment. When this was mentioned by her mother – she didn't seem to agree. In fact she is intelligent enough to know what's happening to her insides – over 2 years. It wasn't as if it was a sudden problem.

No Trippers – it ain't that easy.

We have to face the simple and appalling fact the kindest, most honest, and most beautiful woman ever to walk into our life, is still there like the crescent moon hanging over this bay – now known to be the only moon – suspicions that there could be a new one each day have recently been found unfounded. But now – from absence of sexual desire on the part of this lady – any attempt to touch the said man would burn hand and soul with the awful cell destroying heat of dry ice.

Endgame.

Or at least the final move.

I shall post this.

It is a letter to you Lindsay. It is everything I feel. I have a dream of you and our kids in that house – that your new job is to be a mother to our children – how many times in Sperlonga have I looked at mothers and daughters and seen that favourite image of mine and imagined you the mother – and you the daughter. And I have a nightmare – that a chemical, hormonal, psychological gate has clicked in your brain, we'll never know why – and never be able to open it. And I am lost. In a pain which has clarified but not died since January.

So time to wake up.

Please write.

If only to say goodbye.

Yours,

As long as this machine is to him, (which was Hamlet's rather witty way of saying 'till death but like me he doesn't wants to sound sloppy)

Anthony

X

Via Flacca — September 1st 1985

I feel I should write something. The existence of this
window, this table, this grey-pink dusk over the
mediterranean. It seems to expect some commitment
to memory by writing. I have several possibilities —
a long critique of an English T.V. quiz show; I'd be
showing interest in my paymasters. But it can wait.
27 pages just to say 'get a real director' can wait
for times of less reality — for times of busyness. Or
I could write the outline for "How to have a dirty
weekend" + show Melony that I can write a book —
even one as trite as that. Though it would be
quite stylish, quite witty. I'd like to show myself
I can write a book. It can't be difficult — but
lets not find out right now. One for 'domani'.
And then I could write a letter — to Lindsay — she has
one for me she says. And if she goes to London — letters
may be all that remains of our tale.
But can I tell her what I'm thinking. How can I
explain the fear I have of her going to London; and yet
my continued refusal to end this separation. How
can I explain anything.
So maybe then just a travel journal for myself.
To open + read in ten years time in my diaries.
I regretted not writing up my first U.S. trip of '73
but the recollection is there — the young negro in
Montgomery, the taxi on Canal Street, the queens in
New Orleans, and the cable cars and two years
later the fleas in Union Square.
So maybe not a travel journal. Do I want
to remember the drive from Rome Airport the

day before yesterday — the frantic search in a provincial
town for a box of matches. The hotels full — 2 nights
in the Amalee pension before moving down the coast
to this white stone serviced palace. The Bay's
beautiful. Screw the other guests. Maybe I resent
their bourgeois natures because, I see my own
reflections.
"This is no country for old men" — nor this for
young ones — "sole" This is a land of families
and couples. There are beautiful women
aged either 14 or 44. Father/Husband nearby.
And I who should be a father/husband — still wear
my wedding band, but read Proust, eat pasta,
drink cappuccino — alone.
I feel perturbed — peered to be accurate — that
Tony Connolly's Moss Side chic has brought the
source of troublesome thought back from an empty
space which she seemed to have insistently +
successfully created — back to the forefront of
my mind just as I didn't need it. This may be
my favourite Summer spot in Europe but I could
do without the memories. Or could I. Probably
I need some conclusion — need to arrive. Somewhere.
Unlike Proust the wound is as damp and wide
as ever. The fact she didn't see me, but behaved
in the final moments cool + honourable — the fact
that I am unable to angle my heart in any other
direction — my appalling peformance with Katy, my
indifference — physical — to Hilary — my fears &
subsequent retreat from Fran — well at
least I was right. My mother thought me wise
+ that afternoon in Disley in the sun, in the dirt

of my little blue racer — looking through the mirror at the
girl getting into the battered MGB — knowing that
I had met my destiny. Well I was right. "The only
girl for me" — its gone from the juke box at the old
beach caff but it hasn't gone from me.
But I knew that at christmas — beneath the anger
+ the pain — I knew it. But forced by the anger to
make a break — by perfect praxis — oh hallowed
process — I discovered why it had ended. Without
that poor tired child Passia my life in Hwall to
this beauty who hated my touch — could only be
continual agony. She never understood that I loved
the beauty of her soul as well. But never saw the
value of the aesthetic side of my feelings. To be
as beautiful as she — can she not expect a man's
sexual adoration; if not as a present given — at
least not as a bore, a duty, a distraction.
And hope: oh yes hope. Her mother said "Perhaps you
were punishing him" in the war of your marriage;
And my heart leapt in the neat little Italian Restaurant.
And don't I know how Kitline, after her affair
with the professors son, found my slightest touch
unbearable, and how, using correct psychoanalytical
method, I painstakingly worked on her mind so
that after one year she had become obsessed
with sex — my sex. Is it the better taste of hew
having won her body back. I chucked her aside
for my poets wife. Or is it fear. Or lack of time
or excess of pain — these lines — the to black
outfit — the "lewd cunt come spewing home" were

quite as horrible as those volcanoes of your youthful
pain – but as a youthful confidence in Kint – now
it has all but run out + the world is as it is.

Sept 4th 1981

And now three days later – Proustian emotion – tears
for Saint hong – worsening illness exaggerated
by massive consumption of L.S.D and resultant
extatic hysteria – pink skin and new insights
into knots + the art of windsurfing – fine to look
back and see if my state of mind has altered
since Tuesday night. For at least 24 hours
following the trip my only desire, more even than
for Roberts hacienda-like dream – was to race
into Lindsays arms – tell her I love her and that
I now know that she is the love of my life and
lets have kids etc etc. Tempered now an this
last but one day by sexual fear – again and
again. Even pain – the black body stocking
loomed into view like one of these blasted
large flying insects escaping the storm in my
room – and merging with all those other
adoring purchases! worn for them not for me,
Why? why? why? Am I back where I started.
Why then did I feel so confident as the acid raged
through my brain. If she had been on the phone
– at the house when I rang – for her – I would
have blurted it all out "lets have our sons
+ daughters and live in each others lives – I will
love you more –" & Why was

⑤

I so confident then – now – so scared – this Sunday – I may even to be perplexed about it all to phone on the pretext of her worries about Tabitha. If I remember rightly there were pieces of acid logic. What.

1) She knows that when passion really leaves – it is the end. She said as much of Michael. That she is still in love with me – since like me here heart seems unable to open to any other – that she never thought it was really over – well then she must know that passion is not gone.

2) She enjoyed it that time ___ And that once in N. York. The fact they were the only two pieces of real lovemaking in 12 bitter months does not affect – it – our two bodies – working. It has happened.

3) The idea that refusal of sex with me was 'punishmnt' – the most painful searing part of her marriage war. My selfishness deserved response perhaps and if she could kick me in the eye then why not the ultimate attack. Nightly castration. In that area of battle it took such little effort – so little planning or thought – to repay me for every wrong I had done – in particular that wrong of saying constantly – 'Go' And since I know that in that I was unfaithful to my love – did not believe that we were tated – treated our life as an experiment yet to be judged. I was guilty – that refusal to commit in terms of children particularly (and that is what sex is for – providing a pointer for that

battleground) may have caused her wrath — wakened that vicious frigidity in our bed. And now that I have seen my destiny. Now after 8 months - know with the shock of a St Paul struck by lightning that - she is the one. Will this not clear matters up.

There are - as I here I ain here in my beautifully sited sickbed - eat your heart out Byron — arguments against. Briefly:

1) That she is not living with another is no proof that she is still in love with you. He may have rejected her. If she is still available it could as easily by lack of opportunity — indifference to passion —lack of direction. There is no proof that she has any passion left at all.

2) As in these two occasions on which a) she may merely have closed her eyes, shut you out, and treated it as masturbation or b) and particularly in N.York, closed her eyes + imagined John Scott (or other) or even felt slightly titillated by coming straight from an adulterous bed to the marriage bed by way of the Atlantic. When your lewd cunt comes spewing home on a Boeing 747

3) 'Will this not clear matters up' indeed !!. What if it wasn't punishment. When this was mentioned by her mother- she didn't seem to agree. In fact she is intelligent enough to know what's happening to her insides — over 2 years. It wasn't as if it was a sudden problem.

No Trippers — it ain't that easy.

We have to face the simple + appalling fact that the kindest, most honest, and most beautiful woman ever to walk into our life, is still there like the crescent moon hanging over this bay — now known to be the only moon — suspicions that there could be a new one each day have recently been found unfounded. — but now — from absence of sexual desire on the part of this lady — any attempt to touch the said man would burn hand and soul with the awful cell destroying heat of dry ice.

Endgame.

Or at least the final move.

I shall post this.

It is a letter to you Lindsay. It is everything I feel. I have a dream of you and our kids in that house — that your new job is to be a mother to our children — how many finely in Sperlonga have I looked at mothers & daughters and seen that favourite image of mine + imagined you the mother — and you the daughter. And I have a nightmare — that a chemical, hormonal, psychological gate has clicked in your brain we'll never know why — and never be

8

able to open it. And I am lost. In a pain which has clarified but not died since January.

So time to wake up.

Please write.

If only to say goodbye.

Yours,

As long as this machine is to him,

(which was Hamlet's rather witty way of saying 'till death' but like me he doesn't want to sound sloppy)

Anthony. X

FACTORY RECORDS
86 Palatine Road, Manchester 20.
Telephone 061-434 3876

There is so much to take in from this letter. The ending saddens me. His drug-addled brain was wrong on many counts but right at the last – 'And I have a nightmare – that a chemical, hormonal, psychological gate has clicked in your brain, we'll never know why – and never be able to open it.' Now, older and childless, I regret that I refused the job he offered – to become the mother he had imagined while in Italy. But he'd once told me, during a row, that I'd make a terrible mother, although he remembers it as 'that refusal to commit in terms of children (and that is what sex is for…)' so he may have been right that this was one cause for rejection of him in the bedroom (or, as he put it, 'wakened that vicious frigidity in our bed'). After all, men and women operate in a very similar way sexually but there is one vast difference, and that is that for a woman before menopause, sex with a man inevitably gets somehow tied up with childbirth, even if it's just to avoid it. It's often part of a woman's sex drive and I'm not convinced it's part of a man's. Then again, it may have been a self-protective survival instinct that stopped me getting pregnant with him. Although we would have been materially comfortable, I doubt I would have coped psychologically with his continual absences at the cost of his family. Also, I'd cared for a friend's baby every Tuesday for nearly a year and found it unutterably boring.

My mum was also right: however much I rejected the idea at the time, I do think I wanted to punish him back.

Tony writes that sex (or the lack of it) was the main stumbling block to our reunion. Yet the 'poor child passion' wasn't dead, as Tony thought; it had just fallen asleep, as Yeats so eloquently put it, and this was to be proven later on.

It's interesting that Tony mostly doesn't address me directly in the above letter but uses instead the third person. It's as if I am one of a larger crowd of characters. Perhaps if he had spoken these words to me (looking in my eyes even) I might have found it easier to respond. I know why he writes, 'she didn't sue' – even though our divorce hasn't happened yet. I remember signing a piece of paper that Tony gave me one night at Old Broadway disclaiming all my rights to proceeds from Factory Records. Not that it would have stood up in court if I *had* sued him. But when he produced this paper it made me think badly of him, because it hadn't even crossed my mind to do such a thing, whereas it had certainly crossed his. He wanted to push me out of any claim to Factory. And he wouldn't, as it turned out, be the only one.

Tony writes, 'This is no country for old men.' Although people would generally now equate this with the 2007 Coen brothers film *No Country for Old Men* – released the year Tony died – he is remembering the line in the Yeats poem 'Sailing to Byzantium'. The poem speaks of the agonies of old age, the remedy being to leave the country belonging to the young and go on a symbolic, spiritual search to Byzantium. However, Tony is also saying Italy is no country for the solo young either, such as he was.

Tony's recalls being in California – in Union Square, San Francisco – in 1975. This

was when he'd just learned his mum had died, hence his tears. He'd travelled across the width of America two years earlier in 1973 and this had made a huge impression on him. The photo above was from that time.

He loved California and San Francisco; that was why he booked our honeymoon there. I came to love it greatly too – years after our split I rented a room in Santa Cruz and survived there for nearly six months before running out of money. I loved driving down the Big Sur and also up into San Francisco, as we'd done on our honeymoon. I wished I could stay there for the duration of my life quite frankly, but back I would come in January 1994, meeting a cold, wet, dark England – and depression.

I'm not sure which quiz show it was that Tony mentions having to write a critique for, but I do remember him being in line for the job as the host of a game show called *The Krypton Factor* – a job he rejected. It ultimately went to Gordon Burns and the show became very successful.

Some parts of the letter make no sense to me now. Tony Connolly was Tony's father's partner after the death of his wife, Tony's mum, and Connolly and I were good friends until he died in 2014, but I don't get the reference to 'Moss Side chic' unfortunately. In the later segment of his letter, Tony admits to having had an acid trip. He tries to itemise some insights and conclusions from the trip but at the end he gets personal and can't fictionalise his feelings anymore. He mentions pink skin and new insights into 'knots and the art of windsurfing'. The knots may refer to wind speed, rope knots or even the poem 'Knots' by R.D. Laing. I'm fairly sure it was rope knots.

His reference to 'Saint Loup' is to a character in Proust's *In Search of Lost Time,* a close friend of the narrator, Marcel, called Robert de Saint-Loup. It's possible Tony was about to read the part where Saint-Loup is killed in combat. Then there's yet another of Tony's favourite quotes from Rochester, 'when your lewd cunt come spewing home'. It's taken from the poem 'A Ramble in St. James' Park'. Tony added 'on a Boeing 747', incorrectly implying I'd had sex with John Scott before flying to New York.

In this letter we also have his first written reference to, and desire for, The Haçienda. He writes that it was Rob Gretton's dream when I clearly remember Tony had had a vision for it years before. Rob was likely more of a driving force while Martin Hannett was totally against it. In the early 1980s there was no thriving rave scene and quite what The Haçienda was *for* wasn't exactly clear, other than as a live venue and Tony wanting to 'give the kids somewhere to go'. The vision was industrial and, as Tony adored the artistic skills of Peter Saville, he trusted him to hire architect, Ben Kelly, to design something spectacular out of a boat showroom on Whitworth Street West. Rob had begun his career in the music business as a DJ and although it took some years for the club to come into its own, The Haçienda eventually found its niche when the DJs entirely took over from live bands. The name 'Haçienda', chosen by Tony, came from a Situationist International slogan: 'The Haçienda Must Be Built'. While Tony was writing his letter from Italy, The Haçienda in Manchester was indeed being built.

CHAPTER 8
The Eastern Mystic and the Western Hustler

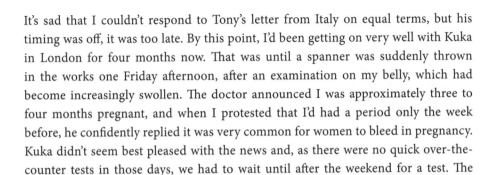

It's sad that I couldn't respond to Tony's letter from Italy on equal terms, but his timing was off, it was too late. By this point, I'd been getting on very well with Kuka in London for four months now. That was until a spanner was suddenly thrown in the works one Friday afternoon, after an examination on my belly, which had become increasingly swollen. The doctor announced I was approximately three to four months pregnant, and when I protested that I'd had a period only the week before, he confidently replied it was very common for women to bleed in pregnancy. Kuka didn't seem best pleased with the news and, as there were no quick over-the-counter tests in those days, we had to wait until after the weekend for a test. The result was negative.

I would receive a diagnosis of an ovarian cyst, for which I was given a surgical referral. Kuka's reaction to the pregnancy announcement made me doubt a relationship that had otherwise been a happy one, up until that point at least. And so began my own confusion, because I did want children eventually – and Tony had asked me to be the mother of his children. Kuka himself never did have children; I asked him recently if he hadn't wanted them: he said he loved children, he just couldn't put up with the wife that went with them! Although affronted by this I took comfort from the fact that he'd never found anyone else to step up to the mark either.

The fact that Tony not only wanted children, but he wanted them with me was a strong pull. But then there was the thorny issue of the house he'd bought. I was scared to bear *his* children in *his* house. I thought I'd be terribly lonely, left holding the baby; although of course, children do grow and speak and become more interesting as time goes on. I had a deep fear, though, of being tied inexorably to the whims of this man. I'd seen a ruthless streak in Tony that bordered on cruelty. For example, there was his treatment of musicians when they didn't agree with him, or his apparent pleasure in the pain I felt while he was punishing me. Kuka was kinder, he showed compassion at least and never tried to manipulate me, unlike Tony. I couldn't trust Tony as his

FACTORY RECORDS
86 Palatine Road, Manchester 20.
Telephone 061-434 3876

Later, much later, that same Sunday night,
full moon, September '81

Dear Lins,
I feel very guilty for having interfered with my romantic irrelevancies at a time when you are trying to make an important
decision about your career. I don't want to confuse your mind with
any more of my garbage but I felt I had to write immediately to
wihhdraw whatever spectors I may have left with you tonight.
It worried me that as you left you seemed worried, sad for me.
Don't be. I don't feel bad at all. It's almost like a weight lifted
from my chest; I know in time now I will be able to breathe more
easily. I lost you many years ago when my lack of committment created
yours. As you say , you are a woman who passes through life and who
passes through loves. I am not, my efforts at adultery over the past
five years have been merely disastrous attempts at ego balance with
the "travelling lady". "'I know I'm just a station on your road" (Cohen).
In that simple difference lies the impossibility, that I have known
deep down inside but never dared to face.
That is who you are...you have passed through my life, I'm very
grateful. Should you ever feel that other feeling, not love...god
knows I felt love for Eithne or Thelma,,,but somethign else which
you would recoginse just as I did...then....que sera....but for now
I want more than you could give....just as before I could not give
what you wanted..
I wish you love and luck. I8d like to think we could be deep friends...
and yet that would mean losing my passion for you...and in a sentiméntal
sort of way I'm quite attached to that passion. I think I would sacrifice
a highly valued friendship with Lindsay Wilson/- just to feel my heart
beat faster in 30 years time if I caight sight of your car in Manchester.
So, my love, look to the future, you have a very beautiful soulá,
accepåt your hysteria like Malcolm accepts his migraines...it is the conditi
of genius...in you of an overflowing spirit. Tho like Mlcolm you coulld
take pills you know.........so here's to your future, with all the love
of five years past. Life is in the end our career; we shared something
unique in our lives together.........bonne chance.   anthony....X
                                                    (X as terrified and as
VAT. No. 305 6301 96   Reg. No. 2340540
A. Erasmus, R. Gretton, M. Hannett, P. Saville, A. Wilson   untidy as our last X tonight)

reactions felt inconsistent and unreliable. But I was 29 then, Tony only 31, and I didn't feel any pressure to rush into having a family whereas, with hindsight, I think Tony did. He knew better than me how fleeting life is.

In this next letter sent from Manchester, he's saying goodbye yet again.

Later, much later, that same Sunday night,

full moon, September '81

Dear Lins I feel very guilty for having interfered with my romantic irrelevancies at a time when you are trying to make an important decision about your career. I don't want to confuse your mind with any more of my garbage but I felt I had to write immediately to withdraw whatever spectors [sic] I may have left with you tonight. It worried me that as you left you seemed worried, sad for me. Don't be. I don't feel bad at all. It's almost like a weight lifted from my chest; I know in time now I will be able to breathe more easily. I lost you many years ago when my lack of commitment created yours. As you say, you are a woman who passes through life and who passes through loves. I am not, my efforts at adultery over the past five years have been merely disastrous attempts at ego balance with the "travelling lady". "I know I'm just a station on your road" (Cohen). In that simple difference lies the impossibility that I have known deep down inside but never dared to face.

That is who you are.....you have passed through my life, I'm very grateful. Should you ever feel that other feeling, not love....god knows I felt love for Eithne or Thelma, , , but something else which you would recognise just as I did..... then.....*que sera*....but for now I want more than you could give.....just as before I could not give what you wanted. I wish you love and luck. I'd like to think we could be deep friends....and yet that would mean losing my passion for you.....and in a sentimental sort of way I'm quite attached to that passion. I think I would sacrifice a highly valued friendship with Lindsay Wilson/ – just to feel my heart beat faster in 30 years time if I caught sight of your car in Manchester. So, my love, look to the future, you have a very beautiful soul, accept your hysteria like Malcolm accepts his migraines....it is the condition of genius....in you of an overflowing spirit. Though like Malcolm you could take pills you know.......so here's to your future, with all the love of five years past. Life, is, in the end, our career; we shared something unique in our lives together.......... bonne chance.

anthony.....X

(X as terrified and as untidy as our last X tonight)

The letter clearly follows a meeting during which no lovemaking took place. I think sex had become the only acceptable means of a reconciliation for Tony. Unfortunately for him, I'd learned the lesson of fidelity by then. For me, being an honest person – or at least unable to lie well – I'd learned that monogamy was essential for my commitment to stay intact. It was unfortunate I'd learned this after all the shenanigans with Tony, and it was too late, because I now felt I owed this newfound faithfulness to my current lover, and not to my husband.

The decision about my 'career' which he mentions was my dilemma over whether or not to go back to nursing. It was the first job I'd trained for in London following my degree, but I'd abandoned it after a year, feeling unable to endure the hierarchical discipline. In the seventies, nursing was worse than school: on one occasion I was told off for talking to a patient, and on another I was chastised for not filling out a fluid chart when I'd been unable to take a break for over five hours. It was strict! I applied again to St. George's Hospital in London and was accepted after the interview, but this time I lasted only a week. It was too late, it no longer felt like the right path to take.

Tony advises me to accept my 'hysteria' and suggests taking pills for it. It didn't occur to me then that Tony's choice of the word 'hysteria' was sexist. Hysteria was a mental disorder attributed to women as long ago as Ancient Egypt, if not before. The Greek physician Hippocrates described hysteria as originating in the uterus, and female hysteria is part of the history of psychoanalysis: Sigmund Freud considered hysteria to be a female disease. Nowadays such assumptions are outdated, recognised as carrying implications of male superiority. That said, I do believe that some female imbalances, such as depression, can be linked to the hormonal menstrual cycle; Tony recognised I had PMS along with volatile moods and outbursts that fluctuated in accordance with my monthly cycle. I couldn't look dispassionately at it then as I can now, and I thought my rages and tears were justified. To a degree, they sometimes were but I have to admit it represented a symptom of a syndrome as well. Mind you, I never acted as crazy with any man as I did with Tony.

Tony had problems handling me and wanted to put me on antidepressants, which I refused to take. Later, in the nineties, he became a fan of Prozac, believing it to be a cure-all of mental illness. He even tried it out himself for a short while but subsequently thought better of it, since, by his own admission, it was making him even more full of himself than usual.

Tony's quote, suggesting that he's 'just a station on my road', is adapted from the song 'Winter Lady' by Leonard Cohen. This illustrates how transitional Tony's imagination was – ranging from West Coast hippy views of women one minute to Yeats and Shaw on the same subject in the next. Such poetic views may seem somewhat patronising and dated today.

The Malcolm mentioned in this letter isn't Malcolm Whitehead who appeared before, but a lovely colleague and friend of Tony's at Granada called Malcolm Clark.

The next letter from Tony came completely out of the blue. In an entirely different vein to the last, he's no longer saying goodbye, nor does he take my new relationship seriously.

FACTORY RECORDS
86 Palatine Road, Manchester 20.
Telephone 061-434 3876

36, Old Broadway.
November 11th, Wednesday, 6-15pm

Dearest Lins,
Wanted to say thankyou for the poem and the song. Sorry it's had to wait ten
days but owing to my incurable optimism/romance(my vain stupidity, I suppose)
I had thought to say these things in person. How silly, how silly; it took
fully to last weekend to let fear and pain decay the hopes. So now I write to
say.
The song is lovely. Vini brought me a copy on Sunday last. Your voice <u>sounds</u>
so good, very delicate.....anyway it really sounds beautful. You must be aware
that on three occasions your phrasing/timing is completely off, and you hit
a wrong note on five occasions. It doesn't subtract from the charm or beauty
of the piece but if you want to have a hit record then you'll have to sort that
out, and those thibgs are easy....lessons, my love...lessons. Take singing
lessons. Alright. As for the sentiments in the song, I can't bear to think
about them. Found the Lew Stone original and made out some of the other
lines.....I don't know about Spring, I can hardly bear to think of Christmas.
But on.
The poem was also lovely. I know that image of the warm house, the cosiness,
that step down into the study at which point I'd first see you in the kitchen,
.........yes. I tried to write a poem about the image which haunted me in
New York last month, but I couldn't get it down in rhyme, it seemed to escape
poetry. Two people, a boy and a girl, they seem to be kneeling...in front
of a window...in this dream everything in the room is white, I can't quite
wwrk out why they're kneeling excebt that they're looking out of a window,
perhaps from under a blind, and it's the rooftops of San Francisco and maybe
it's the moon and maybe it's dawn, and it's the first morning of their honeymoon, and that picture so ill defined, that feeling of shared wonder...in
New York this Autumn it never left me for a second.
Ańd so you don't want to "go back". Funny, you the eastern mystic, me the
western hustler...yet even for me "go back" is too linear too much like
a motorway or plane trip to mean anything in relation to our innermost
life. That "love from above" which we both felt survives ᴍᴀxiᴎ in me despite
the vicious pruning of the last year. In me it is a recógnition that beyond
infatuation and friendship, there is a thing, A kind of relationship that
is rare, almost a twinning of souls in one destiny, that I felt soft ꜰᴍᴎꜱ

VAT. No. 305 6301 96   Reg. No. 2340540
A.Erasmus, R.Gretton, M.Hannett, P.Savile, A.Wilson

intimations of that afternoon in Disley. Since the "going back" that
I have done or tried to do in the last three months is arriving at
knowledge of this thing, well I feel as if I have grown in wisdom and
moved a million miles forward in my understanding of life. I had thought
it was the same for you. To see beneath the outwardly boring nature of
"husband coming home from work", the miracle of two people sharing their
life.....I felt that you too had moved on.....and up....I know that beyond
the games of Granada or Factory,,,the personal life is something holy,
and that throwing it away by negligence and ignorance....my refusal to
accept your depressions for example...is my biggest mistake. Was.
But then maybe you don't see it that way. Maybe. Jesus. The fear.....
the precipitous ups and downs.
When you left, or xix rather when I dropped you at your mum's last week
my heart was full...I felt that I had won your heart back..that in your
eyes and voice I could recognise my own recognition of our fate...that
after all the dangers of our separation I was coming home.....cleansed
seeing more clearly.....that the love I had discovered so deep enbedded
in Italy....was there in you.

And then the week grew on.....maybe it was by the following weekend that
it began to dawn on me. I had assumed that in our friend's talk, you were
being totally honest with me...well I'm sure you were honest....but now
I also know that there must have been things you merely didn't tell me....
..out of kindness....and I realised you had gone to London...and that
the dear car, far from being asymbol of regeneration, was just a nice
way of saying good-bye. My fears were confirmed by a story Alan told me of
what happened to him and Sally once. ....I suppose I deserve everything
I get. Hubris....pride before a fall. I'd be grateful,if you have decided
to "move forward" with your new friend...well I suppose I8d be grateful
to know....so write...and particualrly as when we were getting into the car
you mentioned an inscription you were going to put on the car if you'd
left it for me....it seemed lovely,,,but I can't remember what it was.
I didn't worry at the time because I thought I could ask you soon.....
god what a dunce.........anyway when you write......tell me what it was.

I8ve just found a piece of Yeats which I've been searching for....all
a bit late, mate....but I suppose my way of dealing with a broken heart
(not so much broken as seriously pummelled by constant flurries of hope
and despair) is to fidd these perfect grammatical renderings of my plight"
or feelings more like.

....

VAT.No.305 6301 96 Reg.No.2340540
A.Erasmus, R.Gretton, M.Hannett, P.Savile, A.Wilson

....   I took a break there...Sullivan at the bell...had
tickets for Heartbreak House at the Royal Exchange...so I went. Great. Like
most art there was loads of stuff (it's 12-55 now) about love and marriage
and men and women. Wonderful how personal passion and heart break even
enriches these things with....well....bits of yourself.   You should really
go And see it with your mum before it finishes if you arrive back from
London before the end 'f the month. Much better than that awful Lancashire
piece we saw. Shaw is so good on woman. He shares my view...and that of
the Iroqois Indian nation...wiped out by Columbus etc.....
And where was I...oh yes...Yeats

Well I feel quite guilty now....about this letter.....funny how men with
broken hearts feel so justified in unburdening their soorrows on the
woman who has so captured their heart. No right really. They/you have
enough problems of their own....I'm suppose it's just crying in the
wilderness...before I despair completely....I suppose I'd love to knww if
my case is hopeless....a line to say goodbye and tell me what your line
was for the dear Karrman Ghia. Put the crippled animal out of its
misery.   Oh, god and I nearly lost the full two stone too.

But we might as well do the Yeats as I appreciate your appreciation of the
distilled wisdom of Western European art which you squeeze from my
wandering quotations.....so Yeats.....and that thing that I found with
you.....and cannot quit...and which now I dread has been lost in you......
Lawrences diamond beneath the rose...though there in two souls like
unique jigsaw cuts.

                 "..............it seemed that our two natures blent
                 Into a sphere from youthful sympathy,
                 Or else to alter Plato's parable,
                 Into the yolk and white of the one shell."

I'm sorry if I killed it in you.........still seems to be here in this
heart of mine....in Troilus and Cressida last Saturday night....a
dissappointingly awful production on BBC2......Cressida says to Troilus.
"Will you be true?"....he replies. "Ay; it is my fault, my vice."
And so it seems it is mine....nearly a year from that dread Christmas when
I decided action was required......and no nearer escape.....all that bosh
about Proust and the onset of indifference. Not me so lucky.   You...well
at least tell me for fucks sake.....then I can forget you..."As I should
......but Spring.".....and maybe to end....my mad lady.....for you are that
.....and it has taken me five years to love you as that.....that piece from
Proust......how loving you in the midst of your depressions, your mad

VAT. No. 305 630196   Reg. No. 2340540
A.Erasmus, R.Gretton, M.Hannett, P.Saville, A.Wilson

Ophelia scenes,,,,loving your beauty and your kind and honest soul inthe
midst of the fighting and stilleto heeled assault...how that was...and
may well the be the only......poetry.

          "....people whose own hearts are not directly engaged, always
          regard unfortunate entanglements, disastrous marriages, as
          though we were free to choose the inspiration of our love,
          and do not take into account the exquisite mirage which
          love projects and which xx envelops so entirely and so
          uniquely the person with whome we are in love, that the
          'folly' with which a man is charged who marries his cook
          or the mistress of his best friend, is as a rule, theonly
          poetical action that he performs in the course of his
          existence."

from "The Sweet Cheat Gone"

and shouldn't you really tell me if you are

your slave and former master...........

Anthony

VAT. No. 305 6301 96   Reg. No. 2340540
A. Erasmus, R. Gretton, M. Hannett, P. Savile, A. Wilson

36, Old Broadway.
November 11th, Wednesday, 6-15pm
Dearest Lins,

Wanted to say thank you for the poem and the song. Sorry it's had to wait ten days but owing to my incurable optimism/romance (my vain stupidity, I suppose) I had thought to say these things in person. How silly, how silly; it took fully to last weekend to let fear and pain decay the hopes. So now I write to say.

The song is lovely. Vini brought me a copy on Sunday last. Your voice <u>sounds</u> so good, very delicate.....anyway it sounds really beautiful. You must be aware that on three occasions your phrasing/timing is completely off, and you hit a wrong note on five occasions. It doesn't subtract from the charm or beauty of the piece but if you want to have a hit record then you'll have to sort that out, and those things are easy.....lessons, my love.....lessons. Take singing lessons. Alright. As for the sentiments in the song, I can't bear to think about them. Found the Lew Stone original and made out some of the other lines......I don't know about Spring, I can hardly bear to think of Christmas. But on.

The poem was lovely. I know that image of the warm house, the cosiness, that step down into the study at which point I'd first see you in the kitchen, ...yes. I tried to write a poem about the image which haunted me in New York last month, but I couldn't get it down in rhyme, it seemed to escape poetry. Two people, a boy and a girl, they seem to be kneeling....in front of a window.....in this dream everything in the room is white. I can't quite work out why they're kneeling except that they're looking out of a window, perhaps from under a blind, and it's the rooftops of San Francisco and maybe it's the moon and maybe it's dawn, and it's the first morning of their honeymoon, and that picture so well defined, that feeling of shared wonder...in New York this autumn it never left me for a second.

And so you don't want to "go back". Funny, you the eastern mystic, me the western hustler...yet even for me to "go back" is too linear, too much like a motorway or plane trip to mean anything in relation to our innermost life. That "love from above" which we both felt survives in me despite the vicious pruning of the last year. In me it is a recognition that beyond infatuation and friendship, there is a thing, a kind of relationship that is rare, almost a twinning of souls in one destiny, that I felt soft intimations of that afternoon in Disley. Since the "going back" that I have done or tried to do in the last three months is arriving at knowledge of this thing, well, I feel as if I have grown in wisdom and moved a million miles forward in my understanding of life. I had thought it was the same for you. To see beneath the outwardly boring nature of "husband coming home from work", the miracle of two people sharing their life.....I felt that you too had moved on.....and up....I know that beyond the games of Granada or Factory... the personal life is something holy, and that throwing it away by negligence and ignorance....my refusal to accept your depressions for example....is my biggest mistake. Was. But then maybe you don't see it that way. Maybe. Jesus. The fear.....the precipitous ups and downs.

When you left, or rather when I dropped you at your mum's last week, my heart was full....I felt that I had won your heart back....that in your eyes and voice I could recognise my own recognition of <u>our</u> fate....that after all the dangers of our separation I was coming home.... cleansed, seeing more clearly.....that the love I had discovered so deep embedded in Italy.... was there in you.

And then the week grew on....maybe it was by the following weekend that it began to dawn on me. I had assumed that in our friend's talk, you were being totally honest with me....well I'm sure you were honest....but now I also know that there must have been things you merely didn't tell me.....out of kindness.... and I realised you had gone to London.....and that the dear car, far from being a symbol of regeneration, was just a nice way of saying goodbye. My fears were confirmed by a story Alan told me of what happened to him and Sally once. ......I suppose I deserve everything I get. Hubris.....pride before a fall. I'd be grateful, if you have decided to "move forward" with your new friend...well I suppose I'd be grateful to know.....so write....and particularly as when we were getting into the car you mentioned an inscription you were going to put on the car if you'd left it for me.....it seemed lovely....but I can't remember what it was, I didn't worry at the time because I thought I could ask you soon.....god what a dunce..... anyway when you write......tell me what it was.

I've just found a piece of Yeats which I've been searching for....all a bit late, mate.....but I suppose my way of dealing with a broken heart (not so much broken as seriously pummelled by constant flurries of hope and despair) is to find these perfect grammatical renderings of my plight or feelings more like.

....

I took a break there.....Sullivan at the bell....had tickets for Heartbreak House at the Royal Exchange.....so I went. Great. Like most art there was loads of stuff (it's 12.55 now) about love and marriage and men and women. Wonderful how personal passion and heartbreak even enriches these things with.....well...... bits of yourself. You should really go and see it with your mum before it finishes if you arrive back from London before the end 'f the month. Much better than that awful Lancashire piece we saw. Shaw is so good on woman. He shares my view.....and that of the Iroquois Indian nation.....wiped out by Columbus etc.....

And where was I....oh yes.....Yeats

Well I feel quite guilty now.....about this letter.....funny how men with broken hearts feel so justified in unburdening their sorrows on the woman who has so captured their heart. Not right really, they/you have enough problems of their own....I suppose it's just crying in the wilderness.....before I despair completely....I suppose I'd love to know if my case is hopeless.... a line to say goodbye and tell me what your line was for the dear Karmann Ghia. Put the crippled animal out of its misery. Oh, god and I nearly lost the full two stone too.

But we might as well do the Yeats as I appreciate your appreciation of the distilled wisdom of Western European art which you squeeze from my wandering questions.....so Yeats....and that thing that I found with you..... and cannot quit.....and which now I dread has been lost in you..... Lawrence's diamond beneath the rose.....though there in two souls like unique jigsaw cuts.

"...............it seemed that our two natures blent
Into a sphere from youthful sympathy,
Or else to alter Plato's parable,
Into the yolk and white of one shell."

I'm sorry if I killed it in you.......still seems to be here in this heart of mine....... in *Troilus and Cressida* last Saturday night.....a disappointingly awful production on BBC2......Cressida says to Troilus, "Will you be true?"......he replies, "Ay, it is my fault, my vice." And so it seems it is mine.....nearly a year from that dread Christmas when I decided action was required....and no nearer escape.....all that bosh about Proust and the onset of indifference. Not me so lucky. You .....well at least tell me for fucks sake....then I can forget you..... "As I should..... but Spring."...... and maybe to end......my mad lady....for you are that.....and it has taken me five years to love you as that......that piece from Proust.....how loving you in the midst of your depressions, your mad Ophelia scenes......loving your beauty and your kind and honest soul in the midst of fighting and stiletto heeled assault....how that was.....and may well be the only......poetry.

"..........people whose own hearts are not directly engaged, always
regard unfortunate entanglements, disastrous marriages, as
though we were free to choose the inspiration of our love,
and do not take into account the exquisite mirage which
love projects and which so envelops so entirely and so
uniquely the person with whom we are in love, that the
'folly' with which a man is charged who marries his cook

or the mistress of his best friend, is as a rule, the only
poetical action that he performs in the course of his
existence."
from 'The Sweet Cheat Gone'
and shouldn't you really tell me if you are
your slave and former master..............
Anthony

Quite why Tony had such a sudden change of heart, I'm not sure. It may have been because he'd found out I was going into hospital for surgery, and he was convinced I'd got terminal cancer. Since he thought his life was running in tandem with Marcel's life in Proust's *The Sweet Cheat Gone* and I was Albertine, perhaps he imagined her untimely death would mirror my own. Or maybe it was the demo he'd received of 'I Get Along Without You Very Well', which I sang accompanied by Vini Reilly's musical backing. I wondered, when I received this strangely affectionate letter (sent just before I went into hospital), if Tony had taken the words of the song demo literally. The true meaning of the lyric, of course, is that the author isn't getting along very well at all – thinking of spring could break his/her heart in two. As we'd married in spring it could perhaps be taken that way. Tony may have construed it to mean I wanted him back, and a big part of me did, although I wouldn't admit it. Tony wasn't the only one to be inconsistent. Although I'd gathered my mum hadn't been wild about me marrying Tony, it was her enthusiasm for the song that made me suggest to Vini that we try a version of it. She knew I was in denial about how much I really cared for Tony. She never interfered in my private life, but I wonder if she was nudging me, knowing the lyrics to be somehow appropriate? The recording obviously helped bring Tony around. Alas, not me.

I couldn't respond to him in the same way. My relationship with Kuka had by no means run its course. We'd made plans, we were going to India together, I couldn't just walk away from him and, in any case, I wasn't ready to.

Tony was quite right about me hitting the wrong notes. I think singing is the best of all careers but unfortunately, I wasn't gifted in that department. When I eventually came to terms with that fact, I planned on hiring a choirboy for my next Factory release (FAC 96 'Telstar' by Ad Infinitum) but unfortunately, the music publisher blocked an addition of lyrics to the tune, so we had to settle for putting my voice through a vocoder.

I must have sent Tony a poem, probably thanking him for the good times but, despite telling him I didn't want to go back, it didn't put him off his quest to make me return to him and end my relationship with Kuka. This quest of his, and my own confusion, continued for nearly two years. He'd said in the letter that the personal life is something holy, so perhaps, being a Catholic boy, he simply wanted to stay married to his first wife.

In the Catholic religion, there is, after all, only one wife. But I agree that there is something more holy about the personal life than work – Granada and Factory, in his case.

It was perhaps symbolic that Tony went to see *Heartbreak House* at the Royal Exchange. An apt title at any rate. This George Bernard Shaw play is actually a comedy about the pointless pursuits of the upper middle classes. Tony says it was about 'love and marriage and men and women' and that Shaw shares his own view 'and that of the Iroquois Indian nation'. My understanding of the Iroquois women is that they were honoured members of the tribe, decision-makers with other important roles, plus the lineage and family name was passed down through the women's family. Sounds like the complete opposite of Factory Records at this time but, then again, three of the four main directors have died, not to mention Ian, leaving several wives, ex-wives and girlfriends behind.

Shortly after mentioning the GBS comedy, Tony speaks about the doomed lovers in one of his favourite tragedies – Shakespeare's *Troilus and Cressida*. Cressida, despite loving Troilus, is unfaithful to him when they are apart. She hadn't wanted to leave Troilus whereas he brings it about, or at least doesn't stop it from happening. Thus, he takes the blame for her consequent loneliness and a situation that leads her to be unfaithful. Tony is intimating in the letter that he also blames himself and apologises, despite my fighting and 'stiletto-heeled assault'. That was the worst thing I ever did (in my whole life) in terms of a physical attack. We were in his car, I was on the back seat with Alan Wise beside me, and Tony was in the driving seat with someone else in front. Tony turned round and said something nasty to me – to my shame I don't even remember what – but it made me so angry I kicked him in the forehead. He was okay, the kick had no force in it, but, as he rightly pointed out, the forehead is quite close to the eye. Tony calls me 'mad', referring to my 'mad Ophelia scenes', another allusion to Shakespeare, and indeed I hold my hands up. I was as mad as hell with him at times. Unfortunately, I retaliated every time Tony insulted me and not always with words. Once he had me pinned to the floor to stop me from punching him – a flyweight fighting a heavyweight, so he always had the advantage except in the above case.

His quote from *The Sweet Cheat Gone* by Proust may somewhat over-romanticise the poetry of a disastrous love. But it is also a beautiful quote and speaks of the humbling nature of a love that bears no relation to logic. It is true that there's no accounting for love, or passion. Passion is generally little thought out. I think passion always meant more to Tony than love – not to say that he didn't love, I know he did.

Tony was rarely logical when in love. Perhaps when one part of the brain is highly developed (the intellectual one in his case) then another part, such as the emotional area, suffers and pays a price. Tony was often led by fantasy rather than reality. He was in denial of the true circumstances of our situation, as this letter shows, and he wanted the beautiful woman that he'd continue wanting all his life, (in this case, to provide a fantasy family).

People tell me I've had an interesting life but I've sometimes wished I'd married a more ordinary (but kind) man. It might have been more boring, with less 'poetical action' to quote Proust, but I suspect there would have been more stability. And children. Tony's letters to me had poetry and spoke of love but was this really how he felt or was he merely showing off his literary knowledge? In the above letter he's still trying to impress but is now trying to write in a more literary way in an attempt to analyse our lives. Bob Dickinson, aforementioned Granada director and author, who has read Tony's letters to me, commented that, 'Tony thinks of himself as a kind of stream-of-consciousness writer, much influenced by the Beats like Kerouac and Ginsberg. Then he goes Proustian, and his tone is more serious, but his long sentences still sound like his TV scripts – he writes like he knows he's being watched, and not just read.'

In *24 Hour Party People*, I liked the scene where Tony (played by Steve Coogan) is taking me (portrayed by Shirley Henderson) to Manchester Piccadilly Station for her departure to London. He asks her twice, almost begs her, not to leave him. I met the scriptwriter, Frank Cottrell-Boyce, whose brain lit up like a light bulb when I told him the story of how Tony and I broke up. He loved the idea that it was the wife who left this slightly comic character version of Tony. But what we see next in the film is how Tony bounces back almost straightaway after she gets out of his car. While admitting to it being a low point for him, he immediately launches into a literary reference – of course – and says:

'I think it was F Scott Fitzgerald who said, "American lives don't have second acts". Well, this is Manchester and we do things differently here.' Then he smiles to camera and says, 'this is the second act,' before pulling on his joint.

Tony's character is expertly drawn here. People really believe that Tony said, 'This is Manchester and we do things differently here' – the sentence has practically become Tony's slogan, appearing on wall decor art prints amongst other things. Little do people realise that in fact it was the perceptive screenwriter Frank Cottrell-Boyce who came up with it! But, words apart, this was precisely how Tony dealt with emotional trauma. His brain drove him forward, he had an uncanny ability to put emotional upset to one side while he got on with the important business of living. That's how he was when Ian Curtis died, and that's how he eventually was when he gave up waiting for me to return to him.

CHAPTER 9
How Love Fled

I'd barely come out of surgery when Tony came to visit me in hospital. It seemed an odd thing to do under the circumstances, given that the operation was in London, and I was staying there with my boyfriend. I must have arranged it so that the two men wouldn't cross paths. That said, Kuka didn't object to Tony's visit even though there was clearly a subtext other than friendship to Tony's appearance at the hospital. Tony was a busy man and, if he'd moved on from me, there was no way he'd have travelled all the way to London for a short meeting – hospital visiting hours were strictly adhered to in 1981.

His visit didn't go too well as he confronted and interrogated me about my relationship with Kuka. He reacted badly to my answers and, clearly irritated, told me about a woman he was seeing. Then Tony sent a handwritten letter via my mum, who brought it with her a day or two later.

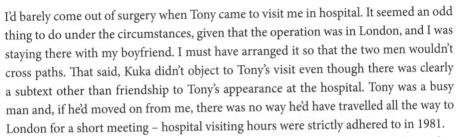

8-15 pm.
Friday night.
on the train

Oh my love,
What a stupid bastard I am. If you cast me aside now – you will be so right! I behaved abysmally. And now I can't ring you or take back any of my stupid comments. What a dolt. Oh god I feel so angry with myself.
As I walked across harlow earlier on, I felt all that irritability-jealousy of the unnamed man – the aftermath of all the tension. I knew I'd say something or cause trouble – and I told myself to cool it. And I tried + I failed! I behaved like a pig. To mention some irrelevant Didsbury cow in order to provoke some truth from

②

you about your life in London .. I know
your silly, gentle, paranoiac mind + to
put that crap into it was utter stupidity
on my part. A desperate attempt to
dispell some of my confusion. Most
inglorious. Most petty. And I
deserve to pay the price of loneliness
that I offered as my own small "bit" in
the prayers for your health.

I have no intention of approaching
any woman until my fate is sealed.
I know you find marriage boring + the
kind of scene I provoked tonight — typical
of the petty problems contained within
that institution. I will not argue for
marriage — I will make no claims

③

— I swore on my mother's grave that I
would make no attempt to win you
back — I wonder if my gifts break that
vow — but for myself — for myself
— I want marriage — in this case I
want you as my wife + mother of my
children — and until you seal the
death of real happiness — I see no
point in chasing the empty foolishness
of fancy. You find it fun - romance -
I find it too unreal — too lacking in soul -
all heart — no soul; and while there is
still the slightest hope that you'll come
back to me — I will avoid contact with
such things — which while marriage is
a possibility - even a faint one — seems

④

to me no more than a putrescent sore —
a vain and fantastical obstacle to
real + lasting happiness. For God's
sake read Lawrence's poem —
"Fidelity".

Does /oving that poem mean I am
grown old. If so, I thank God for
each year that adds on. Forgive me
but I find your espousal of romance —
childish — immature. Hence perhaps
my irritability. I have seen too many
people — ███████-█████ who have
chased romance — I have seen that
strange emptiness of soul grow in
their eyes as the years pass and

⑤

'romance' leaves them emptyhanded and
so little at peace.

That's why there will be no woman for
me now — or for some time to come. With
'romance' now I can smell the dead
corpse even with the first thought of
a body desired.

And so I wait.

And after my performance tonight
I expect to wait in vain.

And still I love you to distraction.

Yours.
your husband.

Anthy x

8.15pm

Friday night on the train

Oh my love, What a stupid bastard I am. If you cast me aside now – you will be so right. I behaved abysmally. And now I can't ring you or take back any of my stupid comments. What a dolt. Oh god I feel so angry with myself.

As I walked across London earlier on, I felt all that irritability – jealousy of the unnamed man the aftermath of all the tension. I knew I'd say something or cause trouble – and I told myself to cool it. And I tried and I failed. I behaved like a pig.

To mention some irrelevant Didsbury cow in order to provoke some truth from you about your life in London. I know your silly, gentle, paranoiac mind and to put that crap into it was utter stupidity on my part. A desperate attempt to dispel some of my confusion. Most inglorious. Most petty. And I deserve to pay the price of loneliness that I offered as my own small "bit" in the prayers for your health. I have no intention of approaching any woman until my fate is sealed.

I know you find marriage boring and the kind of scene I provoked tonight – typical of the petty problems contained within that institution. I will not argue for marriage – I will make no claims – I swore on my mother's grave that I would make no attempt to win you back – I wonder if my gifts break that vow – but for myself – for myself – I want marriage – in any case – I want you as my wife and mother of my children – and until you seal the death of real happiness – I see no point in chasing the empty foolishness of fancy. You find it fun – romance – I find it too unreal – too lacking in soul; and while there is the slightest hope that you'll come back to me – I will avoid contact with such things – which while marriage is a possibility – even a faint one – seems to me no more than a putrescent sore – a vain and fantastical obstacle to real and lasting happiness. For God's sake read Lawrence's poem – "Fidelity".

Does loving that poem mean I am grown old. If so; I thank God for each year that adds on. Forgive me but I find your espousal of romance – childish – immature. Hence perhaps my irritability. I have seen too many people who have chased romance – I have seen that strange emptiness of soul grow in their eyes as the years pass and 'romance' leaves them empty handed and so little at peace.

That's why there will be no woman for me now – or for some time to come. With 'romance' now I can smell the dead corpse even with the first thought of a body desired.

And so I wait.

And, after my performance tonight, I expect to wait in vain.

And still I love you to distraction.

Yours, your husband,

Anthony

x

Tony later admitted it was a 'hysterical note'. So, hysteria wasn't confined to women after all. I probably played down my relationship with Kuka because I didn't want to hurt Tony unduly. In truth, though, being confused I also wanted to keep my options open, especially now that Tony apparently wanted me back, and doubts had recently arisen about a long-term future with Kuka. How exactly I played it down I'm not sure, but clearly, judging from Tony's letter, I must have spoken about Kuka in fun, romantic terms rather than long-term marriage. When Tony told me, between gritted teeth, about someone he was seeing himself, I wondered what he was doing visiting me in that case? Perhaps he felt jealous of Kuka and probably felt guilty getting angry with someone who'd just had fairly major surgery.

In his letter Tony reduces romance to a thing of fancy, but the fact was that my relationship with Kuka hadn't been a passing dalliance, it had depth. It was also fresh and surprising, and we had adventures. We shared weekdays as well as weekends together, and he introduced me to cultural activities, art galleries and art house films, none of these things had happened with Tony. By comparison my marriage had become stale and I'd either been sidelined from Tony's adventures or found them dull. Mostly the former.

Tony's letter is very emotional, and his handwriting becomes increasingly shaky. It suggests he began writing when the train was stationary – probably at Euston station – with his hand becoming more unsteady due to the movement of the train. The contrast between Tony's earlier letters and this and two recent ones revealed a total turnaround. Now he loved me to distraction? He'd told me so many times he didn't want us to continue. I couldn't get my head round it but felt a pull in his direction.

He mentions D.H. Lawrence's poem 'Fidelity', which is about the way a marriage can create what Lawrence calls a 'gem' underneath all the chaos of romance and love, and that gem is fidelity. The letter is a bit of a lecture but also an appeal, and there are a number of strong feelings swirling around in his head which don't find any resolution in words. Is this the same man who earlier wrote that being in love was everything? Love is all very well, he'd added, but it is merely happiness. Given what became of my life, I well know the truth in his words about the differences between marriage and foolish fancy. That I'd been prone to such had already been demonstrated with my juvenile crush on Howard. But it wasn't accurate in my current situation.

FACTORY RECORDS
86 Palatine Road, Manchester 20.
Telephone 061-434 3876

                                    36, Old Broadway.......Sunday afternoon end of
                                                 this long November '81

Dearest Lins,
Thought I'd wrote you a letter...nothing in particular...just a load of
stuff to help you pass the time in your "lying in". I seem so unable to
control my over-anxious love ("She bad me take love easy..as the leavese grow
on the tree...but I was young and foolish/ and with her could not agree.")
at your bedside, that here, cool, calm, and tender even, in front of my
typewriter, and that little picture of the unicorn being variously stabbed,
I feel I can do a much better job of helping you pass your time.
So my love, some general chit-chat. Got the train home...full of anxiety
which was at least a little dispelled by penning that hysterical note
your mother sent down....(ah, detente when it comes is so sweet..)and that
too may have passed an amused ten minutes for you.....Alan was late at
Stockport station.....you know...like you were sometmes....hmph..hmph...
went round to see Rob and Lesley(first time since Gretton's return from
the states)....they're lovely and so untroubled....Lesley said of my
horrors and shakings in Madrid...that she found it strange that tragedy.
..insane jealousy...fights with the loved object...had never crossed her
path....a charmed life...could it last...probably will for them....I pray
so for it.....though she finds Ian even harder to deal with now and
even more upsetting than a year ago..strange. Rob wanted to go out...NewYork
time, but I put him off.....emotionally drained was little Wilson. Funny
how Gretton is the one person I know who can make trimuphant self coffidence
appear charming and neuer tedious.
Saturday;;;;slept in. Went shopping in Didsbury in the afternoon. Met Penny
Bowers little kid..who seems very grown up on his bike...I think Penny's
gping to do the door at the Hacienda (What a fucking name). ...met Steve
one of the nice young Granada researchers....and at the bus stop, Nobby Carr
the big bodied fourty five year old Manchester raconteur....he's lovely...had
a nice ten minute chat at the bus stop about the state of the new british
comedians who he'd just done some work with...he didn't think their cracks
about Lady Diana..."I get morning sikness too....every morning I feel sick jus'
thinking about them"...would go down well in the Northern clubs.
Home to cook my dinner/tea....stew.....nearly as good as you and my mum's...
nearly...I can get it to taste really meaty but I think I get the proportions

VAT. NO. 305 6301 96 Reg. No. 2940540
A.Erasmus, R.Gretton, M.Hannett, P.Savile, A.Wilson

Tony was quite melodramatic in this letter, the stuff about the 'emptiness of soul' that grows in their eyes 'as the years passed' is like something out of a 19th century novel, and the ending with its 'corpse' reference also seems rather gothic, or perhaps surrealist. The irony in Tony's repudiation of romance is that romance was the very thing he was always caught by. Despite having five serious relationships in his life, he tended to romantically fixate on just one woman at a time and, once fixated, found it almost impossible to move on, even when the situation called for it. He knew it himself and told me it was as if he was a fish caught by a hook in its mouth. At this point in our history Tony was fixated on me, and all the girlfriends he was going through couldn't replace me.

Then, in the latter period of his life, for seventeen years he was fixated on Yvette and couldn't move on from her even when he tried.

Tony reminds me that he's sworn not to try to win me back. When he wrote: 'I deserve to pay the price of loneliness that I offered in my own small "bit" in the prayers for your health,' he's referring to a recent time when he visited his mother's grave in Hollins Green. Throughout his life he went to her grave, usually in times of trouble, or if a decision was required of him. Given his belief that I was terminally ill, he prayed for my health there and, as he says later in the letter, swore on his mother's grave that he'd give me up in exchange for it. It seemed to me a ridiculous vow, and a ridiculous belief, but I appreciated his concern.

Then I received another loving letter, sent directly to the hospital. He addresses me by my maiden name although we were still married, and yet a few weeks before he died in 2007, he referred to me as Lindsay Wilson.

36, Old Broadway.....Sunday afternoon end of this long November '81
Dearest Lins,
Thought I'd write you a letter....nothing in particular....just a load of stuff to help you pass the time in your "lying in". I seem so unable to control my over-anxious love (She bad me take love easy...as the leaves grow on the tree.... but I was young and foolish....and with her could not agree.") at your bedside, that here, cool, calm, and tender even, in front of my typewriter, and that little picture of the unicorn being variously stabbed, I feel I can do a much better job of helping you pass your time.
So my love, some general chit-chat. Got the train home... full of anxiety which was at least a little dispelled by penning that hysterical note your mother sent down...(ah, *detente* – with your ma – not you yet – when it comes is so sweet..) and that too may have passed an amused ten minutes for you.... Alan was late at Stockport station.... you know....like you sometimes.... hmph ....hmph...went round to see Rob and Lesley (first time since Gretton's

2/

of Bisto wrong. Tesco's actually had NO cornflour..thought you'd like
to know that.
Sage gave Rpb and Lesley a lift over on 'our' way out...he seems very
well....chirpy...rude. Everybody very pleased that you're well by the
way.
Went out to meet Barney and Sue in a pub in town..Danish Wine bar,,,one
drunken seven year old(looked like Roger five years ago) fell off his
chair four times..very entertaining. Sue is five months pregnant.
I think Barney's pleased.
Rob insisted we had to go to a club....no-one else ever wants to but
he insists on 'checking out Manchester'...jeesus. We were on our way
to the Zoo Club...a redecorated Slack Alices...until I remmebered that
on Thursday's What's in I had described it as " a rich man's watering hole2
and hence felt far too embarassed,,,not to say unenethusiastic to go.
So we crossed Cross Street to Quentins.....Chris (you now..Brian Tilsley)
Rob was annoyed that I refused to hustle Free drinks out of said
Coronation Street Star. It is though hysterically funny when chris/Brian
ascends the DJ box..."And it's Angelas birthday..great...come on everybd...
..lets have a party..." christ..it's embarrasing...but also very funny.
Got bored within minutes, and left the fab four to go to a party whoch
had to be better....in Didsbury..some friend of Alan and Annies's. Alan
the asshole..typically never showed and I felt very peculiar until In
npticed some familiar faces......Annie...your Annie...what a surprise when
we had just been talking about her....I said that we'd just been talking
about her.   She looked well..very well...young...pretty(not my type but)
and on her own.....um mmmmmm....she was chatting to some fellah most
of the time....when she left she took his phone number. Well.. gossip
gossip gossip...sends her love and says get in touch if you come back
north. I told her you were going to decide what to do about me according
to what an Indian mystic was going to tell you. She laughed a lot...
"that's my Lindsay...mad...quite mad" And mine too.
And who else was there??????Graham (leather coats) with arm firmly
around Nicky.....the girl I know from the Dobsons....you from the
Hebden Bridge lot perhaps...and 8th day etc...seem quite a pair..though
Graham seems listless about his job....Sarah has opened a shop on the
Fulham Road......and Michael is in Paris...though on his last trip to
the south of France he took a van load of funiture and then didn't get
paid. Now trying to open a shop in gay paree the story goes.
And the remains of the party...till well after everyone else was gone
was filled with a fascinating conversation with a man called Richard Teal
or Dick or sometiing....he's an academic of some sort...30...eccentric
but trim looking....small bow tie....and he's a cabalist..and totally
devoted to the occult and atsrology...and the occult...and all tjosr
things...and very knowledgeable, and lots of fun......told me that Pisces

VAT. No. 305 6301 96 Reg. No. 2340590
A.Erasmus, R.Gretton, M.Hannett, P.Saville, A.Wilson

return from the States)... they're lovely and so untroubled.....Lesley said of my
horrors and shakings in Madrid.....that she found it strange that tragedy.....
insane jealousy....fights with the loved object.....had never crossed her path....a
charmed life.....could it last.....probably will for them....I pray so for it..... though
she finds Ian even harder to deal with now and even more upsetting than a
year ago.... strange. Rob wanted to go out.....New York time, but I put him off.....
emotionally drained was little Wilson. Funny how Gretton is the one person I
know who can make triumphant self- confidence appear charming and never
tedious.

Saturday; ; ; ; slept in. Went shopping in Didsbury in the afternoon. Met
Penny Bower's little kid...who seems very grown up on his bike....I think Penny's
going to do the door at the Hacienda (what a fucking name)....met Steve, one
of the nice young Granada researchers..... and at the bus stop, Nobby Carr, the
big bodied forty-five-year old Manchester raconteur.....he's lovely....had a nice
ten minute chat at the bus stop about the state of the new British comedians
who he'd just done some work with....he didn't think their cracks about Lady
Diana....."I get morning sickness too.....every morning I feel sick just thinking
about them".....would go down well in the Northern clubs.

Home to cook my dinner/tea.....stew.....nearly as good as you and my
mum's.....nearly.....I can get it to taste really meaty but I think I get the
proportions of Bisto wrong. Tesco's actually had NO cornflour....thought you'd
like to know that. Sage gave Rob and Lesley a lift over on 'our' way out....he
seems very well .....chirpy....rude. Everybody very pleased that you're well by the
way. Went to meet Barney and Sue in a pub in town.....Danish Wine bar, , , one
drunken seventeen year old (looked like Roger five years ago) fell off his chair
four times....very entertaining. Sue is five months pregnant. I think Barney's
pleased.

Rob insisted we had to go to a club.....no-one else ever wants to but he
insists on 'checking out Manchester'.....jeesus. We were on our way to the Zoo
club..... a redecorated Slack Alices..... until I remembered that on Thursday's
What's On I had described it as "a rich man's watering hole" and hence felt far
too embarrassed.....not to say unenthusiastic to go. So we crossed Cross Street
to Quentin's....Chris (you know....Brian Tilsley). Rob was annoyed that I refused
to hustle Free drinks out of said *Coronation Street* Star. It is though hysterically
funny when Chris/ Brian ascends the DJ box...."And it's Angela's birthday....
great....come on everybody.....let's have a party..." christ...it's embarrassing....
but also very funny. Got bored within minutes, and left the fab four to go to a
party which had to be better....in Didsbury...some friend of Alan and Annie's.
Alan the asshole...typically never showed and I felt very peculiar until I noticed

was not in fact two fish swimming in opposite directions....aparrently the real suymbol includes a whale constellation and the two fish are connected by ropes to this massive whale, and they are the way they are because they are moving with this whale.....the whale being all the dreams,,and idealism, and ambitions of the Piscean. (like my romanticism about marriage...it sure takes a lot of pulling and swimming...particularly with my pro-romance wife) Sometimes they can pull it..sometimes they can't. He said a galvanised Piscean was a fascinating character.....Al Capone for example. Al Capone for God's sake.

Cancer....I suppose you know that the crab's claws don't just mean that you bite....OUCH....but that your arms spread out wide like the crabs, to cobtain and to hold in mother fashion....children or even groups of people but there is this desire to take care, to control even with those enclosing arms.

Sp he was great.......went home feeling that the bottle of Rioja which gained admittance to the party was far better spent that the many pennies delivered into the clutches of the Cprontaion street celeb. Had a cooked breakfast this morning..spoilt myself. Have done some accounts......then your mom rang. We shared our mutual amazement at how well you are.........discussed philosophies of romance....the correct use of the London train...the state of the bookmaking on the chances of Lindsay and Anthony Wilson....decided to follow your recommendation.... let it work itself out.......and with much more confidence resolved to have a chat agin mid-week.......Evens is the real call..tho me being me I'd only give 6-4 against....not on the chat..that's defo.

And now..as the afternoon winds on.....and in your health at least life seems so much clearer...the falling leaves now regain their delicate shades and their promise of the beauty of the seasons change.....lose that feeling of death and compketion that they have taken on in past weeks ....the darkening light no longer cold and fearful.....more misty..... vague and reassuring as the story of the crib draws near.

And so before I take walk out the Boradway....is there anything else... not really....I was going to talk to you a little bit about this house. How it will go if you so require it....and how if your life continues anyway aprt from me...then it should go anyway.....I searched for A house to replace Charlesowrth for three years....and I looked all the time for a FAMILY HOUSE....and if that isn't to be the case then this lovely palace will contain only the shades of the family I once imagined....not sure I could stay..........and then there's the connection of material objects and tjeir loyalty with certain women. I remember my old Sunbeam Stilletto.....it was loayl to Eithne.. When I tried to take a girl called Jane out from Girton...it wouldn't start..refused....I used to kick it.........when I tried to take Fran Landsman out..it dropped it's

VAT. No. 305 630196   Reg. No. 2340540
A.Erasmus. R.Gretton. M.Harnett. P.Savile, A.Wilson

some familiar faces......Annie....your Annie.....what a surprise when we had just been talking about her. She looked well....very well....young....pretty (not my type but) and on her own.....um mmmm....she was chatting to some fellah most of the time....when she left <u>she took his</u> phone number. Well...gossip gossip gossip...sends her love and says get in touch if you come back north. I told her you were going to decide what to do about me according to what an Indian mystic was going to tell you. She laughed a lot..."that's my Lindsay...mad...quite mad." And mine too.

And who else was there?????? Graham (leather coats) with arm firmly around Nicky ... the girl I knew from the Dobsons....you from the Hebden Bridge lot perhaps....and 8th day etc.... seem quite a pair....though Graham seems listless about his job....Sarah has opened a shop on the Fulham Road....and Michael is in Paris....though on his last trip to the south of France he took a van load of furniture and then didn't get paid. Now trying to open a shop in gay paree the story goes.

And the remains of the party...till well after everyone else was gone was filled with a fascinating conversation with a man called Richard Teal or Dick or something....he's an academic of some sort....30....eccentric but trim looking.... small bow tie....and he's a cabalist....and totally devoted to the occult and astrology....and the occult....and all those things....and very knowledgeable, and lots of fun....told me that Pisces was not in fact two fish swimming in opposite directions....apparently the real symbol includes a whale constellation and the two fish are connected by ropes to this massive whale....the whale being all the dreams, , and idealism, and ambitions of the Piscean. (Like my romanticism about marriage...it sure takes a lot of pulling and swimming...particularly with my pro-romance wife). Sometimes they can pull it...sometimes they can't. He said the galvanised Piscean was a fascinating character......Al Capone for example. Al Capone for God's sake.

Cancer......I suppose you know that the crab's claws don't just mean that you bite....OUCH...but that your arms spread out wide like the crabs to contain and to hold in mother fashion....children or even groups of people but there is a desire to take care, to control even with those enclosing arms.

So he was great.......went home feeling that the bottle of Rioja which gained admittance to the party was far better spent than the many pennies delivered into the clutches of the Coronation Street celeb. Had a cooked breakfast this morning....spoilt myself. Have done some accounts......then your mom rang. We shared our mutual amazement at how well you are......discussed philosophies of romance.....the correct use of the London train....the state of the bookmaking on the chances of Lindsay and Anthony Wilson....decided to follow your

propshaft halfway down my street...and when I tried to take Hilary out it
overheated and then speqed boiling radiator water all over my chest...I
screamed...I screamed so much...but delighted in the starnge inanimate
loyalty of that silver machine to a woman.
And this house.....well did it stop me making love to the Belgian boiler.....
it made it feel impossible though our relation had soured while still staying
at Alans.....but I thought I knew enough of its vibrations not to bring
Fran back here when I sought to take solace in someone elses xxxx arms......
.....but that night....when I stayed first at her house...I returned to
36 Old Broadway the next morning_ to find the cellar flooded and the
video equipment destroyed....and it hadn't just leaked in in an impartial
way...we found from the debris and smell that foul sewage water had erupted
as out of the mouth of hell...at great speed and with much power from out the
depths of the basement toilet.......and I felt it was accusing me of
disloyalty to the cause for which the house was bought.......I then got
very annoyed with the hoise...just as I had with the Stilleto...told it to
leave me alone...and it's not my fault if they don't want me and what th
fuck does it expect me to do....................and the funny thing is.....
these loyal inanimate objects don't say a word...they just stand there aNd
stare back at you....as if allpowerful in their immuatability.
It8s funny that the only act of sexual congress that has taken place under
these rovves in several years.....cost £20.00
Though it was, dare I say....worth every penny.

"Ypu took me on the road to Paradise.......
....and though we lost our way........I must convey my thanks.

Take care.......rest yourself........don't get impatient to get out.....
.....don't fiddle with your dressings or your stitches or whatever.....
..and I'll pop 9n on Tuesday night.....and I'll even behave myself.

Love

Anthony   or if you w nat it the way I do it now for Factory...

                      yours,

                                  Daft isn't it.   And so are you.

                                              See yah.

VAT. No. 305 6301 96   Reg. No. 2340540
A. Erasmus, R. Gretton, M. Hannett, P. Saville, A. Wilson

recommendation.....let it work itself out..... and with much more confidence resolved to have a chat again mid-week.....evens is the real call....tho me being me I'd only give 6-4 against.....not on the chat....that's defo. And now....as the afternoon winds on....and in your health at least life seems so much clearer... the falling leaves now regain their delicate shades and their promise of the beauty of the seasons change....lose that feeling of death and completion that they have taken on in past weeks. ....the darkening light no longer cold and fearful.....more misty....vague and reassuring as the story of the crib draws near.

    And so before I take walk out the Broadway.....is there anything else.....not really.....I was going to talk to you a little bit about this house. How it will go if you require it.....and how if your life continues anyway apart from me.....then it should go anyway.....I searched for a house to replace Charlesworth for three years....and I looked all the time for a FAMILY HOUSE.....and if that isn't to be the case then this lovely palace will contain only the shades of the family I once imagined....not sure I could stay......and then there's the connection of material objects and their loyalty with certain women. I remember my old Sunbeam Stiletto.....it was loyal to Eithne.... when I tried to take a girl called Jane out from Gorton.....it wouldn't start...refused....I used to kick it........when I tried to take Fran Landsman [sic] out....it dropped it's propshaft halfway down my street.... and when I tried to take Hilary out it overheated and then spewed boiling radiator water all over my chest.....and I screamed.....I screamed so much...but delighted in the strange inanimate loyalty of that silver machine to a woman.

    And this house....well did it stop me making love to the Belgian boiler..... it made it feel impossible though our relation had soured while still staying at Alan's....but I thought I knew enough of its vibrations not to bring Fran back here when I sought to take solace in someone else's arms.....but that night..... when I stayed first at her house......I returned to 36 Old Broadway the next morning to find the cellar flooded and the video equipment destroyed.....and it hadn't just leaked in an impartial way....we found from the debris and smell that foul sewage water had erupted as out of the mouth of hell.....at great speed and with much power from out depths of the basement toilet....and I felt it was accusing me of disloyalty to the cause for which the house was bought......I then got very annoyed with the house.....just as I had with the Stiletto....told it to leave me alone....and it's not my fault if they don't want me and what the fuck does it expect me to do...................and the funny thing is..........these loyal inanimate objects don't say a word.....they just stand there and stare back at you......as if all powerful in their immutability.

    It's funny that the only act of sexual congress that has taken place under

First Class

POSTCODE IT

Be properly addressed

Lindsay Reade,
Ward E,
National Temperance Hospital,
Hampstead Road,
LONDON N.W.1 2LT

these rooves in several years.......cost £20.00. Though it was, dare I say......worth every penny.

"You took me on the road to Paradise........ ....and though we lost our way..............I must convey my thanks.

Take care........rest yourself.......don't get impatient to get out.......don't fiddle with your dressings or your stitches or whatever.....and I'll pop in on Tuesday night.....and I'll behave myself.

Love Anthony or if you want it the way I do it now for Factory....

yours,

(FCL Stamper with signature Anthony H.Wilson)

Daft isn't it.

And so are you. See yah.

In this chatty letter, Tony begins with yet another quote from his favourite poet, Yeats. The line is actually, 'She *bid* me take love easy,' from the poem 'Down By The Salley Gardens'; Tony used the word 'bad' as an abbreviation for 'bade'. The poem's protagonist had been too insistent with his lover and, in the next stanza, now grown older and wiser, he is 'full of tears'.

Then Tony mentions the word *detente* – meaning the easing of hostility or strained relations – in reference to my mum, but not me yet. My mum had judged Tony quite harshly and, without ever directly saying so, hadn't really approved of him. She'd have preferred me to tie the knot with a rather nicer person called Mark, to whom I'd previously been engaged. (The trouble was that Mark, being *too* nice, couldn't stand up to me, and I didn't want to end up as some kind of shrew.) As a result, Tony and my mum were a bit awkward with one another initially but, the fact that, at this point in the story, she's at least communicating with him suggests she thought he could now be my better option. Nothing was said; she was wise enough to know I wouldn't have taken advice, or would have rebelled against it.

It strikes me as strange that my main bone of contention – namely 36 Old Broadway – is referred to by Tony as if it was bought with me in mind. Such a shame we never talked about it and shared the search. Much to my amazement, despite his attachment to it, Tony offers in this letter to let the house go (if I require it). When he uses the capitalised words FAMILY HOUSE it goes further than ever towards explaining where his main mental difficulty was at this juncture: he was now more than ready for a family and he wanted it with me, his wife. The search he'd been on to find such a family house – for three years, he writes – was unbeknownst to me. His other occupations seemed to take his (and our) full attention, so as far as I knew another house wasn't on his agenda.

If only he'd said all this to me sooner. 'If only' … two of the saddest words in the world. But, as ever, the timing was out. Later, while attempting a reconciliation, we did go and view other houses in Didsbury together, but nothing seemed right. These big houses felt frightening, as if they represented a giant trap to be set for me. This wasn't just the fear of being stuck alone with a baby, but also a discomfort I felt around big, expensive houses. From the get-go neither of us were materialistically minded; Tony was very ambitious but, speaking for myself, that was the very reason I was happy for Tony's savings to be used to create Factory Records rather than to buy us a bigger, better house than the two-up/two-down we lived in.

In describing his adventures, Tony includes many people he knows and bumps into on one night. It's almost as if he's trying to escape his worries by becoming socially overactive. On his return from visiting me in hospital (after which he penned the 'hysterical' note), he sees two Factory partners – Alan (Erasmus) who picks him up from the station and Rob (Gretton), whom he visits in Chorlton. Tony declines joining Rob for a night on the town on account of feeling 'emotionally drained'. The next day Tony sees Penny (Henry) who did indeed run the door at The Haçienda (I remember she previously ran the door at Rafters for Alan Wise) and her 'little kid' – her young son, Ben. Then there is Nobby (Carr), a compere at nightclubs such as Rotters (on Oxford Street and now a car park). 'Sage' is Jon Savage, a Cambridge-educated writer and music journalist. Best known latterly as the author of *England's Dreaming*, an award-winning book chronicling the Sex Pistols and the rise of punk rock, Jon was working at Granada in those days, as I remember. He hung around Tony a lot, frequently visiting us in Charlesworth. At this juncture, he's taking Tony to Rob and Leslie's flat, where they meet up with Barney (Bernard Sumner, singer of New Order) and his girlfriend, Sue. Then there's a mention of the clubs they go on to: the Zoo club and Quentin's (owned by Chris Quentin, who played Brian Tilsley in *Coronation Street*). Tony leaves to attend a party of a friend of Alan (Erasmus) and Annie, Alan's girlfriend at the time. Tony then meets another Annie – the sister of my ex-boyfriend Michael, and other friends of mine from

FACTORY RECORDS
86 Palatine Road, Manchester 20.
Telephone 061-434 3876

Late Tuesday night. 36, Old Broadway. Dec 1st '81

Darling Lins,
Another letter then, a last one maybe, who knows, life seems so uncertain
these days. Perhaps I am better to learn to live happily in the arms
of uncertainty.
You were very pretty tonight, fidgeting around your bed like a young
schoolgirl, smiling with those flashing eyes. And the train journey was
fine....again a corridor train and a compartment in blue old velvet to
myself. The guard was most solicitous. making sure he would wake me up
at Stockport should I fall asleep. He sat most of the trip in the next
compartment..he had his wife with him...they were about fifty. Somewhere
near Stafford she came into my compartment laughing saying her husband, "the
guard" was worried that their laughing and talking would disturb my sleep.
I showed her my book, and laughed with her saying I was not sleeping, and
that he was "silly". She laughed and returned next door, scolding her husband
in a playful voice that he was indeed "silly." One of those little pieces of
passing human contact that make the soul smile.
And Proust made me smile....as I recap the last volume I founD pages of
wonderment about love and pain and literature....fabulous stuff that obviously in my highly excitable state in Italy I had not relished to the full. Was
it you or the windsurfing?
And one matter arising. Sorry to be so deathly.....when I was leaving...the
German romantic always full of weltscmerz or is it schmalz. Particularly
as when walking away down those particularly dark and unhospitable back
streets between your bed and the railway, I realised that I should not have
reacted with such (hidden) shock and horror to your saying that you could
not imagine ever sleeping with me again. I realised that I had never really
asked myself that question. I base my vain attempts to recapture you too on
a philosophical committment to true love, and a rational faith in marriage
'contra mundum'. But can I really see us back togrher again....sharing
a bed.   No.   Just like you that picture seems impossible. I don't
think it means anything in particular.....just that I can't imagine it..
that it does NOT seem possible.
And then a few minutes later as I boarded the train, my mind returned to
this thing one could not think of. "Why then we should do it...spend a
night together.....beacuse it seems it cannot exist". I laughed and settled

VAT. No. 305 6301 96 Reg. No. 2340540
A. Erasmus, R. Gretton, M. Hannett, P. Savile, A. Wilson

my time with him, one being Graham, who'd made me a fabulous leather coat and jacket which I wore constantly. This explains Tony's 'leather coats' reference.

The 'act of congress' Tony refers to ironically helped put paid to our reconciliation. It was a sore point with me, and Tony was unwise to remind me of it. It took place at Old Broadway just before I embarked on the relationship with Kuka. Tony suggested paying me for sex. It's a pity he didn't just say he wanted to make love to me, that he wanted us to make try to make a go of things again. It was play-acting of course but, all the same, there was an undertone of truth to it. The fact I went along with his suggestion makes me cringe to this day. It was as if he was tacitly showing me that my money worries would cease if we got back together (which they would have done), that all I had to do was have sex with him, but I ultimately chose the money worries over being a whore. Following this charade, we both felt strangely happy. There was a kind of tangible relief that we were still a couple, that now we could get on with the business of sharing our lives again. But my happiness was brief and was almost immediately replaced by shame. The experience exacerbated my impression that I was a possession of Tony's, to be bought and sold, to be shipped to his new house like a piece of furniture. It was to be another seven years before the next 'act of congress' would take place between us.

Tony's first visit to me in the London hospital was quickly followed up with another. It seemed incongruous to me that Tony was being so kind and loving to me while I was virtually living with another man quite happily. I wondered if he liked the challenge, or if he just chose to be blind to my situation.

Or was it simply a final appeal? Real this time? Perhaps it was, because when Tony arrived home from his second visit to the hospital, he typed and sent me the following letter. Unlike the rather comedic previous letter, this one is not funny. He seems more resigned and indicates it could be his last letter to me.

Late Tuesday night, 36 Old Broadway, Dec 1st '81
Darling Lins,

Another letter then, a last one maybe, who knows, life seems so uncertain these days. Perhaps I am better to learn to live happily in the arms of uncertainty.

You were very pretty tonight, fidgeting around your bed like a young schoolgirl, smiling with those flashing eyes. And the train journey was fine .....
again a corridor train and a compartment in blue old velvet to myself. The guard was most solicitous, making sure he would wake me up at Stockport should I fall asleep. He sat most of the trip in the next compartment....he had his wife

down to my conversation with the guard......but the joke......this more
than flippant idea....kept reappearing....like a challenge.
Why don't we. Just one night. Sometime when you are back up North
convalescing. Your mum won't mind you being off. Have dinner, a bottle of
wine....and then sleep together in our old bed,....and then have
coffee...toast even in the moʊning.....and return to the real world.
Since there seems no jealousy in your world, and you wish to behave like
a free agent....and since the delicate state of your body precludes any
entry of the disturbing notion of sexuality.....it would become merely
the acting out of the unthinkable. As I type it,it seems as ludicrous
as it no doubt is. For us to share a bed seems so much a part of the
past...locked away with all those other things.....and yet I feel as
I did on the train....a fascination with the idea of just doing it. As if
soemone had offered me this exotic drug...it was completely harmless,
and had an effect which could not be described or even imagined. Except
by taking it.
I imagine it, like biting into time, not knowing whether you will taste
the sweet but cloying past or a fresher flavour of future times. Or
would it be the present, and a sense of moment....or would the sheer
unthinkability scare us back down the stairs......well there it goes....
.....it would not throw light on our confusion but in encountering
confusion provide at least a fascinating experience. And are we yet too
old for fascinating experiences.   Enough.   It's mad. Feel free to
reject this suggestion quite out of hand.   Interesting as an idea though.
And so......whatever.....we will live on through all this.....if as seems
likely we will continue on our separate ways for at least the next short(?)
period of our lives.....well though I may lose hope or faith...or you
lose even more than you've lost now....yet I will always believe that
the spirit of our marriage will never fade.....we have had some bad
times....and then nearly a year apart with other people.....and still
for all I could scream "out" and for all you can quietly disclaim
marriage and posession and a shared life.....for all of that and after
all of that........we are still very much in love....in that love
into which we sank that first summer. If that is all that is left.....
the tenderness in the ꭓ spaces between us from eye to eye....then that
is an achievment of fantastic height.....it is a base and a foundation
which should we some day both decide at the same time to return to.....
.....well I believe that it will always be there. We should never be
friends. There was too much passion and love to degrade it like that.
So for now.....I thank god that you are well.....compared to all my
dire imaginings,,,,my going out again into the cold of 'not-you' is
easily bearable.   And since I will not write again.....and since,
this could be my last opportunity.........the poem which I have

with him....they were about fifty. Somewhere near Stafford she came into my compartment laughing saying her husband, "the guard" was worried that their laughing and talking would disturb my sleep. I showed her my book, and laughed with her saying I was not sleeping, and that he was "silly". She laughed and returned next door, scolding her husband in a playful voice and saying that he was indeed "silly". One of those little pieces of passing human contact that made the soul smile.

And Proust made me smile...as I recap the last volume I found pages of wonderment about love and pain and literature.....fabulous stuff that obviously in my excitable state in Italy I had not relished to the full. Was it you or the windsurfing?

And one matter arising. Sorry to be so deathly.... when I was leaving.....the German romantic always full of *Weltschmerz* or is it *schmalz*. Particularly as when walking away down those particularly dark and unhospitable [sic] back streets between your bed and the railway, I realised that I should not have reacted with such (hidden) shock and horror to your saying that you could not imagine ever sleeping with me again. I realised that I had never asked myself that question. I base my vain attempts to recapture you on a philosophical commitment to true love, and a rational faith in marriage '*contra mundum*'. But can I really see us back together again....sharing a bed.   No.   Just like you that picture seems impossible. I don't think it means anything in particular..... just that I can't imagine it.....that it does NOT seem possible.

And then a few minutes later as I boarded the train, my mind returned to this thing one could not think of.

"Why then we should do it....spend a night together......because it seems it cannot exist". I laughed and settled down to my conversation with the guard..... but the joke.....this more than flippant idea.....kept reappearing......like a challenge. Why don't we. Just one night. Sometime when you are back up North convalescing. Your mum won't mind you being off. Have dinner, a bottle of wine....then sleep together in our old bed.....and then have coffee....toast even in the morning....and return to the real world. Since there seems no jealousy in your world, and you wish to behave like a free agent.....and since the delicate state of your body precludes any entry of the disturbing notion of sexuality.... it would become merely the acting out of the unthinkable. As I type it, it seems as ludicrous as it no doubt is. For us to share a bed seems so much a part of the past.....locked away with all those other things.....and yet I feel as I did on the train.....a fascination with the idea of just doing it. As if someone had offered me this exotic drug....it was completely harmless, and had an effect which could not be described or even imagined. Except by taking it.

sometimes mentioned to you.....and which ....well it says all I have
to say. I've loved Yeats since he was my 'first' poet when I was
sixteen......nice somehow that my expreience in life should lead me
to feel so deeply&exactly those great commonplaces of love and
experience and pai n which he sets forth to the love of his youth...
who incidentally and for him,like me,in vain, was to be the only
love of his life, Maud Gonne;

> "When you are old and grey and full of sleep
> And nodding by the fire, take down this book,
> And slowly read, and dream of the soft look
> Your eyes had once, and of their shadows deep;
>
> How many loved your moments of glad grace,
> And loved your beauty with love false or true,
> But one man loved the pilgrim soul in you,
> And loved the sorrows of your changing face;
>
> And bending down beside the glowing bars,
> Murmur,a little sadly, how Love fled
> And paced upon the mountain overhead
> And hid his face amid a crowd of stars."

With all my love,
Anthony.   X

VAT. No. 305 6301 96   Reg. No. 2340540
A.Erasmus, R.Gretton, M.Hannett, P.Savile, A.Wilson

I imagine it, if at all, like biting into time, not knowing whether you will taste the sweet but cloying past or a fresher flavour of future times. Or would it be the present, and a sense of moment....or would the sheer unthinkability scare us back down the stairs......well there it goes.....it would not throw light on our confusion but in encountering confusion provide at least a fascinating experience. And are we yet too old for fascinating experiences.   Enough.   It's mad.   Feel free to reject this suggestion quite out of hand. Interesting as an idea though. And so.....whatever......we will live on through all this.....if as seems likely we will continue on our separate ways for at least the next short (?) period of our lives.....well though I may lose hope or faith....or you lose even more than you've lost now.....yet I will always believe that the spirit of our marriage will never fade.....we have had some bad times....and then nearly a year apart with other people.....and still for all I could scream "out" and for all you can quietly disclaim marriage and possession and a shared life......for all that and after all of that........we are still very much in love.....in that love into which we sank that first summer. If that is all that is left.....the tenderness in the spaces between us from eye to eye....then that is an achievement of fantastic height..... it is a base and a foundation which should we some day both decide at the same time to return to.....well I believe that it will always be there. We should never be friends. There was too much passion and love to degrade it like that. So for now....I thank god that you are well......compared to all my dire imaginings, , , , my going out again into the cold of 'not-you' is easily bearable. And since I will not write again.....and since, this could be my last opportunity.....the poem which I have sometimes mentioned to you.......and which.....well it says all I have to say. I've loved Yeats since he was my 'first' poet when I was sixteen.....nice somehow that my experience in life should lead me to feel so deeply and exactly those great commonplaces of love and experience and pain which he sets forth to the love of his youth....who incidentally and for him, like me, in vain, was to be the only love of his life, Maud Gonne;

"When you are old and grey and full of sleep
And nodding by the fire, take down this book,
And slowly read, and dream of the soft look
Your eyes had once, and of their shadows deep;

How many loved your moments of glad grace,
And loved your beauty with love false or true,
But one man loved the pilgrim soul in you,
And loved the sorrows of your changing face;

And bending down beside the glowing bars,
Murmur, a little sadly, how Love fled
And paced upon the mountain overhead
And hid his face amid a crowd of stars."

With all my love,

Anthony. X

He'd said he wouldn't write again – which he actually did, but not for another seven months. Why though? Was he giving up because I'd told him I couldn't imagine sleeping with him again, or even having one last try at this? It would transpire though that, letters or no letters, he wasn't about to give up. He wrote that I wished to behave as a free agent, but this simply wasn't true. I felt committed to my other relationship. I was not immune to the kind of fixation that Tony had with certain partners. The sad fact at this stage was that I was in a sexual relationship with Kuka and therefore, bonded and loyal to him physically. I couldn't imagine sex with Tony, his body felt wrong to me. But this was to be temporary, as most things are.

When he writes of 'a philosophical commitment to true love, and a rational faith in marriage *contra mundum*', it's almost as if he's making the same kind of appeal that Roger McGough made to him years earlier over Thelma. A Catholic principle. I wish I hadn't been dismissive of such a sentiment, not especially being a fan of marriage, as he points out. I think intellectually he was correct.

I couldn't bring myself to accept Tony's suggestion of sharing a bed – I felt it was something only a couple would do. Yet it was something we would do again and again (once my relationship with Kuka was wrecked and I was free again). We slept together later that decade with passion; then, in 2007, when his illness had aged him from 57 to 87, we chastely slept side by side in his loft apartment most weekends for the last three months of his life.

There are elements of self-pity contained in the letter – the very idea of it being the 'last letter', although he takes the piss out of himself with the *weltschmerz/schmalz* joke. But there's also powerful writing, such as the part about 'taking a bite out of time' and seeing what it would taste like. Clearly this was a Proustian influence but powerful, nonetheless. Reading his words in later life, I regret that I didn't experiment with him and take that bite out of time.

Tony's comparison between his love for me and Yeats's for Maud Gonne was romantic, but the idea that I was the only love in his life was delusional. I didn't know it then, but he'd also already compared Thelma to his Maud Gonne. And he was young then, more loves were to follow. All the same, there was something powerful between Tony and me and always a connecting thread – fainter than an umbilical cord, but ever felt. I feel it following his death and know I always will.

It's strange to think that now I have become old and grey (or would be, without hair dye), that I'm slowly reading his words and trying to make sense of how our love fled. Yeats's poem 'When You Are Old' says everything and more about a lost love when viewed from an older and wiser perspective. It is deeply sad, but also intensely romantic.

CHAPTER 10
That's the Deal

It was January 1982 and Kuka and I had booked a six-week trip to India for after I left hospital. This left me free from the stress of having to make an immediate decision about Tony and our future. Tony knew about this trip and accepted it, and I felt comfortable letting things just be as they were. While I was away, Tony embarked on another relationship, this time with a girl called Ros, who seemed a genuinely good prospect for him. Despite my misgivings about losing him to someone lovely, I came to terms with it. No longer torn, I was able to properly embrace my role as Kuka's girlfriend. But this transpired to be only a lull; pressure from Tony would eventually return.

The experience of India was so overwhelming that I thought of little outside of it. My focus was on adapting to life there, which I found both outstandingly beautiful and disturbing in equal measure. We arrived in Bombay, now renamed Mumbai, but failed to find anywhere to stay, at any price, in the whole city. We spent the whole night wandering the streets. As dawn broke, we found ourselves watching these figures slowly arise around us on the pavements, figures we'd earlier assumed to be bin bags that had been dumped by the side of the road. The population was huge – it made London seem like a quiet suburb – and the poverty was overwhelming. We visited a shanty town called the Colaba district; open sewers ran through it while 3-year-olds wandered about holding babies or taking care of toddlers. But the children and the people were colourful and beautiful, they wore rags with broad smiles.

We travelled as far south as Khajuraho and saw the magnificent temples and erotic sculptures. We saw burning bodies on the *ghats,* the riverfront steps that ran down to the River Ganges of Varanasi and watched the sunrise over the Ganges. I felt a deep connection to the rich cultural heritage of the country, but Kuka and I were struggling to compromise on our differing desires there, with him wanting to buy as many antiquities as possible while staying in cheap dives, whereas I was keener on hot water and some degree of comfort. He generally won since I had little money, and so I had to resign myself to the nightly buzz of mosquitoes in my ear. All the same, India was a mind-blowing experience. Despite some of the horrors we'd seen there, the most depressing sight of all was driving into London from Heathrow Airport; it was March, cold and harsh, and the bleak roads we drove along teemed with depressed-looking people battling against driving rain. My diary note for that day: 'Everywhere people look blue with cold and drawn with worry. There's no lepers, no filth, no starvation and yet somehow the picture has a bleakness you can't find in India'.

As soon as I got back to Manchester, Tony was back on my case again, ostensibly as friends but it was fairly obvious that there was more to it than that. Despite having told me he was going to marry Ros, which admittedly upset me – although I didn't show it – he asked me to stay at Old Broadway to take care of the cat while he was in New York. He'd told my mum in April 1982 that he was having doubts about his relationship with Ros, and there were other indications he was still working on our reconciliation. He'd taken me the previous year to see the cavernous boat showroom where The Haçienda was to be built, and invited me again to see the work in progress before the grand opening. He took Ros to the opening night of The Haçienda on 21 May as he was still seeing her, but he took me there the following night. Also, the very night before The Haçienda opened, he took me to a literary dinner with the television host David Frost. We weren't sitting together but Tony insisted we change places, whereupon I discovered I was sitting next to the evening's star, David Frost himself. This was a mistake. Tony probably thought I'd be impressed but I hated every moment. Frost, despite being a fantastic broadcaster with great skill at interviewing people, showed zero interest in talking to me at all and it felt cold. Little did I know that he was just like that with anyone he didn't know – unless he had to interview them. My older self wouldn't have been so sensitive to Frost's disinterest in me, but either way, he seemed removed, and didn't so much as touch the meal on offer that the audience had paid quite a lot for. It felt to me that he lacked the human touch, there was almost an emptiness of soul, and I wondered if this was what became of products of the TV world. It compounded my misery over the situation I was in. I burst into tears in the bathroom between courses. I couldn't let Tony go but didn't want him back either.

When Tony took me to The Haçienda on 22 May, the place seemed half empty, as it would be for years to come. My outstanding memory of that night is of the two of us dancing arm in arm to 'Me and Mrs Jones' by Billy Paul. The irony of the lyrics, describing a couple who were meeting behind the backs of their partners, was not lost on me. It was as if we were in a seventies disco, not the ultramodern, industrial and trendy nightclub it was supposed to be. In my diary note for that day, I wrote that 'it felt like a prison', that 'the music was absolutely terrible', and that 'the miserable people there do not deserve all that money being spent on them'. I also observed that 'Tony was ill – he looked a wreck – and we went home early'. My first impressions of The Haçienda mirrored the way I felt about LA at the beginning, and yet I came to love and appreciate both places.

In addition to our night at The Haçienda and that awkward literary dinner, Tony and I had been out for a meal earlier that month to mark our wedding anniversary on 14 May. No wonder Ros was getting fed up. It must have been horrible being with someone who was still carrying a torch for another, particularly when he had been considering marriage with her. Ros would have been a good match for him but inevitably they broke up. Then, as soon as that happened, Tony's focus was well and truly back on me.

Why hadn't I refused all contact and continued with my life in London? Perhaps I would have done if we hadn't been married. Perhaps if I wasn't still fascinated by Tony and his drive or still felt a strong attachment to him. The fact was that I felt completely torn. Kuka was terribly decent about this, even suggesting Tony and I give it a try. This only compounded my confusion and drew me nearer to Kuka if anything. Tony, meanwhile, was being outrageously manipulative in trying to pull me away from Kuka, which tended to have the reverse affect.

Tony had earlier expressed viable doubts about my singing ability after hearing the demo I'd made with Vini of 'I Get Along Without You Very Well'. He pointed out, 'You must be aware that on three occasions your phrasing/timing is completely off, and you hit a wrong note on five occasions'. Nonetheless, he'd also written to me, 'Your voice sounds so good, very delicate … beautiful … if you want to have a hit record then you'll have to sort that out, and those things are easy … lessons, my love … lessons.' We were either both fooling ourselves or it was another example of Tony's manipulation, or both: the lessons, paid for by Tony, took place in Manchester and drew me away from London – and Kuka. I naively went along with this and took the lessons, but Tony's money didn't buy me a great singing voice unfortunately. Subsequently, Tony enthused about putting the track out as a Durutti Column single, and Vini and I duly went into Revolution studios in Cheadle Hulme during May 1982 for the recording. I actually recorded the vocal on the very day The Haçienda opened. All this time I was spending away from Kuka was yet more of a compromise to our relationship. But I still wouldn't give Kuka up.

And then came the arrival of this next extraordinary letter from Tony.

May 24th 1982
WHAT I WANT FROM A WIFE
1) A Partner: one of the most important points of all and one where we both fell down.......and the hill was so long. It's not just a question of being supportive, but more that feeling that though you may remain two people in your everyday appearances to other people, there is inside the light, glowing softly, hidden from many perhaps, but there so strongly inside, that there is one other person who is as important to you as yourself, and that other person is not exactly the other, the wife, but the two, the single personality that is your partnership.....through life

My 24th 1982

WHAT I WANT FROM A WIFE

1) A Partner; one of the most important points of all and one where we
both fell down....and the hill was so long. It's not just a question
of being supportive, but more that feeling that though you may remain
two people in your everyday appearances to other people, there is inside
the light, glowing softly, hidden from many perhaps, but there so strongly
inside, that there is one other person who is as important to you as
yourself, and that other person is not exactly the other, the wife but
the two, the single personality that is your partnership...through life
until death does part you from your breath.

2) Children. I should _need_ to _want_ to tke be the father of HER children
It's deep and complex but contained within that statement. Much more
complete and serious than it sounds. Inside your bones.

3) Destiny; yes I should need to feel that too. I suppose I come near
to some of your ideas about fate and the spirit/sould, and would add
as a footnote that Yeats thing from Plato about feeling like two halves
of one sphere.....as if I had always been, in times of not knowing her
that jagged edged half shell, and the jagged edges of hers the only
ones that fit and have fitted even when we didn't know each other...just
waiting in time; waiting on time. And I need to know AFTER infatutaion.

4)Beauty; this is the one I'm embarassed about; I find it demeaning to
my spiritual self respect that the flesh could be important in this
mystical context, but I have learnt...Eithne....Katy...and many more, that
lack of artistic wonderment on my part saps away the strength from the
possible growth. To be nice to myself I put it down to my obsession
with art is beauty is truth....to live in the presence of female beauty
that is alive, thinking, changing like an ever flowering rose, each day
new petals , new colours....is like beaing Botticelli....to be able to
watch in the artists minds eye, or in your bed beside you each night,
the wonder of creation...form, shape, line, colour....art...and for me
a horny little schoolboy...a lady of beauty. I would want this from
a wife.

5) My mother; the great discovery of my mid twenties...I have never budged
since from thsi particular piece of knowledge. The way in which I would
require my wife to be like my mother is a subtle one. No simple question
of looks or the way she cooks stew.....Completely different...to do with he
attitude to people around her...the way she deals with sertain aspects
of life. The way I knew Thelma was wrong because of the way she talked
to her dog; the way you used to take Mrs Wild to the shops on a Saturday..
...things that mean little on tye surface but present a world view...I
should need a wife who had my mother's world view,,in its essence not in
its million ramifications.

6) I would need a wife who really loved me; not essential, but less pa

until death does part you from your breath.

2) Children. I should <u>need</u> to <u>want</u> to be the father of HER children. It's deep and complex but contained within that statement. Much more complete and serious than it sounds. Inside your bones.

3) Destiny; yes I should need to feel that too. I suppose I come near to some of your ideas about fate and the spirit/soul, and would add as a footnote that Yeats thing from Plato about feeling like two halves of one sphere.....as if I had always been, in times of not knowing her, that jagged edged half shell, and the jagged edges of hers the only ones that fit and have fitted even when we didn't know each other......just waiting in time: waiting in time. And I need to know AFTER infatuation.

4) Beauty; this is the one I'm embarrassed about; I find it demeaning to my spiritual self respect that the flesh could be important in this mystical context, but I have learnt....Eithne......Katy.... and many more, that lack of artistic wonderment on my part saps away the strength from the possible growth. To be nice to myself I put it down to my obsession with art is beauty is truth.... to live in the presence of female beauty that is alive, thinking, changing like an ever flowering rose, each day new petals, new colours.....is like being Botticelli.....to be able to watch in the artist's mind's eye, or in your bed beside you each night, the wonder of creation.....form, shape, line, colour......art......and for me a horny little schoolboy.......a lady of beauty. I would want this from a wife.

5) My mother; the great discovery of my mid twenties.....I have never budged since that particular piece of knowledge. The way in which I would require my wife to be like my mother is a subtle one. No simple question of looks or the way she cooks stew.....Completely different..... to do with her attitude to people around her......the way she deals with certain aspects of life. The way I knew Thelma was wrong because of the way she talked to her dog; the way you used to take Mrs Wild to the shops on a Saturday.......things that mean little on the surface but present a world view.....I should need a wife who had my mother's world view, , in its essence not in its million ramifications.

6) I would need a wife who really loved me; not essential, but less painful.

Tony

x

It seemed like a draft contract or a job advert for something I didn't feel minded to apply for. Who did he think he was, wanting this and wanting that? I also felt reprimanded somewhat, as if I should pull my socks up and get on with the job of being a good wife. And yet he blamed himself as well as me for our marital failure. The final paragraph about his mother has significance. Tony's mum was the great love of his life, and he frequently drew comparisons between the two of us – the way I cooked stew was one of them. I wonder why stew was so important to him; he often referred to it, was it a metaphor for something else? The slowness of the cooking compared with fast food, the mother at the hearth and the warming smell of stew signifying love? It's now a dated way of thinking about food but is maybe symbolic of a stay-at-home mum compared to an absent one. The last meal I ever made for Tony was stew and, more than any other gift I could bring him, it felt very much tied up with my love and care for him. It was sad that, being so poorly, he could only manage a mouthful. A mate of his was only too happy to wolf it down.

Actually, Tony's letter is quite a good document in and of itself but, needless to say, I didn't react favourably to it.

I'm dubious about Tony's statement that it's 'not essential' for his wife to love him. Was he trying to make the facts different by joking about them, to make it easier for me to leave the man I was with? But, if he was joking, then the whole document becomes a joke. As well as demeaning to him if she doesn't love him, it's also not very nice for her to be with someone she doesn't love. Why would she? To use him for some other reason?

The fact that he wanted a beautiful wife was all very well but what happens when the wife grows old? Is she to be replaced by a younger model? This he did to his second wife, leaving her for a woman twenty years his junior. I'm not without sympathy for men who desire younger, beautiful wives and can understand those with power choosing them, given the magnetic pull of sexual attraction. I still wonder if it's somewhat emotionally immature and superficial.

I'm fairly sure this was the envelope containing the 'What I Want From A Wife' document:

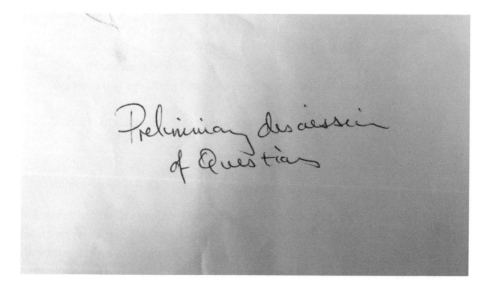

As mentioned earlier, Tony had admitted he'd been wrong to buy Old Broadway in the way he had and promised he'd happily sell it. Hence he suggested we go out together and look for another property. If he'd been this contrite before I'd embarked on a significant relationship things might have turned out differently. One of the houses we did look at was on Central Road, Didsbury, next door to Bruce Mitchell who, as stated earlier, had joined up with Vini Reilly in 1981. He's still involved with The Durutti Column to this day, especially in a managerial capacity. It would have been fun living next door to Bruce, an interesting and funny guy. Also, this house actually felt right to me, that was until I fell down the stairs on the way out.

All the houses Tony and I viewed were lovely and very much designed around having a family but, in every case, I could sense a fear of being trapped in them. I felt like a wild bird that didn't want a cage, however gilded. Neither of us were fully committed to this move; Tony hadn't even put his own house up for sale, which is usual practice before looking for another, or ought to be.

For my thirtieth birthday that July, Tony gave me a beautiful painting of cows. During our honeymoon, he couldn't understand why I wanted a plastic cow milker we'd seen, and he refused to buy it. He wrote that he'd made the 'second fatal mistake of holiday', failing to buy 'a moo-cow milker – an extremely tatty plastic milk jug with a brown plastic cow's head which slurps out milk; and yours for only $3.50 at this tourist trap'. He was oblivious then to its significance to me, not having taken on board the story of how I'd fallen in love with a cow being starved for slaughter, leading me to vegetarianism. But now he understood and gave me something infinitely more tasteful. These cows looked exactly the same as the one I loved, with brown ears and a white face. The gift meant a lot, it was as if he now appreciated

something deeper within me than my looks. The picture fell off my wall with a sudden crash twenty-five years later, three weeks before Tony's death.

With the painting he sent me the above card with poetic words on the other side suggesting a resolve to accept what comes:

2nd July 1982

My darling Lins,

A gift for your 30th birthday – may you be happy in the coming decade. These cows, a perfect image of the dream we've sadly lost. I love the little calf on the left – as faint and removed as our hopes. When we are older – our lives quite removed from each other, that little dream will still be there just as the paintings still hang on the walls of our rooms. There will always be a corner of our souls in which we are for ever husband and wife. It isn't Catholicism – just the condition of what we were to each other that cannot be erased. Good luck with your – our – record and with dispelling the Boethian mists that cloud your wheel. All is as it should be if only we could see beyond that mist.

My love in all its ages.

Anthony

x

And now my life is quite removed from him, but the painting still hangs on the wall of my room.

Boethius appeared as a beggar in the film *24 Hour Party People;* Steve Coogan, the Tony character, is seen walking away from a catastrophically deserted night at The Haçienda when he passes the beggar sitting under an archway, who tells him he is Boethius, author of *The Consolation of Philosophy.* It is his belief that history is a wheel; that it rises up on spokes, but then is cast back down into the depths. Good times pass away, but then so do the bad. Mutability is tragedy but also hope. The worst of times, like the best, will always pass away.

Tony, of course, replies: 'I know. I know'.

Frank Cottrell-Boyce, had obviously picked up on something Tony had said for this particular storyline.

When Tony refers to the Boethian mists that 'cloud my wheel' I expect he's probably referring to the depressions I felt, suggesting that they cloud over an appreciation of positive change and good times. It is poetic even though mists are not strictly Boethian, rather it's the wheel that is.

It was shortly after my thirtieth birthday that Tony started giving me ultimatums, wanting a 'final' chat. When I repeated that I couldn't go back he said it was 'the end' but, again, he wasn't consistent, apologising the next day and, yet again, leaving the option open. This gave me *carte blanche* to return to my boyfriend in London, although that relationship was obviously souring given my pull towards Tony and consequent turmoil. In fact, my peace of mind was destroyed. The pressure to go back to Tony wasn't just coming from him, I felt it from all sides somehow. Being a bit of a rebel, this only made me go the other way, but my indecision was agonising.

Then Tony left for a holiday to China, perhaps wanting an adventure to match my own to India. I drove him to the station and saw him off. As he remarks in his letter, our farewell was an emotional one. His handwritten letter from China this time was addressed to Lindsay Wilson at Old Broadway, even though I wasn't living there.

东方宾馆
TUNG FANG
BINGUAN

Wednesday, August 25th 1982
Canton, China

Dearest Lins,

On this dramatic day, I need to write a letter
of sorts and who is there for me to address but
you, my wife; though estranged - still the only
person I can read Proust to, the only recipient
then of this letter from China.

I just need to put down on paper how
excited I feel tonight. This holiday had been
a suddenly arranged, little dreamt of, and
therefore potentially disappointing expedition.
Until I finally get you out of my system I'm
not really fit to go to the pictures let alone go
on holiday. But, pale and tired, I went that I
should, this autumn, be less pale and tired. That
strange - tight - neurotic - near to tears - full eyelidded
farewell at Stockport was almost worth the
fare in itself; what strange reactions we provoke

2

东方宾馆
TUNG FANG
BINGUAN

in each other – are you sure you're not my
mother – and was that graveside vow my
undoing – and can we find ourselves apart
and – forget that maudlin stuff – the
holiday's the Thing.

Well Hong Kong is just fine. Fabulously
different, exciting peculiar. Brian is good to
me in his way. Last night we talked from
midnight till 4 about our loves. I feel sad for
him. Judy is divine, beautiful, Chinese – capricious
wilful, only 23, and right now back in Taipei;
and he loves her. Poor sod. In this death-bound
romance I almost think he begins to appreciate
you. His enmity towards you I think comes from
the disrespect shown by wife to husband – in public.
It was a sin both committed, but Brian only
witnessed your commission. He remembered your
attack on (racially) mixed marriages – in the Stables –
and said he didn't agree they were impossible – but
did that there were great difficulties. He asked

3/

东方宾馆

TUNG FANG
BINGUAN

me to do the Tarot for him. Sun + Moon, World
and Devil at opposite quarters - one up - one
down - making the wheel at the Centre. Brian had
been looking for "some kind of resolution" - of
course it was exactly the opposite. Me; "the
ineluctable modality of life, Brian" — "More of
the same you mean." I fear he will be hurt by
Judy. If it be so - then so it be.

And the modality of Hong Kong - lots of
fun. Though if I had intended to make this
the start of my "Lindsay is dead - get on with
living phase" (Brian's wisdom from Castaneda
— 'live like a warrior') then it was the wrong place.
More beautiful dresses in one town than I have
ever seen before. If the only remnant of my
hunger for you is to be this dreamlike window
-shopping for you - it will be devotion enough.
The designs here - both cheap + expensive - are
stunning - something to do with their approach to
the shoulders + hips as a plane. In the last

4

东方宾馆
TUNG FANG
BINGUAN

week I have bought you 142 dresses – they
suit you. What was that Proust stuff about
forgetting you I wrote last summer. In time –
on time.

And there has been time – for windsurfing –
found a beach on the south side of the Island,
a crazy 45 minute bus ride from town. I am
absolutely at home – an O.K. exotic holiday –
but – that was until today.

TODAY

I arrived in Canton – I crossed the border
into Red China at 12.00 – it is now 10.30 pm. And
I just cannot believe that this land which has
fascinated me on and off for fifteen years is more
wonderful than I could ever have imagined. Crazy,
bustling, bemusing, exhilarating, wildly alone,
unique, happy, — a joy to be in. The streets of this
city of 3 million are full of bikes – thousands with
smiling careering bright faced Chinese. Buddhist
temples with towers that make Kew seem insignificant

5

东方宾馆
TUNG FANG
BINGUAN

look down on the triumph of Socialism and
Daoism. The honeycombed city full of people and
wierd shops — strange 7 storey restaurant —
street teenagers selling cassettes to the flood of
cyclists who swarm over the Pearl river
bridge — deliciously shaped gardens in honour of
revolutionary dead, great peoples auditoriums
— ideograms on hoardings that paint the words
"China belongs to the people — dark thronged
streets cause theyre saving on public electricity,
department stores of crumbling concrete and
bizarrely simplistic products — and the cultural
parks where — hundreds of people listen to
amplified folk concerts — ride primitive ferris
wheels — watch a girls floodlit basketball
match, an open air movie, a pair of T.V. sets
in an open amphitheatre — an acrobates/
ballet theatre, tea gardens, trees and
crowded park benches, lovers on the boating
lake and even a story-telling place where
perhaps 200 or so old men loll on pews and
fan themselves in the evening heat while

東方賓館
TUNG FANG
BINGUAN

other old men take it in turn to sit at the raised table and bell into the microphone – stories – old folk tales of heroes and wars and lovers and antiquity.

My dream come true. And if my other dreams are to be rudely wakened from – this teeming revolution and strange asia nation – the oldest surviving culture in the world – if it has to be enough that China be everything I ever dreamt China could be – then it is enough. And of course I miss you. Soon and sadly I will be able to miss China as well. But all of feeling of loss requires great gains to have first been had. And tonight I sit in the heart of China, and tonight I am a husband writing to his wife from far away. Like my mum said; I am a lucky boy.

All my loving.

Anthony

xxxx

Wednesday August 25th, 1982

Canton, China Dearest Lins,

On this dramatic day, I need to write a letter of sorts and who is there for me to address but you, my wife; though estranged – still the only person I can read Proust to, the only recipient then of this letter from China.

I just need to put down on paper how excited I feel tonight. This holiday had been suddenly arranged, little dreamt of, and therefore a potentially disappointing expedition. Until I finally get you out of my system I'm not really fit to go to the pictures let alone go on holiday. But, pale and tired, I went that I should, this autumn, be less pale and tired. That strange - tight – neurotic – near to tears – full eye lidded farewell at Stockport was almost worth the fare in itself; what strange reactions we provoke in each other – are you sure you're not my mother - and was that graveside vow my undoing – and can we find new selves apart and – forget that maudlin stuff – the holiday's the thing.

Well Hong Kong is just fine. Fabulously different, exciting – peculiar. Brian is good to me in his way. Last night we talked from midnight till 4 about our loves. I feel sad for him. Judy is divine, beautiful, Chinese – capricious, wilful, only 23, and right now back in Taipei; and he loves her. Poor sod. In this death-bound romance I almost think he begins to appreciate you. His enmity towards you I think comes from the disrespect shown by wife to husband – in public. It was a sin both committed but Brian only witnessed your commission. He remembered your attack on (racially) mixed marriages – in the Stables – and said he didn't agree they were impossible – but did that there were great difficulties. He asked me to do the Tarot for him. Sun and Moon, World and Devil at opposite quarters – one up – one down – making the wheel at the centre. Brian had been looking for "some kind of resolution" – of course it was exactly the opposite. Me; "the ineluctable modality of life, Brian" – "More of the same you mean". I fear he will be hurt by Judy. If it be so – then so it be.

And the modality of Hong Kong – lots of fun. Though if I had intended to make this the start of my "Lindsay is dead – get on with living phase" (Brian's wisdom from Castenada – 'live like a warrior') then it was the wrong place. More beautiful dresses in one town that I have ever seen before. If the only remnant of my hunger for you is to be this dreamlike window shopping for you – it will be devotion enough. The designs here – both cheap and expensive – are stunning - something to do with their approach to the shoulders and hips as a plane. In the last week I have bought you 142 dresses – they suit you. What was that Proust stuff about forgetting you I wrote last summer. In time – in time.

And there has been time – for windsurfing – found a beach on the south side

of the Island, a crazy 45 minute bus ride from town. I am absolutely at home –
an O.K. exotic holiday – but that was until today.

TODAY

I arrived in Canton – I crossed the border into Red China at 12.00 – it is now
10.30 p.m. And I just cannot believe that this land, which has fascinated me on
and off for fifteen years, is more wonderful than I could ever have imagined.
Crazy, bustling, bemusing, exhilarating, wildly alone, unique, happy – a joy to be
in. The streets of this city of 3 million are full of bikes – thousands with smiling,
careering, bright faced Chinese. Buddhist temples, with towers that make Kew
seem insignificant, look down on the triumph of Socialism and Daoism. The
honeycombed city full of people and weird shops – strange 7 storey restaurants
– street teenagers selling cassettes to the flood of cyclists who swarm over
the Pearl River bridge – deliciously shaped gardens in honour of revolutionary
dead, great peoples auditorium – ideograms on hoardings that paint the words
"China belongs to the people" – dark thronged streets cause they're saving
on public electricity, department stores of crumbling concrete and bizarrely
simplistic products – and the cultural parks where – hundreds of people listen
to amplified folk concerts – ride primitive ferris wheels – watch a girls floodlit
basketball match, an open air movie, a pair of T.V. sets in an open amphitheatre
– an acrobatics/ballet theatre, tea gardens, trees and crowded park benches,
lovers on the boating lake and even a story-telling place where perhaps 200
or so old men loll on pews and fan themselves in the evening heat while other
old men take it in turn to sit at the raised table and tell into the microphone –
stories – old folk tales of heroes and wars and lovers and antiquity.

My dream came true. And if my other dreams are to be rudely wakened from
– this teeming revolution and strange nation – the oldest surviving culture in
the world – if it has to be enough that China be everything I ever dreamt China
could be – then it is enough. And of course I miss you. Soon and sadly I will be
able to miss China as well. But all of feeling of loss requires great gains to have
first been had. And tonight I sit in the heart of China, and tonight I am a husband
writing to his wife from far away. Like my mum said; I am a lucky boy.

All my loving,
Anthony
XXXX

When Tony writes, 'until I finally get you out of my system, I'm not really fit to go
to the pictures let alone go on holiday', my insecurity made me read this not as him
wanting me back but as him *wanting* to get me out of his system. And yet, clearly, I

can now see he was in pain and that he really wanted us to continue. It's strange that I couldn't comprehend this then. Where was my empathy? I'd felt heartache but hadn't seriously thought that Tony felt that for me. This was partly because of all the things he'd said in rejection of me and partly because my insecure self never imagined I was someone men would feel heartache over. I should have trodden more lightly on their souls because I was, and they did.

I could forgive all of Tony's earlier treatment of me – as I hoped he'd forgive my own treatment of him – but I couldn't forget. I felt that if I went back I might suffer from it all over again, the neglect and punishment equating almost to abuse.

He wrote, 'Love to Nabs & Tabs' on the back of the envelope: 'Nabs' for Nathan McGough and 'Tabs' for Tabatha of course. Nathan had moved into Old Broadway and ended up staying almost two years.

Nathan remembers: 'I enjoyed living there, I was working the bars at The Haçienda most evenings, we weren't under each other's feet as housemates, and we got along well as we always had done since we first met in 1973. I think he really loved the house and was happy there. He had all the classic Factory Records posters framed and covered the hallways with them.

'It was peaceful, except for the Factory board meetings. Tony and Rob fighting, and Alan mediating. He had a good work ethic and liked his routines (as you know). He was a busy man but knew how to relax. Fifteen minutes for a coffee, a spliff and a chat. Then back to work with that incredible energy he had.'

Tony initially stayed with an old friend of his, Brian Eads, who lived in Hong Kong. I'd met Brian when he'd stayed with us in Charlesworth for a week or so. He struck me as highly intelligent but abrupt to the point of rudeness. He probably felt justified to be rude to me because I'd rowed with Tony in public and he'd witnessed this. I agree that this was wrong (but hadn't been able to control my anger). Brian wounded me one day during his stay because he said that the meal I'd made, one of many as we never ate out, was 'boring'. This particular meal was hotpot. I suppose he was used to more East Asian flavours but in those days the only cooking from Asia we were all that familiar with was Vesta Chow Mein (similar to a Pot Noodle). My cooking tending to be basic meat and two veg, which Tony liked best.

I feel ashamed and apologise for the suggestion I made to Brian regarding racially mixed marriages: I must clearly state that this had no basis in racism whatsoever, but rather to do with couples who've grown up from birth in different countries and cultures. I'd read an article, probably in *Cosmopolitan* or such like, providing statistics that indicated the nearer couples are born and raised to one another, the better their compatibility – the boy next door being a girl's best chance of success. It also said that interracial couples who were born and had grown up far apart from one another had much less chance of succeeding, usually because of cultural differences. Brian agreed with Tony on the difficulties these differences can present but it was an insensitive and stupid thing that I'd said, nonetheless. I probably wanted to hit back at Brian as he'd hurt my feelings about my boring hotpot. It's that stew thing raising its head again. I thought that his chances of happiness with the girl he was in love with, were, in any case, low mainly because he was opinionated and rude and bit the hand that fed it. Plus, she seemed out of his league, being a good deal younger and stunningly beautiful. I actually believe the biggest factor for success in marriage is if both partners have had a happy childhood. In other words, probably just luck.

Tony mentions the 'ineluctable modality of life', a phrase he was very fond of and a line that he adapted years later for the film notes of *24 Hour Party People*: 'There is an ineluctability about the way we go up and then down,' the Wheel of Fortune. 'Ineluctable' means that which cannot be escaped from. Tony had read James Joyce's *Ulysses* at Cambridge where he'd likely have first come across the phrase. In the book, the protagonist Stephen Dedalus reflects on whether or not what he sees is real, and this is followed in turn by a consideration of what he hears (the ineluctable modality of the audible) and its ability to deliver truth.

There are a few mystical references in this letter, things Tony knew I was interested in, such as the Tarot and the writings of Carlos Castañeda. We'd both read *The Teachings of Don Juan* by Castañeda, it being one of the few books that endorsed the taking of drugs for a spiritual quest.

As for the Chinese dresses, I wish Tony had brought at least one back for me, but he didn't. He gave me something more lasting though – a Chinese Buddha. He knew that if I were to ascribe to any religion it would be Buddhism. I fancied getting married at a Buddhist centre in the Lake District and we'd visited it with this in mind, but Tony really had his heart set on his childhood Catholic church. Catholicism was more significant to Tony than just this church. Perhaps because it was handed down by his mother, it, like she, was always in his heart somehow. The religion does bring with it certain rules and ritual. Catholics believe that only death can end a marriage, and Dennis Clinch, the priest who held Tony's funeral service, told me as much when I rang him a few days later to confess how furious I felt towards Tony for preferring fantasy to reality, even at his own funeral. That day I'd wanted to cry for the loss of him, but I couldn't, as it felt as if his false public persona was on show rather than the real person he was underneath. Yes, it was showtime again, and this was not instigated by the press, who behaved with dignity, but by Tony; it was as if he'd stage-managed the whole thing.

Despite our history and despite sleeping beside him, most Saturday nights for the last several months, I was banished to the upstairs of the church. The mother of his children was also banished somewhere out of sight. The young and beautiful Yvette was centre stage, just as Tony would have wanted it, even though she was then living with someone else. I looked down at all the other strange faces milling around upfront, near his coffin, and wondered why they were there and not me. They hadn't been with him when he was throwing up, or were sitting by his side as his tears fell at the loss of everything. Even the priest bought into the make-believe story.

Tony had little cash flow: we'd been out for dinner together the previous New Year's Eve and he'd asked me to stop en route to the restaurant so he could check his balance as he wasn't sure that his bank card could bear the cost. I'd told him not to worry, if it came to that I'd pay (the waitress was unable to get the card machine to work for either of us after all, but he promised to go back, they knew him anyway). Despite his apparent impecunity that night, there were nine large black limousines for the funeral standing outside the church. Thelma stepped out of one of them to greet me and I envied her tears as mine were stuck well down beneath my fury. I wondered as to the cost of these, and also why there was no seat for me in any of them, making me late to his burial as well. I was mad as hell with Tony for two days afterwards. So mad I rang the priest and told him so. It felt wrong being so angry with Tony when he was dead, but the priest seemed to totally understand it and he forgave it as quite natural. He was so very kind that my anger instantly evaporated and, at last, I was instantly able to cry. As I mentioned in the introduction of this book, confession is one Catholic tradition that I like and, on that note, I can't really take the high moral ground over Tony's love of fantasy, having engaged in it fully myself.

There was wisdom in Tony's line: 'But all of feeling of loss requires great gains to have first been had.' It reminds me of another line I like, from the film *Shadowlands:* 'The pain now is part of the happiness then. That's the deal.'

Trust Tony to end the letter on a positive upbeat note when he was writing to a woman who was with another – 'tonight I am a husband writing to his wife from far away. Like my mum said; I am a lucky boy.' He was always irrepressibly optimistic, and even described having cancer as an adventure.

Tony's gift from China

CHAPTER 11
Is You Is Or Is You Ain't (My Baby)?

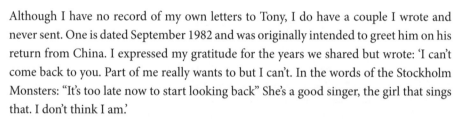

Although I have no record of my own letters to Tony, I do have a couple I wrote and never sent. One is dated September 1982 and was originally intended to greet him on his return from China. I expressed my gratitude for the years we shared but wrote: 'I can't come back to you. Part of me really wants to but I can't. In the words of the Stockholm Monsters: "It's too late now to start looking back" She's a good singer, the girl that sings that. I don't think I am.'

The song I made reference to is 'Miss Moonlight' by the Stockholm Monsters. Although Tony France sang lead on most Monsters tracks, this was sung by his sister, Denise France. The Monsters had released a single on Factory called 'Fairy Tales' in 1982, which had been recorded the year earlier. This was a Martin Hannett production but the relationship between Martin and Tony – and Martin and Factory – had soured by this point, so this record marked the end of Martin's productions for Factory for the foreseeable future.

My letter continued (referring to 'I Get Along Without You Very Well'): 'I heard the mix Hooky [Peter Hook] had done and I hated the vocal so much I did it again. Perhaps it was because that time I sang it to Kuka, thinking I was staying with you, but this time I sang it to you and it sounded better. I also didn't like the way Vini's guitar had been wiped off in favour of the xylophone. After an hour with Stewart (Pickering, in Revolution, Cheadle Hulme), the result sounded almost exactly like the first version, which you didn't like. I think perhaps you had better not put it out, so that no more money is wasted.'

I closed the letter by wishing him well, from the bottom of my heart.

Tony did release 'I Get Along Without You Very Well' in June 1983, as a double A-side with 'Prayer'. Amazingly it went into profit, not that I got paid anything. It was probably because of 'Prayer', which is a hauntingly melancholic piece. I love the Cor Anglais, played by Maunagh Fleming, and Vini plays piano with just as much skill as guitar. As I mentioned in the introduction of this book, the cover was a still from a video Tony filmed of me, applying make-up to my bare face, at Old Broadway.

FACTORY RECORDS
86 Palatine Road, Manchester 20.
Telephone 061-434 3876

Thursday night, beginning of December, '82.

Dearest Lins,
Here's le brochure...with Paul Smith's
adress....and the Filofax....and the
cheque from me.....if you haven't got a
bank account you can countersign it with
someone or I can get you cash. Get Him a
red one....(sorry about the 'H') as "the east is
red".......if not red then black and so on.
The boy's adress is.
Brian Eads,
2,Castle Road.
HONG KONG
Please insert any Christmas message of your own
choosing.....but be sweet, my love, he's a
much battered child of the universe...with
a slightly overweening personality, but
a lotta women problems...so you've gotta be nice.
I enclose an extra quid for postage and
a little card which I'd be grateful
if you would insert.
Ta.
Hope you get lucky, Sunday night.
See yah after Christmas...or for traditional
Itaàian lunch before.
Love and handshakes,
Yours,

VAT. No. 305 6301 96   Reg. No. 2340540
A.Erasmus, R.Gretton, M.Hannett, P.Saville, A.Wilson

Tony had been unwilling to settle with Ros, and was aware that he'd treated her dreadfully. Now that they'd broken up, he perhaps decided just to enjoy some light-hearted relief. He began seeing yet another girl and this time I was glad: a) because the pressure was again off me to be with him but b) because, for now, the option of a return still held, and I wanted to keep it open. Or, at least, didn't want to lose him entirely. This new girl, although good fun, didn't seem to be a long-term prospect in the way that Ros could have been. Her friendliness to me suggested it was just fun for her too.

Meanwhile I was still calling round to Old Broadway when Tony was at work. Nathan was often there with his girlfriend, and Tabatha of course. By now the cat was very frail and barely eating, tinned cat food remained untouched in her bowl.

In Tony's next letter he gives me a small 'job' to do, preparing the way for a more important job; it wouldn't be long before I'd be employed by Factory. My relationship in London was inevitably faltering. Still, it would be a few months yet before I'd be on the Factory payroll.

Thursday night, beginning of December, '82

Dearest Lins,

Here's le brochure.....with Paul Smith's address.....and the Filofax....and the cheque from me.....if you haven't got a bank account you can countersign it with someone or I can get you cash. Get Him a red one.....(sorry about the 'H') as the east is red.......if not red then black and so on.

The boy's address is,

Brian Eads,

2, Castle Road

HONG KONG

Please insert any Christmas message of your own choosing.....but be sweet, my love, he's a much battered child of the universe....with a slightly overweening personality, but a lotta woman problems.....so you've gotta be nice.

I enclose an extra quid for postage and a little card which I'd be grateful if you would insert. Ta.

Hope you get lucky, Sunday night,

See yah after Christmas......or for traditional Italian lunch before.

Love and handshakes,

Yours,

Anthony

In the early 1980s, the Filofax, a kind of desktop organiser, became all the rage. They were perhaps a forerunner to the mobile phone, and they became a trendy status symbol, particularly with busy businesspeople and yuppies. They were also expensive (I couldn't afford one, for instance). Tony loved them and used his constantly (although he would still write notes in biro on his hands). It seemed to give him an air of importance, which I expect was partly why people used them. I mean, you wouldn't need one if you weren't busy. But, then again, he *was* busy.

During 1982 I wrote in my diary: 'I have to stop seeing either Tony or K. Feel today it has to be Tony if that's what I want most, or K if it's what "they" want most. Feel bloody miserable either way. I wish I could be a better person. My guilt is enormous.' As the year wore on Kuka became increasingly disturbed by the situation. At the end of November, I wrote that he was 'at the end of his tether, does not want to know'. We were now understandably having rows. He told me 'The fuck's off', meaning it's the end, and he told me to 'clear my things.' The following day I wrote: 'I'm clinging on to something that cannot be. Feel calm about it but a little sad. I'm off to seek my independence – nothing and nobody else'.

I'd been fairly distant from the machinations of Factory Records during 1982, but I was aware that Martin Hannett had brought a legal case against them. I was fond of Martin and he of me but, being out of touch with him during this particular phase of his life, I didn't get involved. I hadn't realised how self-destructive Martin had become, he was off the rails with drugs by this point, although I could empathise with his animosity towards Tony and Factory. He said that Tony was impossible to talk to, being 'that one way mirror, the chairman of the board[1].'

Martin presented his lawsuit in March 1982, requesting that Factory be wound up and assets shared equally between the directors, or his own share be bought out. He had several complaints and claims; one of them was that 14 per cent of Peter Saville's shares had been bought out by the other directors without Martin's knowledge or agreement. Tony told me that Saville felt it fair to relinquish most of his shares since he'd moved to, and was now working in, London.

According to Martin's legal suit, Factory shares became divided 23.5 per cent to Rob, Tony, Alan and Martin with 6 per cent remaining to Peter. Although this meant Martin's shares had been bumped up from 20 per cent to 23.5 per cent, the purchase of the 14 per cent of shares from Saville cost £22,000, or so he claimed. On Tony's next letter to me, written in January 1983 while in a lawyer's meeting over Martin's case, he scribbled across the top of it '23.5 per cent and 6 per cent'. Tony calls this 'legal graffiti'. It is possible Tony had to be reminded about such a split and payment. According to Peter Saville, he was never paid anything for his shares and only kept 5 per cent of them. Maybe this

---

1 *Play at Home* video, Factory Records, 1984.

was why Tony also added the figure 5 per cent to his scribble, and a mathematical brain better than mine may be able to work out why he added the figure 1.4 per cent.

Other complaints of Martin's were that money was being mismanaged, again without his consent, such as £13,000 on video equipment at Tony's new house. As mentioned earlier, as well as equipment, the cellar of 36 Broadway was fully refurbished – it was the nicest part of the whole house for the first year.

Martin also objected to the fact that he didn't get notifications of director's meetings and that at one such, in October 1981, Factory changed the nature of the company into a 'night club venture' (FAC 51) without his knowledge or consent ('to which [he] never would have assented'), at an initial cost of £50,000. While at Rabid, Tosh said Martin would slam his fists on the desk and shout, 'Don't fuck with my budgets.' Martin commented that said budgets 'suddenly vanished down a hole in the ground called The Haçienda.'

Tony always made out that Martin's main complaint was that Factory wouldn't provide him with a Fairlight synthesiser. According to Martin's then partner Susanne O'Hara, Tony had agreed to buy this for him on a hire purchase arrangement. Despite Alan Erasmus's advice to her not to call Tony when he'd just returned, exhausted, from New York, Susanne did call him, asking why the deposit for the hire purchase still wasn't forthcoming. The timing of this call was bad, and Tony never responded well to being pushed in any case. Susanne said she walked away from working at Factory that day, and believes Martin would have stayed if he'd got the Fairlight. She told me that Tony blamed her later on for the break-up between Martin and Factory: it was soon after her *contretemps* with Tony over the Fairlight that Martin began litigation.

Tony believed Martin was also hurt that both New Order and ACR wanted to try another producer; an additional complaint Martin levelled was that he hadn't been allowed to produce records for Factory since August 1981. But a crucial factor was that Martin had become a liability due to his heroin addiction. Shan Hira, then drummer of the Stockholm Monsters, told me: 'Hannett was a bit difficult to work with and aloof. When we did our only song with him, 'Fairy Tales', it took him about twelve months from recording it to actually getting round to mixing it.'

While producing records for Factory, Martin also produced three albums for the poet John Cooper Clarke. Cooper Clarke's third album, *Zip Style Method*, was released in 1982 by CBS, but it transpired that Martin had spent the entire budget with only half the album's uncompleted monitor mixes to show for it. Martin then asked CBS for the same advance again – in the region of £50,000. This ploy of Martin's had worked with the previous two albums, with CBS agreeing to pay more, but this time they called his bluff and refused. Instead, they approached keyboard player Steve Hopkins and engineer Laurence Diana, who worked with Martin as part of the Invisible Girls production team. The nucleus of The Invisible Girls was Martin and Steve Hopkins, but others did join at various points.

Re 6'0":
1.4'11":

The 24th of January, 1983.

23.5% →   ← 5°c.   Legal Graffiti

Dearest Lindsay,

A day of splendid possibilities. It's only 11.15 a.m. + already. My eyelids are heavy with exhaustion from last night's "Martin Hannett leaving party", chez Portobello, avec Erasmus, Gretton + dotted Miss Sanderson (looking unique), and here I find myself in a smoke-filled room off Baker St - across the table - directly - Martin Hannett, to his left, the poison harpie O'hara, then Hannett's lawyer - droning on - as he has been for some time + hopefully will for some time further - reviewing the case - god, we know all this shit anyway - and on our side of the table the noble threesome (that's to make you laugh) plus Adams + Mortlock, our lovely solicitors - much less boring than Hannett's. And here I am - just looked up + met a withering stare from the harpie - whoops! Ah - our man's started - he's giving an elaborate philosophical precis of Factory idealism - great - 12 mnths ago he was just a litigation solicitor - oh the coffee's arrived.

And the point is, I am bursting with the possibilities of the day. You see I have decided to be decisive - or perhaps I have decided that I should decide to be decisive. And since my sometime wife plays some role in this denouement, a letter seems in order. For old times sake - or is it because you say my prose is occasionally eloquent.

To begin - I have decided to have a child. It came to me like a flash at around 4.30 a.m. this morning. To say the least - I was excited. I've only really felt it twice before - once in a hotel car park in Disley and then again in a hotel room overlooking an Italian bay

What is it woman in man most requires
    The lineaments of gratified desire " (W. Blake)
    It may indeed be a problem – perhaps our bodies
are incapable of following our hearts – who can tell –
as long as we have this seemingly undying flame – it
seems that our emotions deserve the benefit of the
doubt and let them test our sexuality. Not even
with discussing or theorising – let fall what leaves
will come – if the tree is dead wood – then the
hopelessness of our dreams of nappies and bottles must
be – then – when tried by chance – by occasion as
arising – and from my experience videoing you
in Old Broadway – rising for me will not be
an immediate problem – the camera viewfinder is
meant to distance one from reality – my experience
then was most strange. But let it happen, flow, be
or not be as we meet at the proverbial crossroads.
    And so – my proposal and my desires – lie
before you – framed by that pen from the Chinese
Department store – I wish to wear your ring and you
mine – I want to be your partner in life – to find that
elusive mutual esteem – the Woodward-Newman syndrome –
the deepest of our joint failure of the long gone
Seventies – I want to fill your womb, I suppose,
to hold you in the nights – back turned of course
my girl – we none of us change so much.
    So will you be my wife – we never find out
if Scarlett in the scene after the end credits – when
Butler finally turns again – does she fall into his
arms – has your – "I'll get him back" of five days
ago already faded – in the time it has taken me
to say "Frankly my dear" walk out the Garden gate

— on this 3rd Flash of inspiration I arose, smoked a joint, and proceeded to learn a Shakespearian sonnet of strictest relevance. 4.30 a.m. I must be crazy. And I'm suffering now — God I'm killed — and Hannett's lawyer is thick and the two across the table are really appalling — still — to my child — and maybe the sonnet before the end — in particular to put against that old Proustian bit about love being able to die because we become new people every day — each day, a little changed from the previous day — till after a multitude of days we are completely new — and so in Proust's mind incapable of freeing us from love's chains.

So I am a new person — and I do not want to go back to my first marriage — I want — for this moment with all my heart — to marry anew — a woman who is my life and to whom I was wed in an earlier incarnation — and engender a family. Funny, I realise now that this weekend — our two years is up — I had viewed it vaguely as Xmas 80 — but of course my departure for Brussels + yours for London was the 3rd weekend. And only now has the wheel come full circle. Louise for years.

This is then a proposal of marriage. If it is to work it will be fresh. "Starting over" like our forerunners Lennon-Ono. Can we really make the same mistakes again — do we now know how much we have deceived ourselves, how we have at times lost sight of destiny in the midst of pain + other afflictions. If ever we are ready — it is now — oh, I know there is a stumbling block —

What is it men in Women most require?
The lineaments of gratified desire.

- a little way along the street — before turning back with hope & thoughts of true love.

A once only offer, this my love, — at different intervals in the past 18 months I have suffered great turmoil on account of the love I bear you — there is now no yesterday, no tomorrow — the pain of those days fell from living in past & future + one must act now — for only today exists.

Ooops — had to get into the legal stuff. But have I made myself clear — I'm so whacked — its now 2.15pm — I'll leave off + complete when I get back North. And you're probably in London now as I write. What else for now — oh yes do you want a lawyer for Sunday — I mean that in the nicest possible way ———— I do like my bagels but probably they taste as good early on.

Will Jerein send this letter — the other half of this fateful day is yet to be undergone — accomplished.

Tuesday Afternoon —

Hi — well still haven't quite sorted phase two + with my delay — who knows about phase one — will you ever return to Tara again.   Last night — turned aside to sleep — already we're asexual — she said "You don't love me any more?" and I after a pause replied "Well that's a complicated question" — and after a further silence — we went to sleep. Jesus.

But I'll deal with that — while you must make your mind up about my proposal. I will NOT wait — Hope deferred hath made my

heart sick for too long — a reply to the "Do
you want any help on Sunday?" and "Do you
wish to share bed, life, children, pain + happiness
with your former lover/husband?" — required
by Saturday latest.

I remain — yours, if you
can be mine.

John

X

"Let me not to the marriage of true minds
Admit impediments — for love is not love
Which alters when it doth alteration finds —
— — Oh no it is an ever fixèd mark
Which looks on tempests + is never shaken —
— — Love's not Time's fool, though rosy lips + cheeks
Within his bending sickle's compass come
Love alters not, with his brief hours + weeks,
But bears it out even to the edge of doom"

If this be error, and upon me proved, then
I never writ nor no man ever lov'd.

And while we're quoting. "Had we but
world enough + time — this coyness lady were
no crime" — but we don't.
Respondez s'il vous plaît.
And does it please you?

They provided musical backing for John Cooper Clarke's records between 1978-1982 and, in 1980, they worked on an album with the punk vocalist Pauline Murray, who'd recently wound up her band Penetration. This album, entitled *Pauline Murray and the Invisible Girls*, represented her movement away from punk. Steve Hopkins and Laurence Diana agreed to the task of finishing the John Cooper Clarke album. This they did in a week or two, even writing three or four tracks from scratch.

Martin's case against Factory dragged on for nearly two years, finally being settled out of court in January 1984. The legal fees were substantial, as you can imagine. Tony told me that Martin settled for £32,000 but, in doing so, he acceded his rights to all his production royalties. This turned out to be extremely unwise in the long run, although Martin only lived another seven years following the payout. Thirty-two thousand pounds was a lot of money in 1984 – the big house on Old Broadway cost £50,000, for instance. However, how much Martin was really left with remains in question, since his legal fees have been quoted at £16,000 – half his payout. Whatever the amount was, it didn't last very long; he was forever calling at the homes of Tosh and others, asking for money, presumably for heroin. Tosh remembers him calling round every day 'for a fiver'.

Martin's attempt to wind Factory up didn't happen, although if I'd sued Tony following our divorce it's unlikely Factory would have survived yet another large payout. A legal aid lawyer told me in 1984 I was entitled to half of Factory's assets, as the company had been built with our money during the time of our marriage.

The 24th of January, 1983
6%: 1.4% 23.5% —→ 5% ←—— Legal Graffiti
Dearest Lindsay,
A day of splendid possibilities. It's only 11.15am and already my eyelids are heavy with exhaustion from last night's "Martin Hannett – leaving party", chez Portobello, avec Erasmus, Gretton and sloshed Miss Sanderson (nothing unique) and here I find myself in a smoke-filled room off Baker St – across the table – directly – Martin Hannett – to his left the poison harpic O'Hara, then Hannett's lawyer – droning on – as he has been for some time and hopefully will for some time further – reviewing the case – god, we know all this shit anyway – and on our side of the table the noble threesome (that's to make you laugh) plus Adams and Mortlock, our lovely solicitors – much less boring than Hannett's. And here I am – just looked up and met a withering stare from the harpic – whoops. Ah – our man's started – he's giving an elaborate, philosophical precis of Factory idealism – great – 12 months ago he was just a litigation solicitor – oh the coffee's arrived.

And the point is, I am bursting with the possibilities of the day. You see I have decided to be decisive – or perhaps I have decided that I should decide to be decisive. And since my sometime wife plays some role in this denouement, a letter seems in order. For old time's sake - or is it because you say my prose is occasionally eloquent.

To begin, I have decided to have a child. It came to me like a flash at around 4.30 a.m. this morning. To say the least – I was excited. I've only really felt it twice before – once in a hotel car park in Disley and then again in a hotel room overlooking an Italian bay. On this 3rd flash of inspiration I arose, smoked a joint, and proceeded to learn a Shakespearian sonnet of strictest reference. 4.30 a.m. I must be crazy. And I'm suffering now – God I'm tired – and Hannett's lawyer is thick and the two across the table are really appalling – still – to my child – and maybe the sonnet before the end – in particular to put against that old Proustian bit about love being able to die because we become new people every day – each day, a little changed from the previous day – till after a multitude of days we are completely new – and so in Proust's mind capable of freeing us from love's chains.

So I am a new person – and I do not want to <u>Go Back</u> to my first marriage – I want – for this moment with all my heart – to marry anew – a woman who is my life and to whom I was wed in an earlier incarnation – and engender a family. Funny, I realise now that this weekend – our two years is up – I had viewed it vaguely as Xmas 80 – but of course my departure for Brussels and yours for London was the 3rd weekend. And only now has the wheel come full circle. Louise's two years.

This is then a proposal of marriage. If it is to work it will be fresh. "Starting over" like our forerunners Lennon and Ono. Can we really make the same mistakes again – do we now know how much we have deceived ourselves, how we have at times lost sight of destiny in the mists of pain and other affections. If ever we are ready – it is now – oh, I know there is a stumbling lock –

"What is it man in woman most requires
The lineaments of gratified desire
What is it woman in man most requires
The lineaments of gratified desire "
(W.Blake)

It may indeed be a problem – perhaps our bodies are incapable of following our hearts – who can tell – as long as we have this seemingly undying flame – it seems that our emotions deserve the benefit of the doubt and let them test our sexuality. Not even worth discussing or theorising – let fall what leaves will come – if the tree is dead wood – then the hopelessness of our dreams of nappies and bottles must be – then – when tried by chance – by occasion as arising – and from my experience videoing you in Old Broadway – rising for me will not be an immediate problem – the camera viewfinder is meant to distance one from reality – my experience then was most strange. But let it happen, flow, be or not be as we meet at the proverbial crossroads.

And so – my proposal and my desires – lie before you – framed by that pen from the Chinese Department store – I wish to wear your ring and you mine – I want to be your partner in life – to find that elusive mutual esteem – the Woodward-Newman syndrome – the deepest of our joint failure of the long gone Seventies – I want to fill your womb, I suppose, to hold you in the nights - back turned of course my girl – we none of us change so much.

So will you be my wife – we never find out if Scarlett – in the scene after the end credits – when Butler finally turns again – does she fall into his arms – has your – 'I'll get him back' of five days ago already faded – in the time it has taken me to say 'Frankly my dear' walk out the garden gate – a little way along the street – before turning back with hope and thoughts of true love.

A once only offer, this my love, – at different intervals in the past 18 months I have suffered great turmoil on account of the love I bear you – there is now no yesterday, no tomorrow – the pain of these days fell from living in past and future and one must act now – for only today exists.

Ooops – had to get into the legal stuff. But have I made myself clear – I'm so whacked - it's now 2.15pm – I'll leave off and complete when I get back North. And you're probably in London now as I write. What else for now – oh yes do you want a humper for Sunday – I mean that in the nicest possible way. I do like my bagels but probably they taste as good early on.

Will I even send this letter – the other half of this fateful day is yet to be undergone – accomplished.

Tuesday afternoon ——
Hi – well still haven't quite sorted phase two and with my delay – who knows about phase one – will you ever return to Tara again. Last night – turned aside to sleep – already we're asexual – she said "You don't love me any more?" and I, after a pause, replied "Well that's a complicated question" – and after a further silence – we went to sleep. Jesus. But I'll deal with that – while you must make your mind up about my proposal. I will <u>NOT</u> wait – Hope

deferred hath made my heart sick for too long – a reply to the "Do you want me to help on Sunday?" and "Do you wish to share bed, life, children, pain and happiness with your former lover/husband?" – required by Saturday latest.

I remain —— yours, if you can be mine

"Let me to the marriage of true minds
Admit impediments – for love is not love
Which alters when it alteration finds —
Oh no it is an ever fixed mark
Which looks on tempests and is never shaken — ——
Love's not Time's fool, though rosy lips and cheeks
Within his bending sickle's compass come
Love alters not, with his brief hours and weeks
But bears it out even to the edge of doom."

If this be error, and upon me proved, then
I never writ nor no man ever lov'd

And while we're quoting. "Had we but world enough and time – this coyness lady were no crime" – but we don't.

Respondez s'il vous plait
And does it please you?

I didn't know it but, we really were reaching a 'denouement' as Tony called it – the final part of the drama. He opens the letter by describing events as they were unfolding at the meeting. I'm an additional item on his agenda. But his announcement, 'I have decided to have a child,' sounds not just dictatorial but also desperate in the context of what has preceded it. But then he can't help being melodramatic – all that Scarlett O'Hara/*Gone with the Wind* stuff, for instance. Tony would indeed father a child within the next year or so.

Perhaps Tony had had a premonition of this at his 4.30 a.m. awakening, just as we'd both strongly felt our future together when we met that day in 1976 in a car park in Disley. Or maybe it came solely out of his determination to orchestrate his life the way he wished. His announcement to me about his forthcoming child seemed removed from my own situation and feelings. I hadn't even gone back to him and he's discussing having a child with me, something I never remember him doing during the years we were together, when it would have been romantic. Now he was putting the cart before the horse. When we'd been an active partnership he never once spoke in these terms, so focused was he on his career. Here he's offering full blown commitment which, although I didn't know it when young, is a rare thing in a lifetime. Yet, we'd virtually been separated for two years by this point. I'm not sure why Tony calls it 'Louise's two years'. It was poetic of Tony to suggest a completely fresh start but idealistic rather than realistic. Note that he was still with a girlfriend while writing this.

I regret that I felt unable to accept his offer, and that we couldn't go the Woodward-Newman route in life. Tony was referring to Joanne Woodward and Paul Newman, who shared a rare and wonderful marriage that lasted fifty years until Newman's death from cancer. I take some consolation that I was with Tony in his final days when he was ill with cancer, and that we always remained in touch. The sonnet of strictest reference that Tony learned (and quotes at the end of the letter) is Sonnet 116, written by Shakespeare, and the way we were together at the end of his life meant that, to some extent at least, our love wasn't entirely subject to time's fool. The other quote, following this one, is from Andrew Marvell's poem 'To His Coy Mistress'.

I didn't care for his authoritarian ultimatum in the letter, particularly as it wasn't the first one, nor would it be the last: 'A once only offer, this my love' and 'I will NOT wait,' and a reply required by Saturday latest. It sounded like a business deal rather than a relationship. But, then again, I could hardly blame him, I'd prevaricated so long (and would for a while longer yet). I sympathised and felt guilty about his quote from the bible (Proverbs) – 'Hope deferred makes the heart sick, but a longing fulfilled is a tree of life'. I've no idea what his offer of help for the forthcoming Sunday refers to. Perhaps I had some furniture item I wanted transporting to my parent's house since I felt moved, literally and metaphorically, to return.

I've mislaid Tony's next letter to me but know it existed. Dated 5th February 1983, he sent another ultimatum – a more threatening one this time – stating that we'd be finished if I wasn't back with him within the week. This time I believed him. Although Kuka had said it was over, it had only been during a row and so I decided there and then to drive down to London to end it with him once and for all, saying it was now my intention to go back with Tony. This upset us both and I left in tears, taking the last of my things with me. Inevitably, therefore, I wasn't happy or celebrating being back with Tony when we went for a meal and on to The Haçienda: I got totally drunk as a way of coping. Nor could I bring myself to live in his house which, grand though it was, gave me the creeps (although I slept there that night after collapsing in a drunken heap upon entering it). I'd preferred our little cottage. And I didn't have sex with him. So really it wasn't the reconciliation he was looking for, but he'd won a battle if not the war: he'd got me away from London and my boyfriend.

Perhaps I couldn't forgive him, as reflected in his Valentine's card:

And on the reverse:

I should have been won over but, somewhere along our tangled route, my heart had slowly, sadly, turned to stone. Surprisingly, Tony was understanding and seemed prepared to wait. It was enough for him, for the time being, that I'd finally broken up with Kuka and left London.

CHAPTER 12
A Horse to Water

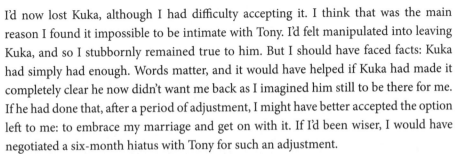

I'd now lost Kuka, although I had difficulty accepting it. I think that was the main reason I found it impossible to be intimate with Tony. I'd felt manipulated into leaving Kuka, and so I stubbornly remained true to him. But I should have faced facts: Kuka had simply had enough. Words matter, and it would have helped if Kuka had made it completely clear he now didn't want me back as I imagined him still to be there for me. If he had done that, after a period of adjustment, I might have better accepted the option left to me: to embrace my marriage and get on with it. If I'd been wiser, I would have negotiated a six-month hiatus with Tony for such an adjustment.

Instead, I felt I was being pushed into intimacy with Tony, but I temporarily dodged the issue. I wasn't ready for it, and I was desperate to delay it. I objected to it taking place in the Didsbury house (pure subterfuge) and suggested Portmeirion, knowing full well it would be closed until March. Tony liked this idea, thinking it a romantic gesture, as Portmeirion had always been 'our' place; our very first magical weekend away together was there during the famously hot summer of 1976. The suggestion was a mistake because it created a build-up, an expectation that was inevitably doomed to disappoint. There is a film called *Play At Home* about Factory and New Order, released in 1984. The film at one point features Tony sitting naked in the bath at Old Broadway with a fully clothed Gillian Gilbert, who had recently joined New Order. It looked almost a reenactment of 'Venus and Mars'. Tony is asked when he last had sex. He replied, 'Seven months, three days ago. I'm saving it for something very special.' He then gave his familiar yet phony laugh. This speaks of an emotional naivety to me, like a child waiting for Father Christmas. Choosing fantasy over reality yet again. Reality can never live up to that.

The next letter of Tony's is undated, but I think it was either late '82 or early '83. He was going away to New York, and I don't recall why. It was doubtless something to do with Factory, although Tony needed little encouragement to visit that city. The letter couldn't have been sent any later than February '83, as that was when our cat, Tabatha, died.

FACTORY RECORDS
86 Palatine Road, Manchester 20.
Telephone 061-434 3876

Dearest wife,

How confusing things are....i don't even care to think about them...
...just get more confused...as you said...not yet whatever....time
to think...etc.....but youARE my wife...anyway business simpler.

A: Will leave fifty pounds with this to pay bills....milk, gardener,
and window cleaners all owed if they call.

B: Herewith also some money from your building society account.

C: People who'll be around. Sandra comes every monday morning to do
the bookkeeping in me office....she's lovely...very easy going etc...
....since the cheque book for Factory stays here for her to go through,
Alan may well need it at various points in the week so keep in touch
with him....as much as it is ever possible....never here or pnly
there Mr Erasmus...Rob and Malcolm will be around in the basement
now and again...don't worry about them...they come and go via the
basement/garden door. The door to the basement needs to stay locked
and the key in pisition on the butchers hook as ever. But don't
put the snick down on the B door as they come up into the kitchen
occasionally to make a cup of tea.

D: Tabitha is still shitting up here in the spare stroe room...and as
you left the door to your room open,...she's done one in your room..
..hah...the love of dumb animals.....and me and me....

D: Coffee machine....teach you to listen to me.....fill thing with
ground beans...only high roast or Italian if you run out....your/our
old style pale beans don't work in the Gaggia. Then...three buttons
BUTTON ONE...turn on it will light up red light...as soon as the red
light goes off press button three to make it happen....when you've got
half a cup of Expresson..turn off button three and press butto n two

VAT. No. 305 6301 96   Reg. No. 2340540
A. Erasmus, R. Gretton, M. Hannett, P. Savile, A. Wilson

FACTORY RECORDS
86 Palatine Road, Manchester 20.
Telephone 061-434 3876

down to bring red light on again for the steam mode....as soon as
the red light goes off bring the milk jug near (the one in the same
pattern as the little cups....before putting milk under, press
button three down...you are now ready...slowly twist the big top
thing...button four lets say...clockwise.......let the first
two seconds of hot water and steam come out of the nozzle...then shove
the milk under and jiggle about...as soon as milk gets up high and befo
loss of pressure turns the steam back to hot water withdrwa and take
every button to the off position and that's it.
The big danger is getting hot water and not steam....to avoid this..
....all activities must happen immediately the red light goes off..
..i.e. when it's at its hottest...if you miss the moment (how
apropos that sounds,,,but there are more memants to come)wait for
3 or 4 minutes till it comes on again of its own accord and then hit
it. The secret is the immediacy on the red light....and you know
how bad our timing is.......will think of you in NYC....strange
how it seems to be your town....urination at the twin towers...
strange girl....love to your mom.

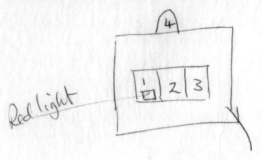

VAT. No. 305 6301 96   Reg No. 2340540
A.Erasmus, R.Gretton, M.Hannett, P.Savile, A.Wilson

I was able to be with her at the end, and I stroked her and she purred as she passed away. Nathan was in the room but removed from it. I cried my eyes out but, when Tony got home from work, he simply accepted the news without emotion and hugged me, smiling at my tears. To me it had a deeper connotation than the ending of the life of our cat, although that was upsetting in itself. Tabatha had been our only dependent together. For that reason, it felt more significant in terms of loss: it was a shared responsibility, now broken. Factory didn't need or appreciate me like Tabatha did. It felt like a final nail in the coffin.

---

36 Old Broadway
Dearest wife,

How confusing things are.....I don't even care to think about them.....just get more confused .....as you said....not yet whatever....time to think...etc......but you ARE my wife.....anyway business simpler.

A: Will leave fifty pounds with this to pay bills....milk, gardener, and window cleaners all owed if they call.

B: Herewith also some money from your building society account.

C: People who'll be around. Sandra comes every Monday morning to do the bookkeeping in me office.....she's lovely.....very easy going etc........since the cheque book for Factory stays here for her to go through, Alan may well need it at various points in the week so keep in touch with him......as much as it is ever possible....never here or only there Mr Erasmus.....Rob and Malcolm will be around in the basement now and again.....don't worry about them....they come and go via the basement/garden door. The door to the basement needs to stay locked and the key in position on the butchers hook as ever. But don't put the snick down on the B door as they come up into the kitchen occasionally to make a cup of tea.

D: Tabitha is still shitting up here in the spare store room.....and as you left the door to your room open,....she's done one in your room.....hah....the love of dumb animals.....and me and me.....

D: Coffee machine....teach you to listen to me....fill thing with ground beans.....only high roast or Italian if you run out.....your/our old style beans don't work in the Gaggia. Then.....three buttons BUTTON ONE....turn on it will light up red light....as soon as the red light goes off press button three to make it happen.....when you've got half a cup of Expresso....turn off button three and press button two down to bring red light on again for the steam mode..... as soon as the red light goes off bring the milk jug near (the one in the same pattern as the little cups....before putting milk under, press button three

down.....you are now ready.....slowly twist the big top thing...... button four let's
say.....clockwise.....let the first two seconds of hot water and steam come out
of the nozzle.....then shove the milk under and jiggle about....as soon as milk
gets up high and before loss of pressure turns the steam back to hot water,
withdraw and take every button to the off position and that's it. The big danger
is getting hot water and not steam.....to avoid this....all activities must happen
immediately the red light goes off.....i.e. when it's hottest....if you miss the
moment (how apropos that sounds, , , but there are more moments to come)
wait for 3 or 4 minutes till it comes on again of its own accord and then hit
it. The secret is the immediacy of the red light....and you know how bad our
timing is.....will think of you in NYC......strange how it seems to be your town ......
urination at the twin towers......strange girl......love to your mom. P

.S. Plant in front room needs new big pole. Cane broke in half last week. Ta
Love
AHW XX

Tony goes into great detail about his new gadget, a Gaggia coffee machine – his pride
and joy. He never drank tea, only copious cups of coffee. The machine was significant to
him in his new home, a symbol of trendiness and prosperity as well as coffee worship.
Believe it or not, espressos and cappuccinos were not that readily available in the early
eighties. They were rare at home and not even all that common in cafes outside of the
city centre. Tony wasn't bothered by, or sensitive to, the vibrations that I could feel in the
house. I sensed depression, loneliness and abandonment. I thought this was something
to do with the old occupants of the house but maybe this feeling represented my own
fears as a potential future occupant. I felt disturbed by it, but Tony was steadfastly able
to leave his own mark there.

He mentions leaving me money from 'your' building society account. It wasn't even
in my name. I did trust him with it, but why did he have to 'daddy' me? I wanted to
be his equal. He ends the letter by mentioning 'urination at the Twin Towers'. This
occurred on one of our better days while in New York together. Tony had been showing
me around lower Manhattan where the World Trade Center complex then stood. The
Twin Towers, when first built, were the tallest buildings in the world. Impressive though
they were, at the time of our visit I was desperate for the loo. There wasn't a cafe or public
toilet anywhere near. No one was about, office workers had all left for the evening, the
building was closed and so I took my chances on the road outside.

The first two months of 1983 were ostensibly good between us; a respite before the
looming Portmeirion visit. In February, we were platonic yet very friendly and had a
lovely trip to Lisbon, where The Durutti Column played the Coliseum to the biggest

audience they've ever had. Thus began my passion for Lisbon and its environs, and I would visit several years running in the 1980s. This trip also instigated a lifelong, albeit distant, friendship with Miguel Esteves Cardoso, an esteemed writer who co-founded Portugal's first independent record label, Fundação Atlântica. The label licensed several Factory acts and also arranged the recording of Durutti's *Amigos em Portugal*, which sold very well.

March '83 was significant on two counts. First of all, New Order had found their niche with their release of 'Blue Monday', having been sufficiently inspired by the New York club scene to move into the dance arena themselves. They'd learned a great deal at the feet of gadget genius Martin Hannett, and as a result were able to create their own dance music with electronic sequencers, samplers and drum machines, and they produced this record by themselves. This would be their ticket to success, despite a slightly inauspicious start.

'Blue Monday' got into the charts soon after its release, but the band made the mistake of performing it live on *Top of the Pops*. It simply didn't work, and likely dented sales slightly for a week or so. Although 'Blue Monday' is now noted to be the best selling 12-inch single of all time, especially following two re-releases, its success wasn't so apparent back in 1983. Saville's original, brilliantly inspired, die-cut sleeve for 'Blue Monday' was so expensive it ate into profits, reputedly even causing a loss with each sale. However, Factory's bank account was generally diminished, particularly with The Haçienda costs draining resources, so such losses were nothing new.

The other significant thing about March '83 was that our reconciliation was not consummated during our visit to Portmeirion. Our stay was, in fact, a nightmare, the polar opposite of our first romantic tryst there in 1976. We took LSD, a bad idea and a bad trip (all round). Tony often unwisely suggested taking LSD at critical moments, such as before going to a bullfight in Spain. That was traumatic for me, to put it mildly, and I'm forever utterly opposed to bullfights. I didn't know that the bull had to die at the end and was equally horrified by the reactions of the audience who cheered as if a goal had been scored every time the poor bull was hurt. It was equally unwise of me to trust and go along with Tony's suggestions: I was freaked out on both occasions. In Portmeirion we could hear a couple in the room above us having sex as their bed banged against the wall. This went down like a lead balloon with us, sitting far apart from each other. I felt uncomfortable with performing to order and I was simply unable to. I think Tony took this to mean the very end, as he behaved rather coldly from then on.

Consequently, when Kuka invited my mum and me to accompany him by road to Paris on one of his antique deliveries, I agreed. Although that relationship had been wrecked, he'd earlier arranged to take my mum to Paris, as he was fond of her, and she'd never been before. She would probably regret going, as things were so strained; I knew deep down I'd now lost Kuka and being with him only compounded my confusion and stress.

To make matters worse, on our return the car broke down in pouring rain, and Kuka got home to find that his mother had Pablo, his beloved dog and soulmate, put down while we were away. Kuka sat on the stairs and wept. I knew just how he felt. It was hell. First Tabatha and now Pablo, the only dog I'd ever felt really close to. Then days later his little yellow canary, Booey, who sang beautifully, got out through his studio window. It felt like an ending of relationships all round. And it was.

In May, Tony gave me a card for our wedding anniversary. He'd wanted to celebrate by going out for a meal, but my mum told me just before I left the house that I'd lost my option with Kuka. Being unready to accept that, I reacted badly and then felt so depressed, knowing she was right and feeling forced into embracing the man who had caused it, that when I arrived at Old Broadway we didn't go for the meal and parted, with Tony saying he was sorry it hadn't worked out, and that he hoped we could be friends.

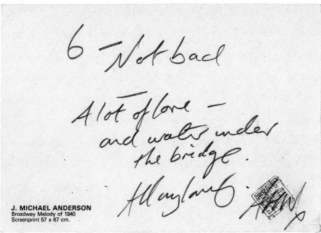

6 – Not bad

A lot of love –
and water under
the bridge.

J. MICHAEL ANDERSON
Broadway Melody of 1940
Screenprint 57 x 57 cm.

东方宾馆

TUNG FANG
BINGUAN

36, Old Broadway, Manchester

Late May, '83

Dear Lins,

A Labour party canvasser called last night; he wanted to know
what way Nathan, Me, and Lindsay Wilson would be voting. From
this I take it you're on the electoral role for the coming festival
of democracy. "G with the W" always placed its endless-but-in-vain
love affair against a background of high politics, and swapping
the decline of the old south for the decline of the good old
north west, I thought it better to let you know in case you
wanted to exerricise your franchise. You can oily vote in one
place in a General election; but I don't know if you're on the
roll in London or Gatley.

I wouldn't bother you but Withington; for that is the fief in
question, might be an interesting seat (I expect a tory landslide
but one must be optimistic...in politics if not in love) as Sylvester
the Tory sitting MP has done little to enhance his name since
1979;;;;it's only a tory marginal, and the labour girl, Frances
Done is apparently a very good candidate. So every vote counts.
The place to vote is down Cotton Lane, opposite Christies on
Wilsmlow Road....down towards the old rabid office...it's the
big primary school....you can't miss it. I know that sometimes
you're not crazy about politics, but there are moments when history
crosses our paths, and it seems a shame not to step into the event

东方宾馆
TUNG FANG
BINGUAN

and share that taste of responsibility for global destiny;

even while personal destinies lie shattered on the ground.

Did you ever have read of War and Peace...all about that...

but some really nice characters...in fact thinking back

Natashas flight of infatutaion with the horrible Kuryagin

has a lot to say about a certain trip to Leeds in the early

hours....and I always thought I was Pierre. In that instance

Natasha fucked up Prince Andrei......but I digress...history

and the rest , tied in with the personal....like this...a

contact that is , I quite understand,both out of time and

out of pla ce.

But anyway...DO vote.

I hope your life is looking up for you.

Yours,

with love,

P.S. Thanks for cleaning up the small bathroom. Whatever

will I do without you?

Then, Tony sent me a somewhat perfunctory letter, typed on his Chinese notepaper, with no romantic attachment suggested therein. But perhaps he hadn't entirely let go.

36, Old Broadway

Late May. '83

Dear Lins,

A Labour party canvasser called last night, he wanted to know what way Nathan, Me, and Lindsay Wilson would be voting. From this I take it you're on the electoral role for the coming festival of democracy. "G with the W" always placed its endless-but-in-vain love affair against a background of high politics, and swapping the decline of the old south for the decline of the good old north west, I thought it better to let you know in case you wanted to exercise your franchise. You can only vote in one place in a General election; but I don't know if you're on the roll in London or Gatley.

I wouldn't bother you but Withington; for that is the fief in question, might be an interesting seat (I expect a tory landslide but one must be optimistic..... in politics if not in love) as Sylvester the Tory sitting MP has done little to enhance his name since 1979; ; ; ; only a tory marginal, and the labour girl, Frances Done is apparently a very good candidate. So every vote counts. The place to vote is down Cotton Lane, opposite Christies on Wilmslow Road...... down towards the old rabid office......... it's the big primary school......you can't miss it. I know that sometimes you're not crazy about politics, but there are moments when history crosses our paths, and it seems a shame not to step into the event and share that taste of responsibility for global destiny; even when personal destinies lie shattered on the ground. Did you ever have read of War and Peace.......all about that ....but some really nice characters........ in fact thinking back Natasha's flight of infatuation with the horrible Kuragin has a lot to say about a certain trip to Leeds in the early hours.....and I always thought I was Pierre. In that instance Natasha fucked up Prince Andrei....... but i digress....history and the rest, tied in with the personal......like this.....a contact that is, I quite understand, both out of time and out of place.

But anyway......DO vote.

I hope your life is looking up for you.

Yours,

with love,

Anthony P.S.

Thanks for cleaning up the small bathroom. Whatever will I do without you?

Tony again refers to the film *Gone With the Wind,* in this letter as "G with the W". Released in 1939, it had a big impact on people for decades afterwards. Tony seems to be tacitly inferring that our love affair was endless but in vain, like that between Scarlett and Rhett. The film's conclusion is somewhat open-ended as, although Rhett tells her he (no longer) gives a damn, Scarlett seems convinced there's hope, and that she'll think of some way to get him back. We never know if she does. Tony also mentions Tolstoy's *War and Peace.* In the story, Natasha, being infatuated with Kuragin, tries to run away with him. When this is thwarted, she attempts suicide. My version of this situation had taken place in May '79, when I went in search of Howard Devoto in the middle of a Magazine tour and found him, but finished up feeling suicidal. Tony writes that he identifies with a central character of *War and Peace,* Pierre Bezukhov. Actually, the nature of this man doesn't remind me of Tony – Pierre is kind and gentle and not especially physically attractive, for instance. Pierre has an unhappy first marriage but eventually finds happiness with Natasha who bears him four children. Prince Andrei on the other hand, who, as Tony wrote, 'Natasha fucks up', maybe resembles Tony more, being handsome, intellectual and somewhat heroic. Tony said in later years: 'I would love to be thin, intense, dark and serious, like Prince Andrei in *War and Peace.* But I'm Pierre Bezukhov – a wally enthusiast[1].' In the novel Andrei is engaged to Natasha but her father insists they wait a year during which time she falls for Kuragin and plans to elope with him. Of course, Kuragin for Natasha, like Devoto for me, was highly unsuitable.

Ostensibly the purpose of Tony's letter was to remind me to vote. Ever the TV link man, he sets this low political agenda against the high political backdrop featured in *Gone With the Wind,* namely the American Civil War. Margaret Thatcher was then in power, a politician who changed the fabric of the country to this day. One example: the Housing Act of 1980 made it possible for council tenants to buy their own homes. This led, in my view, to a chronic shortage of affordable housing, rising house prices, soaring rents in the private sector and a culture of debt and greed, with people forever fixated on house prices. The general election in June 1983 was a landslide victory for Thatcher. Tony and I both voted Labour, but he suspected that the Tories would be re-elected in Withington. Deeply immersed in news reporting for Granada, Tony had the inside track, and his interest in politics remained keen to the end.

It was around this time that Tony sent me the card on the next page that significantly shows a young woman sitting alone. It's clearly me – she's wearing the kind of hat I chose for our wedding and many occasions thereafter. I've always loved hats and wish they weren't so out of current vogue nowadays. Note Tony's use of the custom-made seal of his name in Chinese, stamped over his initials. His question on the other side was never answered.

1The Guardian, 2002, Sean O'Hagan.

Andreolo — Estate
Migneco & Smith editori, Firenze — Tel. (055)263390
AIC/5 — Printed in Italy

CHAPTER 13
On the Factory Floor

Looking back over Tony's notes and letters, it's obvious he still hadn't totally given up on a reconciliation. This was clear even as late as July 1983, despite the fact he had filed for a divorce the previous month. He wrote some ominous words on his card for my thirty-first birthday: the damning line being: 'in these death throe days when separation is almost complete.' I still didn't pay that much attention to it, or even to his divorce petition. Just like the boy who cried wolf, his threats had become meaningless because there'd been so many that he hadn't acted on. I was more focused on the perfume in this note and how he wanted to buy me dresses, and that he'd included a romantic verse and signed it 'all my love': it felt like he was still wooing me. But surely a divorce petition signified the end? I didn't think Catholics believed in divorce. I still thought he might be manipulating me. Surely, we had an indestructible bond that could never be broken? I didn't take it all that seriously and, in any case, if that was what he wanted, it only seemed fair to let him go.

July 2nd 1983

Dearest Lins,

Not really a birthday present; more the traditional duty free, done from duty and tradition; and a little proustian smell adoration. For your birthday, well the tradition there is to buy you a dress. Exactly what I intend to do this 31st occasion. Only in these death throe days when separation is almost complete, I find my taste in your apparel very far from what it seems you wish for yourself. So, rather than get into credit notes etc.... would you care to pick a dress or two for me to pick you....in Manchester or London, and then I'd pick up and give gift.....seems most wholesome solution.....and happy birthday.....

"To me fair friend, you never can be old
For as you were when first your eye I eyed.

July 2, '83

Dearest Lins,
Not really a birthday present; more the
traditional duty free, done from duty and
tradition; and a little proustian smell
adoration.
For your birthday, well the tradition there
is to buy you a dress. Exactly what I intend
to do this 31st occasion. Only in these death
throe days when separation is almost complete,
I find my taste in your apparel very far from
what it seems you wish for yourself. So, rather
than get into credit notes etc...would you care
to pick a dress or two for me to get you....
in Manchester or London, and then I'd pick
up and give gift.....seems most wholesome soluti
on.......and happy birthday.....
        "To me fair friend, you never can be old
        For as you were when first your eye I eyed
Such seems your beauty still."
And so, for this one, and ones to come when I
may not be able to tell you - tho here's hoping
my memory will be that of a lover when each
July comes around - Happy Birthday, sweet
sixteen - and all my love,

X

Such seems your beauty still."

And so, for this one, and ones to come when I may not be able to tell you – tho here's hoping my memory will be that of a lover when each July comes around –

Happy Birthday, sweet sixteen – and all my love,

Anthony x

I never did get the dresses. His reference to our different tastes in 'apparel' may have been based on the fact that I was now resistant to dressing like a dolly bird, in heels and skimpy clothing. I'd been something of a slave to that until meeting Kuka, who referred to my footwear as 'hooker's shoes'. He preferred to see me wear more practical clothes, and shoes I could easily walk in. But Tony did spend a great deal of money on clothes. Once Tony and I were walking along King Street in Manchester and he told me I could have all the clothes I wanted if I went back to him. He was tempting me, knowing they were my weakness when I couldn't afford to buy any. But this felt as if he was my dad rather than my equal. And I'd rejected my dad.

I remained torn. I must have decided to take the line of least resistance, since I still felt unable to embrace the marriage. I felt powerless, incapable of making a decision, nothing felt like the right thing. I stayed in limbo and, if Tony wanted a divorce, so be it. If he wanted me to disclaim all rights to Factory then also so be it. When I signed his document to that effect, which he produced one night at Old Broadway, I should have taken *that* seriously at least. In my experience, I've learned that when it comes down to money one can usually rely on people being deadly serious.

Somewhat surprisingly, that summer I became an employee of Factory. Tony had been waxing lyrical about a wonderful job I could do, organising the overseas licensing for the label. Rob had been managing foreign affairs up to this point but didn't have time to do it any longer, what with New Order's burgeoning success. In May 1983 the band had built on the success of their single 'Blue Monday' and released their second album, *Power, Corruption and Lies*. This was a great album, head and shoulders above their first (*Movement*). *Movement* had felt like part of the band's grieving process for Ian.

I thought the album cover of *Power, Corruption and Lies* an odd choice considering the title, and the electronic nature of the music; it showed a basket of roses, a detail from a painting by the French artist Henri Fantin-Latour. The image seemed better suited to a box of chocolates to me. Still, I came to love the sleeve precisely *because* it was unusual, and because I liked the contents. The story goes that Peter Saville and his girlfriend saw this painting together in the National Gallery, and she jokingly asked him if this painting was to be his next sleeve. Peter latched on to the idea, his thinking being that the flowers were seductive, in much the same way that lies and corruption can infiltrate our lives. Or maybe it was just an easy way out. He is a clever guy, Peter Saville: he and Tony enjoyed many a brainy chat over the years.

It followed that there was quite a bit of stock to license abroad in 1983. Tony said this was a job he'd love to do himself, and I was persuaded to accept it, despite reservations for various reasons. Mainly I suspected his motive; taking this job would end any chance of me visiting London, which of course it did. It seemed kind of primal, like one male animal fighting another and, in this case, Tony had won. My relationship with Kuka was all but over and accepting the job in Manchester – working with my husband five days a week – made it cast-iron certain. I felt Tony's ego was at stake, that winning that score was important to him even if we *were* to divorce. The final *coup de grace*, you might say. It strengthened his power and probably weakened my own, although, divorce or no divorce, at this point he still told me that if I wished to return as his wife then I should. The door was open.

I chose rather to be his employee than his wife but felt uneasy about re-entering the Factory stable. I knew my name was now mud with the likes of Rob Gretton, given my past affairs and therefore, probably to a similar degree, his girlfriend Lesley, who was running the day-to-day office in Alan's flat. On the Monday I began work, Tony suggested operating from Old Broadway so he could show me the ropes. Clearly, Rob didn't want to explain things to me, even though he'd been running the licensing up until this point. Rob had most likely objected to my employment. The workload had become heavier, considerably more than just a few folders to deal with, and now merited the name 'Overseas Licensing Department'. Tony handed me the four or five folders that Rob had kept, jammed with scattered telexes, purchase orders, invoices and contracts, plus he bought me a new red index card box to register contact details in. That was about the extent of the Overseas Licensing Department, and the extent of my training when I took things over. However, I could see at once that income had been lost through the lack of an orderly system. One of the first things I did was to list the licensees in a red notebook.

As Tony thought, it *was* an interesting job, and at a really interesting time in the history of Factory. Prior to this I'd never considered having an aptitude for making money but quickly realised that, given decent product to sell, I was a natural at it. I liked speaking to the licensees all over the world and it was hugely enjoyable making deals and squeezing money out of them. After that first week, Tony set me up at Alan Erasmus's flat on Palatine Road, which had now become Factory headquarters. From then on I worked in a small room, once the second bedroom, which was adjacent to the main office – aka Alan's old living room – where Lesley worked. Alan occasionally slept in the main bedroom, which Ikon had been using during the day before their move to Old Broadway. I initially felt ill at ease in these surroundings; Lesley and I had little to do with one another and I never felt we worked as a team. And yet, despite the many comings and goings, we were the two main constants in the office.

1) Polygram Inc (Michael Theriault)
   6000 Cote de Liesse,
   St. Laurent,
   Montreal, Quebec
       Canada. H4T 1E3

   via Emery Airfreight,
   Building 13. M/C Airport

2) Base Records
   c/o Antonio Fiorelli,
   Via Collamana 26,
   40138 Bologna,
   Italy.
   Tel 010-39-51-534697

   via Caroline
   Unit 6, Tilson Rd.,
   Roundthorn Industrial Est
      M 23

3) Gap Records (Andrew Gardener)
   51, Walker St.
   North Sydney 2060.
      Australia
   Tel 02 922 6649

   via Emery Airfreight .

4) N.M.S (Mario Pacheco)
      Bretou de Los Herreros 48,
      Madrid

   via Emery

5) Virgin France, (Alain)
      65 Rue de Belleville
      75019 Paris

   via European Van Service
   Tel 01 311 5000

6) Rough Trade America (Steve)
      326 Sixth St.,
      San Francisco,
      CA 94103
         USA

   via Rough Trade
   137, Blenheim Crescent
         W11
   Tel 01 221 1100

7) Boudisque . (Kik or Wally)
   Haarlemmerstraat 10-18.
   1012 L.R. Amsterdam

   via Rough Trade

) Gap
   51, Walker St.
   orth Sy
   Aust   a

   n   Airfre

n   Emery

      gin Fran   A1   )
      65 Rue de   lle
            Paris

      a
      T

8) Rough Trade Deutschland
   Marienstr. 17
   4690 Herne 2
   Tel 02325 · 3911 · 12

9) Musikkrätet Waxholm MNW
      Kadhusgaten 12
      Furk   800
         18500 Waxholm
   010 46/   SWEDEN
   Tel 0764/323 45
      Studio 0764/323 29
      Bankgiro 473-2640
      Postgiro 36 11 77-5

10) Spartan Records - Ireland

11) Factory Benelux.
      Michel Duval — 32, Avenue
      (gu Wanes-)   des Phalena
      (12589 Bonda   1050 Bruxelles
   Telex (65146 Wanda. Tel 010 32
               264 9 2729
12) Factory New York . (Home)
            010 32
            219 4450×27
                  (work)

We did have a Monday morning meeting with Tony, Rob and Alan, at which joints were lit and smoked (Lesley was the only abstainer). Other than that, I saw more musicians than directors. Alan was frequently absent and never stayed long when he appeared. Tony was like the visiting MD, who would occasionally swoop in for the all-important cheque signings, or issue instructions over the telephone. Rob was also rarely there and, when he was, he had little to do with me. Rob was humorous and jolly, but he could be a bully. He bullied me for sure. Although gifted with an ability to make people laugh, his comments to me were generally some sort of put-down, rude insults that he thought would be funny to the others in the room. He never once complimented me on my work, even though the overseas licensing income had trebled within six months. Despite that, Factory's bank account was never very healthy during this time, since the outgoings were so huge (thanks to The Haçienda, for instance). The rewards from this creative period would come much later.

How strange that I would be running that department when our divorce came through. I naively imagined Tony would remain loyal to me, married or not, at least in so far as my job at Factory. After all, Factory had been our baby; it certainly took the energy and finances that having a child would have done. But Tony liked to underplay my role. I was only ever going to be a low paid employee unless I slept with him.

Tony submitted his petition for divorce on 10 June 1983. He'd altered the date from 10 April 1983. Presumably he'd had his doubts then. I didn't feel justified to object when I received the papers. I signed the document in front of him although I still doubted that he'd actually go through with it. However, he did. The decree nisi was dated 24 October, 1983. It rattled me that he'd listed my job as 'Antiques Dealer' – my job while living with Kuka. I'd given both that and Kuka up to work full time at Factory, and that was the job I was doing when when the petition went through.

Even with all of this, and against all the odds, I still didn't believe our marriage would ever truly end and, in a sense, it didn't. We were as close at the end of his life as we ever were.

Before completing this form, read carefully the attached *NOTES FOR GUIDANCE*

IN THE   MANCHESTER   COUNTY COURT*   *Delete as appropriate

IN THE DIVORCE REGISTRY*   No.   83D1139

(1) On the   *14th*   day of   *May*   19 *77* the petitioner

Anthony Howard Wilson   was lawfully married to

Lindsay Carole Reade Wilson (hereinafter called "the

respondent") at   *St. Mary's, Marple Bridge, Stockport.* in the

district of *Stockport* in the borough of *Stockport*

(2) The petitioner and respondent last lived together at

45, Town Lane, Derbyshire

(3) The petitioner is domiciled in England and Wales, and is by occupation a

television journalist and resides at *36, Old Broadway, Manchester 20*

and the respondent

is by occupation an *antiques dealer*

and resides at *4, Linksway, Gatley, Stockport*

(4) There are no children of the family now living ~~except~~

(5) No other child, now living, has been born to the petitioner/respondent during the marriage (so far as is known to the petitioner) ~~except~~

     D.8.

(6)   There are or have been no other proceedings in any court in England and Wales or elsewhere with reference to the marriage (or to any child of the family) or between the petitioner
and respondent with reference to any property of either or both of them ~~except~~

(7)   There are no proceedings continuing in any country outside England or Wales which
are in respect of the marriage or are capable of affecting its validity or subsistence ~~except~~

(8)   No agreement or arrangement has been made or is proposed to be made between the
parties for the support of the petitioner/respondent (and any child of the family) ~~except~~

(9)   The said marriage has broken down irretrievably.

(10)   *The parties to the marriage have lived apart for a continuous period of at least two years immediately preceding the presentation of the petition and the respondent consents to a decree being granted.*

(11) PARTICULARS

The relationship broke down in 1980 and on January 15th 1982 the respondent moved out of the family home in Charlesworth. Since then she has lived between Hendon and her mothers home in Gatley. No reconciliation has been effected.

CHAPTER 14
Shown the Factory Door

The decree nisi gave an interim of six weeks before it was made absolute. When I realised Tony wasn't going to call it off, I wrote a letter to the courts. I kept the letter all these years, just as I've kept diaries, simply as a record of how I felt at the time. I never posted it, because I felt I didn't have the right to stand in his way if he really wanted this. Also, I felt a general fear – a fear of getting him back, as well as a fear of losing him. But there was another reason stopping me from posting it; maybe a sense that it was too late, that he'd met someone. Unbeknownst to me, it turned out he had.

> 4 Lindsway,
> Gatley,
> Cheshire
> November 2nd 1983
>
> Dear Sir or Madam,
>
> I am writing to withdraw my consent for the divorce between Anthony and Lindsay Wilson.
>
> I do not believe that the marriage has broken down irretrievably. During the last year – as a result of our attempts at a reconciliation – we have become friends. The main difficulty is that we cannot agree at the same time to go back to the marriage –
>
> since one or other of us has been involved with someone else. This problem has not yet been resolved, but we have both wanted to return to the marriage at different times in the last few months.
>
> Also, I do not agree with divorce as a matter of principle, and I think that a second marriage is likely to have an even poorer chance of survival than a first.
>
> Yours faithfully,
>
> Lindsay Wilson.

It always struck me as ironic that the notification of the decree absolute was addressed to Mrs Wilson.

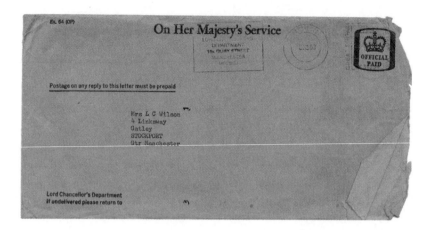

Tony's note to me that Christmas said it all, but I didn't understand or get the reference at the time. I even briefly and mistakenly imagined he might still be wooing me. His line, of course, is taken from *Gone With the Wind*. Ever the romantic, he was saying goodbye to me rather in the same way he'd said it to Thelma – i.e. referencing the end as drama. Only this wasn't Paris, it was the deep south of America. Again, there were parallels to be drawn between Scarlet and Rhett and us. Our marriage was turbulent, and I'd imagined a great love for Howard Devoto that wasn't real, as Scarlett did for Ashley, only realising she'd loved Rhett all along just when she loses him for good. Rhett acknowledges that he and Scarlett have been at 'cross-purposes'; the reason Tony and I were at cross purposes might have been that I'd told him I had doubts about our divorce. In truth I'd just needed more time. Or maybe he could tell that I imagined he still cared – why else had he wanted us to work together? I certainly didn't know I'd entirely lost him.

I continued working at Factory, unaware that, regardless of his note, Tony had not only met someone else but was expecting a baby with her. Tony's son, Oliver, would be born the following September, so, even if I *had* sent the letter cancelling our divorce, it would have been too late. Tony had met Hilary while visiting his friend, Neville, mentioned in Tony's early letters, in a psychiatric unit in Withington. Neville had gone there after losing the plot while taking strong drugs in India. Lacking the funds to escape, several of his musician friends held 'rock 'n' roll jam' gigs in Didsbury to raise the money to bring him home. They were successful, and on returning to the UK Neville was admitted to Withington. Hilary was being treated on the same ward.

Neville told me: 'Tony visited every night for several hours, we got stoned, played guitar, sang and exchanged philosophical views. He loved coming to the funny farm – Tony always had an attachment to craziness and crazy people. He thought madness was close to genius. I took him to Hilary's room and introduced him. He was knocked out by her. They got on really well. The next day when he visited me he told me he was going to marry her – I thought that was premature after one night.'

I knew nothing about Hilary as, unlike other girlfriends, Tony had kept this one quiet. I hadn't realised how strong his desire for a child was and possibly this was a primary goal. Years later Tony told me that, when he fell in love with baby Oliver, he was finally able to fall out of love and cut the cord with me. It was quite a blow to me to learn that Tony was to be a father after I'd entirely given up my life and relationship in London for a life working at Factory in Manchester. Nonetheless I threw myself into the job because I enjoyed it, and because it meant something to me. Actually, it was all I had left.

I liked to get involved with Factory endeavours outside of the licensing, and I started recording music again. My version of 'Telstar', mentioned earlier, received a stark remix from Hooky and was released in 1984 under a name I chose: Ad Infinitum. I prefer the B-side, which was Andy Connell on piano (soon to be part of Swing Out Sister) and Martin Moscrop of ACR on trumpet. The two had been playing around with the tune outside the main Strawberry studio but, when I heard it on my way to the bathroom, I asked them if we could record it. They did it in one take. I bought a job lot of spaceship holograms to be affixed on each record sleeve (which I mostly stuck on myself).

I also began managing the group 52nd Street, who'd released 'Look Into my Eyes'/'Express' in 1982 on Factory. The track of theirs that had really caught my attention was 'Cool As Ice/Twice As Nice' which US label A&M released the previous year. By the time I began managing the group in 1984, the lead singer Beverley McDonald had left and been replaced by Diane Charlemagne – Diane and I were to have a vital friendship for the rest of her life. After 52nd Street she went on to record with Urban Cookie Collective, Goldie and Moby. Sadly in 2015, at the age of 51, Diane would die of kidney cancer – the same disease that killed Tony.

Then there was the aforementioned video I made with Section 25 for their track 'Looking From a Hilltop'. The guys and I were prevented from making tea after being locked out of Tony's main house while working on this video in the basement. Hilary, who was out when I arrived, had seen my car on her return and then 'put the snick down on the B door'. I could hardly go back there again. I wouldn't have gone into the kitchen in any case, but it signified I was a threat, and the writing was already on the wall. I should have parked the Karmann Ghia somewhere else. That particular video at least got finished.

Throughout 1983 and 1984, I continued to keep a close eye on monies from abroad. I negotiated advances with various companies and, once agreed, sent across the necessary parts for them to begin pressing their own releases. Across are examples of original paperwork I kept to monitor monies coming in.

It seems strange now that computers were so uncommon then; there was, of course, no email or internet either. With only occasional access to a typewriter, many documents had to be handwritten. Despite appearances, they constituted an orderly system to me at the time. Bear in mind this was forty years ago. The catalogue numbers illustrate the content. By this point New Order's album *Power, Corruption and Lies* (FAC 75) was visible but not as financially lucrative as it became. FACUS 2, featuring Joy Division's 'Atmosphere; b/w 'She's Lost Control' was released in the UK in late 1980, following an earlier American release. FACUS related to all US releases. I typed up my own copy of

Table 1

MECADISC	FRANCE	N.M.	STOIC	BASE	CAP	MNW
				84 £500	13 £500	
Focus	13 £806 45 48.	Focus	10,	10,	Focus	73
2/10	10 £4,838.70	2 £1,000	28	25 } £5,000	2	75 £2,000 18.4.83
25	Focus	33 £1,500	25	Focus 26.3.81	10, £4,000 17.6.81	93 £2,600 11.4.84
50 } £3,500	2	40 £1,500	40	2	23 £1,800 8.12.80	103 £2,500 11.4.84
63 29.8.83	23 £1,209.68 +81	53 £1,000	50	13 free	25 £4,000 8.12.80	92 £250
65 } £1,008.09	25 £6,451.60	63 £300 £3,000	63	14 £250 15.6.81	11 £270 21.8.81	90 £500
26.83	33 £2,000 28.9.81	44 £500 21.6.84	73	23 £750 15.6.81	14 £1,800 14.81	85
73	40 £11,706.68	55 £500	75	33 £750 15.6.81	33 £600	
75 } £3,700	22 £806.45 4.81	74 £400	103 £500	35 } £2,659 25.21	ACR £750 15.7.81	
93 £3,000	35 £2,419.35	75 £750		42	40	
	50	73 £300		40 £3,000 19.1.82	44	
103 £1,000	53 No advance	79 £200		44 £500	50	
	44 part of	82 £200		45 £1,600 19.1.82	55	
	65 at beginning	93 £300		50 £2,997 3.3.82	72 £450 21.2.84	
	73 £1,500	50 £1,000 *		52 £300	74 £600	
	75 £3,500	103 £800		55 £2,995 25.5.82	79 £500	
	93 £1,500	* Together £1,500		53 free	73	
	55 NJ			63 free	75	
	103 £1,000 2.11.84	25 £400		65 £1,500 31.5.85	93	
	72 £500	10 £400		73 } £6,000 31.5.85	103 £2,000 35.84	
	87 £200 24.10.84	28 £300		75	90 £500	
	92 £250 24.10.84			74 £750 24.2.84	102 £500	
	88 £200 24.10.84			82 £500 24.2.84	108 £200	
	90 £500 24.10.84			93 £1,500 24.2.84	ACR £600	
	Focus			102 £2,000 13.6.84 package		
	8			102 £500 (82-62)		
	74 £500			90 £250 9.10.84		
				Focus 58 £2,000 9.10.84		

Table 2

POLYGRAM	NIPPON C.	R.T. GERMANY	BENELUX	R.T.Z.	METRONOME	DENMARK
13,	50	73		10	10	
Focus	63	75		25	23 } £20,000	
2, } £1,241.70	73 } £13,050 3.4.84	93		23	25	
23, 23.6.81	75	103		40		
25.	93			42		
14 £413.9 23.6.81	90 £2,000 7.9.84	92	90 £550 8.1.84	50		
44 £438.59 17.11.81	10 £3,000 7.9.84	79	79	35		
74, £270 4.9.83	25 £4,000 7.9.84	90	74	43		
40 £2,192.98 17.11.81	40 £4,000 7.9.84		102	53		
50 £2,192.98	23 £1,000 7.9.84 } £11,515.00					
62,	103 £2,000 15.10.84		HIMALAYA			
68,	Focus 2 £800 7.9.84					
65,			84 £550			
73, } £6,169.15	84 £5,000		114 £250			
75, 28.4.83	114 £1,200					
79 £1,088.83 28.11.83						
53 } £1,408.55						
68 14.10.82						
93 £3,780 4.9.83						
103 £3,500 3.5.84						
90 £1,000 28.6.84						
85 £1,000						
90						
108 -						
92 £500 28.6.84 £180						

SHEET 1 OF FACTORY CATALOGUE NUMBERS

Facus 2:   JOY DIVISION 12" "ATMOSPHERE"

FAC 2:   A FACTORY SAMPLE; Joy Div; Durutti, Dowie, Cabs. 7" EP

FAC 5:   A CERTAIN RATIO; "ALL NIGHT PARTY"

FAC 6:   ORCHESTRAL MANOEVRES IN THE DARK; "ELECTRICITY" 7"

FACT 10:   JOY DIVISION; "UNKNOWN PLEASURES" LP

FAC 11:   EXODUS; "ENGLISH BLACK BOYS" 12"

FAC 12:   THE DISTRACTIONS; "TIME GOES BY SO SLOW" 7"

FAC 13:   JOY DIVISION; "TRANSMISSION" 7"

FACT 14:   DURUTTI COLUMN; "THE RETURN OF..." LP

FAC 16:   ACR; "THE GRAVEYARD & THE BALLROOM" Cassette

FAC 17:   CRAWLING CHAOS; "SEX MACHINE" 7"

FAC 18:   SECTION 25; "GIRLS DON'T COUNT"

FAC 19:   JOHN DOWIE; "HARD TO BE AN EGG" 7"

FAC 22:   A CERTAIN RATIO; "FLIGHT" 12"

FAC 23:   JOY DIVISION; "LOVE WILL TEAR US APART" 7" & 12"

FACT 24:   A FACTORY QUARTET; Royal Family, Blurt, Durutti, Hewick.LP

FACT 25:   JOY DIVISION; "CLOSER" LP

FAC 29:   THE NAMES; "NIGHTSHIFT" 7"

FACT 30:   SEX PISTOLS; "THE HEYDAY" Cassette

FAC 31:   THE MINI-POPS; "DOLPHIN SPURT" 7"

FAC 32:   CRISPY AMBULANCE; "UNSIGHTLY & SERENE" 10"

FAC 33:   NEW ORDER; "CEREMONY" 7" & 12"

FAC 34:   E.S.G.; "YOU'RE NO GOOD" 7"

FACT 35:   A CERTAIN RATIO; "TO EACH.." LP

FACT 37:   JOY DIVISION; "HERE ARE THE YOUNG MEN" VIDEO

FAC 39:   TUNNELVISION; "WATCHING THE HYDROPLANES" 7"

FACT 40:   JOY DIVISION; "STILL" LP (Double)

SHEET 2

FAC_41:   STOCKHOLM MONSTERS; "FAIRYTALES" 7"

FAC_42:   A CERTAIN RATIO; DOUBLE 12"

FAC_43:   THE ROYAL FAMILY & THE POOR; "DREAM DOMINION" 12"

FACT_44:   DURUTTI COLUMN; "L.C." LP

FACT_45:   SECTION 25; "ALWAYS NOW" LP

FAC_48:   KEVIN HEWICK; "CATHY'S CLOWN" 7"

FACT_50:   NEW ORDER; "MOVEMENT" LP

FAC_52:   A CERTAIN RATIO; "WATERLINE" 12"

FAC_53:   NEW ORDER; "EVERYTHING'S GONE GREEN" 7" & 12"

FACT_55:   A CERTAIN RATIO; "SEXTET" LP

FAC_57:   THE MINI-POPS; "ISLAND" 7"

FAC_58:   STOCKHOLM MONSTERS; "HAPPY EVER AFTER" 7"

FAC_59:   52ND STREET; "LOOK INTO MY EYES" 12"

FACT_60:   THE WAKE; "HARMONY" Mini-LP

FAC_62:   A CERTAIN RATIO; "KNIFE SLITS WATER" 7" & 12"

FAC_63:   NEW ORDER; "TEMPTATION" 7" & 12"

FAC_64:   DURUTTI COLUMN; "I GET ALONG WITHOUT YOU.." 7"

FACT_65:   A.C.R.; "I'D LIKE TO SEE YOU AGAIN" LP

FAC_66:   SECTION 25; "THE BEAST" 12"

FAC_67:   QUANDO QUANGO; "TINGLE" 12"

FAC_68:   SECTION 25; "BEATING HEART" 7"

FACT_70:   SWAMP CHILDREN; "SO HOT" LP

FAC_72:   A.C.R. "DON'T YOU WORRY 'BOUT A THING" 12"

FAC_73:   NEW ORDER; "BLUE MONDAY" 12"

FACT_74:   DURUTTI COLUMN; "ANOTHER SETTING" LP

FACT_75:   NEW ORDER; "POWER,CORRUPTION & LIES" LP

FAC_78:   JAMES; "FOLK LORE" 7"

FAC_79:   QUANDO QUANGO; "LOVE TEMPO" 12"

FACT_80:   STOCKHOLM MONSTERS; "ALMA MATER" LP

FAC 82:   CABARET VOLTAIRE; "YASHAR" 12"

SHEET 3

FACT 84:   DURUTTI COLUMN; "WITHOUT MERCY" LP

FACT 85:   THICK PIGEON; "2 CRAZY COWBOYS" LP

FAC 87:   KALIMA; "THE SMILING HOUR" 12"

FAC 88:   THE WAKE; "TALK ABOUT THE PAST" 7" & 12"

FACT 90:   SECTION 25; "FROM THE HIP" LP

FAC 92:   MARCEL KING; "KEEP ON DANCING" 12"

FAC 93:   NEW ORDER; "CONFUSION" 12"

FACT 95:   ROYAL FAMILY & THE POOR" "THE PROJECT" LP

FAC 96:   AD INFINITUM; "TELSTAR" 7"

FAC 97:   STREETLIFE; "ACT ON INSTINCT" 12"

FAC 102:   QUANDO QUANGO; "ATOM ROCK" 12"

FAC 103:   NEW ORDER; "THIEVES LIKE US" 12"

FAC 105:   FEVERHOUSE; Soundtrack to Ikon Video

FAC 106:   LIFE; "TELL ME" 7"

FAC 107:   STOCKHOLM MONSTERS; "NATIONAL PASTIME" 7"

FAC 108:   SECTION 25; "LOOKING FROM A HILLTOP" 12"

FAC 109:   CAROLINE LAVELLE

FACT 110:   A.C.R.; LP

FAC 111:   SHARK VEGAS; 12"

FAC 112:   A CERTAIN RATIO; "LIFE'S A SCREAM" 12"

FAC 116:   RED TURNS TO; 12"

FAC 118:   52ND STREET; "CAN'T AFFORD (TO LET YOU GO)" 7" & 12"

<u>Agreed Advances Not paid to date</u>

(all parts received)

<u>Polygram</u>

 85 - $1,000

<u>Nippon C</u>

 84 - 15,000
 114 - $1,200

<u>Himalaya</u>

 84 - £500
 114 - £250

R.T. California

 90 - £400

Virgin - Greece

 25 - $1,000
 23 - $300
 75 - $1,000
 73 - $300
 103 - $300
 10 - $1,000
 50 - $1,000

<u>Base</u>

 84 - £500
 114 - £125

N.M. Spain

 74 - £400
 75 - £750
 73 - £300
 79 - £200
 82 - £200
 93 - £300
 103 - £300
 25 - £400
 10 - £400
 23 - £300

Directors: Alan Erasmus, Robert Gretton, Anthony Wilson.
Consultant: Peter Saville.
Limited Company No: 1524272.
VAT No: 3832 66632

the numbering system as there wasn't one available then. I missed some numbers out as, presumably, they were events or posters or other products that weren't necessary for overseas marketing. It was poignant and perhaps prophetic, that the last number I reached on my typed sheets, was 'Can't Afford To Let You Go'.

I was familiar with all the licensees listed and regularly spoke to the contacts I had for each. On the previous page is a sheet revealing advances for me to chase up.

Once both the pregnancy and Tony's hasty marriage to Hilary was announced, my position at Factory felt somewhat tenuous and awkward. I loved the work and being creatively involved with various musicians but, as mentioned before, I wasn't exactly a popular member of staff and, to add to this, I'd now become something of an irritation to Tony on a personal level. He didn't want his new wife to call round if I was in the office, for instance. There wasn't any strain in our working relationship, not yet at least, but Tony became distant. Polite, but distant. I nobly enquired how his new wife was coping with her pregnancy even though it cut me to the quick. 'Fine, but she gets tired,' was his reply. He was beginning to ignore me.

And then, on 5 December 1984, Tony sacked me.

I wrote to Tony the following, on 8 December 1984:

Dear Tony,

I am writing to seek clarification of my position as your employee.

On Wednesday 5th December, you told me that I was fired and that you would be issuing the customary warning letters.

You were not clear about when this dismissal was to take effect and said that you would like me to stay on and teach my successor the job.

On Thursday 6th, when I arrived for work, I was told by a Director and member of staff (Alan and Leslie) that my return to work was pointless in view of the circumstances. However, I had business to attend to and stayed for the duration of the day.

On Friday 7th you called at the office and I asked you if you had brought my dismissal note. You replied that you thought I had resigned. I said this was not the case. You then suggested that we meet for lunch to discuss the matter but that you would prefer me not to carry on working in the meantime. I asked if you had not been happy with my work. You said that, on the contrary, you had been pleased overall and agreed that the overseas licence revenue had trebled since my management of same. However, you said that I could not continue because of my "disobedience".

I urgently request that you clarify these statements and my position – whether I am dismissed or not, from when such dismissal is to take effect and the said reasons for this dismissal.

Yours sincerely

Ms Lindsay Reade

That letter was ignored until January 1985. I spent Christmas at my parents wondering how Tony could have done such a thing to someone he was supposed to have cared for, and at such a time of the year. Although I'd decided not to sue at our divorce, I was resolved to take him to an unfair dismissal tribunal because that, in my certain opinion, was what it was.

Eventually his long reply came. It gave Tony's side of it, but my own differs. I never got the chance to give my side of the story, and so I have taken this opportunity to break Tony's letter up into three smaller sections with my version of events inter cut between them. My responses are adapted from the defence notes I took with me to the tribunal, which ultimately was never heard. Tony's original letter is, of course, all of a piece:

Factory Records

86 Palatine Road

January 9th, 1985

Dear Lindsay,

You asked for clarification with regard to your dismissal. My apologies that it has been delayed, but as I am sure you will understand we have had to take legal advice, and with the Christmas break intervening, that has been a slow process.

In the intervening time, we have adhered to the loose arrangements made in the throes of our disagreements; necessarily loose owing to the hysterical nature of those confrontations and the absence of reasoned argument or discussion.

As requested by you, I will now briefly itemise the history leading to your dismissal. While generally satisfied with your work for the company, in particular the liaison established with our foreign licensees, there has been, since the early days with the company in the Autumn of 1983, a series of disagreements between yourself and the company's directors over company policy. On several occasions in early 1984 it had to be explained to you that, while you were free to think as you wished, company policy was set out by the directors and had to be adhered to. One particular item of policy was central to the events to come. As well as numerous licensees, Factory Communications Limited has two important foreign operations in which our involvement is as

Factory Records

Factory   30 Palatine Road
Communications Manchester 20
Limited   061 434 3838

January 9th, 1984

Dear Lindsay,
You asked for clarification with regard to your dismissal. My apologies
that it has been delayed, but as I am sure you will understand we have
had to take legal advice, and with the Christmas break intervening, that
has been a slow process.
In the intervening time, we have adhered to the loose arrangements
made in the throes of our disagreements; necessarily loose owing to
the hysterical nature of those confrontations and the absence of
reasoned argument or discussion.
As reque-sted by you, I will now briefly itemise the history leading to
your dismissal. While generally satisfied with your work for the company,
in particular the liaison established with our foreign licensees, there
had been, since your early days with the company in the Autumn of 1983,
a series of disagreements between yourself and the company's director s
over company policy. On several occasions in early 1984 it had to be
explained to you that while you were free to think what you wished, company
policy was that set out by the directors, and had to be adhered to.
One particular item of policy was central to the events to come. As well
as numerous overseas licensees, Factory Communications Limited has two
important foreign operations in which our involvement is as co-owner,
partner and close friend. These two operations are Factory Benelux, in
Brussels, run by Michel Duval, and Factory New York, or OF Factory to give
its correct title, run by Michael Shamberg. By the Summer of 1984 you
had developed a dislike and distrust for both operations. It was explained
on several occasions that the directors of the company had total faith in
both Michel and Michael, and while they had their faults, they were
indispensable parts of the network, and extremely important to the
company. With your responsibility for overseas liason, it was explained to
you again , that whatever your personal feelings, you should represent
the attitude of your company in your dealing with both Benelux and New
York. In the end it was the New York connection which proved the major
problem in the Autumn of 1984.
Throughout the Summer of 1984, Michael Shamberg, in New York, had been
working extremely hard to get american licensing deals for Factory's two
black dance acts, 52ND Street and Marcel King. As Factory's man in New
York, his main function had become liaison man with the major US labels: of
vital importance to the company in this the biggest of all record
markets. .
In the first week in November, in your other role as manager of 52nd
Street you responded to an inquiry from Black Market records of New York,
by saying yes . As is your right as manager of the band , you decided off
your own bat to sign with this company. Fully aware that Michael Shamberg
had spent the last three months trying to sell the band to either A&M
or Electra , you made no attempt to inform Shamberg. In fact he found out
when he went to the Electra Office to again try and tie up the 52nd ST
deal, only to be told, with laughter; "Don't you know.....they've signed

Directors: Alan Erasmus, Robert Gretton, Anthony Wilson.
Consultant: Peter Saville.
Limited Company No: 1524272.
VAT No: 383266652

Factory Records

Factory   46 Palatine Road
Communications Manchester 20
Limited   061-434 3876

to Black Market". The personal embarrassment, and the damage to Factory's
prestige in the States are clear cut.
When the matter surfaced in England, I, as a director of Factory, in a
heated discussion attempted to explain to you why everyone in the
company was hopping mad. It was explained to you that it was not your
job to embarrass Factory operatives merely because you had taken a
dislike to them, that again your personal feelings have no place in
company policy, and that what you had done was seen as extremely
damaging to the company. It was made very clear that such things should
never happen again. Accepting the appaling relationship which now existed
between yourself and Factory New York, I even am offered to act as a go_
between with Michael myself, making it very clear that all American
negotiations were to go through him.
It was around the end of November, I'm afraid I do not remember the exact
date, that I was informed by one of the management Comittee of the Hacienda
club, that the head cleaner, who is also a bass player, had not turned
up for work because he had gone into studio..."for Marcel King" and that
"Tony would know all about it". I did not. I was aware that Michael
Shamberg had been working for three months to get A&M to release a
2nd single by Marcel King. Michael had been responsible for a $6,000 deal
for Marcels first single with A&M, earlier in the year. I was aware
that he had almost negotiated a $1,000 payment for Marcel to complete
demo tracks here in England of two tracks suggested by A&M themselves. But
that money had not yet come through. Having failed to locate you that
evening to discuss the matter, I called Michael Shamberg in New York to
ask if he knew anything about the demo recording. NO. When he had last
talked to them a week before, they were still humming and hawing about
the $1,000. He decided to call A&M immediately, and tell them Marcel was
going in studio, "how about the money?" He called me back twenty
minutes later. A&M knew all about it: apparently you had talked personally
to Nancy Jeffries, of A&M, and set it up, entirely without Shamberg
knowing.
The next day we talked on the phone: my intention then was to minimise
damage; I told you that I couldn't believe you had done it again, but
that "lets finish the tapes today and then think about it".
The following morning I went to see you at your office in Factory.
I began by saying that in the light of the fact that you had been talking
about leaving your job since early Summer, and from the fact that you had
so blatantly ignored all the instructions that had been given you,
and repeated exactly the appaling behaviour of lees than a month ago, by
pursuing a personal vendetta with Michael Shamberg, and again going over
his head and severly embarrassing our US operation: that from such
clearly repeated refusal to do as the company asks, I took it that you
were handing in your notice. You replied that you were not and that
I would have to sack you. I replied that if that had to be the way
it would be, and if you wanted to do it officially, then I would
give you a written warning: since you are as you put it a "free spirit",
it was clear that the official process involving disobedience would
take around three days to get through.

Directors: Alan Erasmus, Robert Gretton, Anthony Wilson.
Consultant: Peter Saville.
Limited Company No: 1524272.
VAT No: 3832 6663?

Factory Records

Factory

Communications

Limited

I suggested that your dismissal be from the end of the year. You replied
that you were owed three weeks holiday pay. I agreed to that. You
asked how much compensation, and I said I would suggest that Factory
norm which is three months salary. You said you wanted much much more and
would sue.
At this point, I am sorry to say, you became violent and abusive. By
violence I refer to the nature of your language. This persisted throughout
the day, and then throughout the next day. You continued to abuse the
lady who is Factory's production manager throughout the two days.
"You fucking cunt" is just a small example of the insults that pesristed
throughout this period.
You also attacked me verbally, though as your loving ex-husband it is
rather like water off a ducks back. However your attacks on my partner
A;lan Erasmus during that two day period were unforgiveable. Mixing
violent language with vicious personal criticism. I got to the point where
if he saw your car outside the office, he was not prepared to go inside.
Obviously your behaviour over this period and the complete destruction
of your personal relationships with other workers and directors within
the company make any suggestion of a return to your post utterly out
of the question.
We will remain loyal to the original suggested terms of dismissal.
Notice, effective as of the end of 1984, three weeks extra holiday pay
to take your salary through to the week ending 19th of January, and then
three months salary as a pay-off.

It is not a happy solution; merely the only solution

Yours,   AHW

AHW.

P.S. Your tax free payoff - 3 mths - comes to
£1,235:00 — please though, return all
Factory Property + papers. P.45 in post.

Anthy.

Directors: Alan Erasmus, Robert Gretton, Anthony Wilson.
Consultant: Peter Saville.
Limited Company No: 1324272.
VAT No: 5032 66632

co-owner, partner and close friend. These two operations are Factory Benelux
in Brussels, run by Michel Duval, and Factory New York, or OF Factory to give
you its correct title, run by Michael Shamberg. By the summer of 1984 you had
developed a dislike and distrust of both operations. It was explained on several
occasions that the directors of the company had total faith in both Michel and
Michael and, while they had their faults, they were indispensable parts of the
network, and extremely important to the company. With your responsibility for
overseas liaison, it was explained to you again that, whatever your personal
feelings, you should represent the attitude of your company in your dealing with
both Benelux and New York. In the end it was the New York connection which
proved the major problem in the Autumn of 1984. Throughout the summer of
1984, Michael Shamberg in New York had been working extremely hard to get
American licensing deals for Factory's two black dance acts, 52nd Street and
Marcel King. As Factory's man in New York, his main function had become
liaison man with the major US labels: of vital importance to the company in this
the biggest of all record markets.

In the first week of November, in your other role as manager of 52nd
Street, you responded to an enquiry from Black Market records of New York,
by saying yes. As is your right as manager of the band, you decided off your
own bat to sign with this company. Fully aware that Michael Shamberg had
spent the last three months trying to sell the band to either A&M or Electra,
you made no attempt to inform Shamberg. In fact he found out when he went
to the Electra office to again try and tie up the 52nd ST deal, only to be told,
with laughter, "Don't you know....they've signed to Black Market". The personal
embarrassment, and the damage to Factory's prestige in the States are clear
cut.

The instructions I'd been given regarding the license of a particular record to a
territory was first to consult with the manager of the group in question. This was why I
rarely had anything to do with Benelux or New York, because either Rob or Tony took
care of the deals regarding their own groups' releases directly, with either Michel Duval
at Benelux or Michael Shamberg in New York. However, as well as licensing manager, I
was also at this stage managing 52nd Street.

In November I received a call from a New York record company called Black Suit,
connected to Profile Records; they wanted to license the latest record by 52nd Street.
This record happened to be 'Can't Afford to Let You Go'. It had already been released
in the UK and, up until licensing, could only be bought at the high import price in the
US rather than standard retail price. The band felt the license was overdue, particularly

since America had been their better market. However, before I discussed terms I first of all rang Michael Shamberg to check if he'd got any other offers. He was very vague, spoke about other interest but no definite offer from any company. I told him about Black Suit, proving that it wasn't true he was unaware of the deal; I remember he offered to call them on my behalf. Admittedly it would have been more diplomatic to agree to this but, as they already had a call booked with me for the following day and, by this point in the proceedings it would only slow negotiations down, I said there was no need. I discussed the deal with the band, and they were very impatient for me to get on with it. Therefore, I verbally agreed terms with the company three days later.

Rob told me that the licence was 'stupid'. I asked him why and he replied, 'If I told you, you wouldn't listen.' I then said, 'Well, tell me, I am listening.' His response to that was to say he wasn't going to waste any more time talking to me. Tony was furious and said I'd destroyed Shamberg's work on behalf of the group. I said I appreciated Shamberg's efforts, but they hadn't so far proved fruitful, and that, as the group's manager, I considered it best to get on with the good deal actually on the table. As far as I knew, I was acting for the good of the group and therefore, the company. No one at Factory had told me Shamberg had been 'working extremely hard throughout the summer of 1984', as Tony letter states, and even if he had, it hadn't amounted to anything concrete and so far he'd brought nothing to the table.

It was also untrue to say that I'd 'developed a dislike and distrust of both operations' – i.e. Michel from Benelux and Michael from Factory US. I have zero memory of ever having a 'dislike and distrust' of Factory Benelux or Michel, whom I didn't even really know. I wrote to Michel to ask him if he could think of anything to concur with that. He replied, 'We had good dealings together as far as I remember'. I also wondered why Tony didn't see fit to mention Annik Honoré, who set up Benelux with Duval? Was she outside of the boys' club, especially – like me – having committed the cardinal sin of adultery? Again, I asked Michel, but he said that 'she was there from the beginning and of course very important, but she left after one odd year for professional reasons.'

I must, however, admit to disliking the way Tony treated Michael Shamberg like royalty while dismissing me as if I was a paid junior when it came to business. It felt to me almost as if they were in a 'bromance'. I took this photo of the two of them in Tony's house, in the room he called the music room. They were working on some kind of Factory business while I was being ignored.

Tony was always wholeheartedly enthusiastic about New York and determined to break Factory on the East coast of America, which partly explained the high value he placed on Shamberg. Yet Shamberg's foray into the music industry had only just begun when he'd made the film of ACR in New York in 1980. Admittedly he then got the licence for 'Cool As Ice' by 52nd Street with A&M but, now several years later and with 52nd Street having a different lead singer, A&M weren't interested in 'Can't Afford'.

More importantly I didn't like the untruths related by Tony in Shamberg's version of events because I <u>had</u> called him and told him about the offer before agreeing the deal with Black Suit/Profile.

Shamberg had recorded an album in 1984 at Strawberry with his then partner Stanton Miranda, along with Stephen Morris and Gillian Gilbert from New Order, under the name of *Too Crazy Cowboys* by Thick Pigeon. Released on Factory, it has been described as 'Artpop minimalism' but I just didn't get it or like it, nor did I care for the expensive, die-cut record sleeve. This could have been another reason Tony levelled the word 'dislike' at me, but I was entitled to my opinion of the record. I probably shouldn't have expressed it, but I often disagreed with Tony's choice of acts and thought he sometimes had cloth ears. If he was enamoured with someone he'd let them record anything – hence why I got to sing with The Durutti Column.

Tony's letter continued:

'When the matter surfaced in England, I, as a director of Factory, in a heated discussion attempted to explain to you why everyone in the company was hopping mad. It was explained to you that it was not your job to embarrass Factory operatives merely because you had taken a dislike to them, and that what you had done was seen as extremely damaging to the company. It was made very clear that such things should never happen again. Accepting the appalling relationship which now existed between yourself and Factory New York, I even offered to act as a go-between with Michael myself, making it very clear that all American negotiations were to go through him.'

Who exactly was this 'everyone' Tony speaks of? Rob Gretton? Rob also developed a close working relationship with Shamberg, who went on to produce many of New Order's videos. Then there was the more relevant issue of Marcel King (in that it was this that prompted my immediate dismissal). Tony wrote:

'It was around the end of November, I'm afraid I do not remember the exact date, that I was informed by one of the management committee of the Haçienda club, that the head cleaner, who is also a bass player, had not turned up for work because he had gone into the studio.... "for Marcel King" and that "Tony would know all about it". I did not. I was aware that Michael Shamberg had been working for three months to get A&M to release a 2nd single by Marcel King. Michael had been responsible for a $6,000 deal for Marcel's first single with A&M earlier in the year. I was aware that he had almost negotiated a $1,000 payment for Marcel to complete demo tracks here in England of two tracks suggested by A&M themselves. But that money had not yet come through. Having failed to locate you that evening to discuss the matter, I called Michael Shamberg in New York to ask if he knew anything about the demo recording. NO. When he had last talked to them a week before, they were still humming and hawing about the $1,000. He decided to call A&M immediately and tell them Marcel was going in studio, "how about the money?". He called me back 20 minutes later. A&M knew all about it: apparently you had talked personally to Nancy Jeffries, of A&M, and set it up, entirely without Shamberg knowing.
    The next day we talked on the phone: my intention then was to minimise damage; I told you that I couldn't believe you had done it again, but that "let's finish the tapes today and then think about it".
    The following morning I went to see you at your office in Factory. I began by saying that, in the light of the fact that you had been talking about leaving your job since early summer, and from fact that you had so blatantly ignored all the instructions that had been given you, and repeated exacting the appalling

behaviour of less than a month ago by pursuing a personal vendetta with Michael Shamberg, and again going over his head and severely embarrassing our US operation: that from such clearly repeated refusal to do as the company asks, I took it that you were handing in your notice. You replied that you were not and that I would have to sack you. I replied that if that had to be the way it would be, and if you wanted to do it officially, then I would give you a written warning: since you are, as you put it, a "free spirit" it was clear that the official process involving disobedience would take around three days to get through. I suggested that your dismissal be from the end of the year. You replied that you were owed three weeks holiday pay. I agreed to that. You asked how much compensation and I said I would suggest the Factory norm which is three months salary. You said you wanted much more and would sue. At this point, I am sorry to say, you became violent and abusive. By violence I refer to the nature of your language. This persisted throughout the day, and then throughout the next day. You continued to abuse the lady who is Factory's production manager throughout the two days. "You fucking cunt" is just a small example of the insults that persisted throughout this period. You also attacked me verbally, though as your loving ex-husband it is rather like water off a duck's back. However your attacks on my partner, Alan Erasmus, during that two day period were unforgivable. Mixing violent language with vicious personal criticism. It got to the point where if he saw your car outside the office, he was not prepared to go inside. Obviously your behaviour over this period and the complete destruction of your personal relationships with other workers and directors within the company make any suggestion of a return to your post utterly out of the question.

   We will remain loyal to the original suggested terms of dismissal. Notice, effective as of the end of 1984, three weeks extra holiday pay to take your salary through to the week ending 19th of January, and then three months salary as a pay-off.

   It is not a happy solution; merely the only solution.

   Yours,

   AHW signed AHW and a hand written

   P.S.: Your tax free pay off – 3 months – comes to £1,235:00 – please though, return all Factory property + papers. P.45 in post.

   Anthony'

This was grossly unfair since I had specifically been asked by Rob Gretton to work with Marcel. Rob had asked me to put together a band rehearsal for Marcel King with a view to then arranging a demo tape. I asked Rob whether to book an eight-track studio or twenty-four-track and he told me that, since Factory were covering the costs, it would be better to go eight-track. Both Marcel and 52nd Street were more Rob's speciality than Tony's since Rob had a keen interest in black music and soul, unlike Tony.

Marcel was a young man who'd had a hit in 1975 at the tender age of 16 as the vocalist on Sweet Sensation's 'Sad, Sweet Dreamer'. Although enormously successful, Marcel only received session singer payments and became very bitter about it, particularly as he became completely broke by the age of 20. Six years later, in March 1984, Factory released his record 'Reach for Love'/'Keep on Dancing' (FAC 92). Presumably this was the $6,000 deal that Tony wrote Shamberg had negotiated, again with A&M.

Marcel sang with the voice of an angel but the devilish side to his nature had a penchant for plenty of drugs. Talented but unfocused, he hadn't rehearsed or made any demos since that first Factory release, nor did he seem the slightest bit motivated to do so. Rob was concerned that Marcel needed a follow up single and soon, and this was why I'd been given the job.

It was no small task getting Marcel down to a rehearsal room with the musicians and equipment I managed to cobble together for him. Somehow I got him there on Monday 3 December; it's entirely possible that a lump of hash was the incentive. But this was outside of my job description of running Factory's overseas licensing, and it was outside of office hours. There was no suggestion of extra pay by Rob, nor did it occur to me to ask for any – I genuinely wanted to do this for its own sake.

We made progress that evening with putting together a song, a track called 'Waiting'. It sounded great and I could see that they were ready to demo it immediately, but we needed studio time to do it. It seemed vital to strike while the iron was hot; Marcel was otherwise liable to become distracted and disappear. Plus, the musicians had lives to live and might drift apart if we didn't get on with it quickly. On the day in question, Factory were overdrawn by approximately £6,000. I'd gathered one of Factory's distributors had apparently gone bankrupt, owing Factory £40,000. This was why, concerned about the expense, I'd told Marcel that we'd record on eight-track. But Marcel insisted he didn't want to bother with that, since the tracks could be master-taped in the same time in a twenty-four-track studio. I told him about the limitations of Factory's budget, but he replied that A&M in Los Angeles were footing the bill, and that he knew this as he'd spoken with them directly two weeks previously. He asked me to telephone the person he'd spoken to – Nancy Jeffries – to verify this.

Rob hadn't told me A&M were to finance this recording and I wondered if, in fact, Marcel was imagining things. I passed by the office that night on my way home and knew it was a good time to phone Los Angeles. I got through to Nancy and it was true. She told me that she'd asked Shamberg to provide a budget for studio costs two months earlier but that he hadn't done so, and that A&M wouldn't OK the payment until this was done. Nancy asked me to work out a budget and said she'd telephone on the Thursday to approve it. She sounded pleased that we were making progress at last.

When I got home, my mum told me that Tony had rung, worried that I was running up a bill in a recording studio. The next morning, I told him it had just been a rehearsal room and that I was going to submit the budget on Thursday. He exploded and said I'd destroyed Shamberg's hard work and that he was negotiating a £3,000 budget for Marcel. Funny, then, that Nancy said she'd been waiting two months to hear anything from Shamberg. The written budget I worked out actually came to £2,000. Tony then asked me to promise I wouldn't communicate with Nancy Jeffries in any form ever again. I didn't agree because she and I had arranged a call and I felt obliged to honour that, even if I had to tell her it was out of my hands. Then he said, 'Well, I take it you have resigned,' to which I replied, 'No, I have not.'

The next day Tony called at the office and said, 'I hope you're going to be sensible about quitting your job.' I reaffirmed that I wasn't resigning. He said that he was going to sack me and give me the official letters of warning. I could see that he meant what he said and became very upset; I cried for the rest of that day. Yet again there'd been no communication. You will note that Rob didn't back me up over his request that I work with Marcel. Instead, he joined forces with Tony to stand against me. Rob had already judged me severely and doubtless was happy to see me removed.

I'd just behaved as if we were one team and hadn't seen it as stepping on anyone's toes. No one had briefed me on the protocol of who talks to who. I'd just been trying to get Marcel's record made, on the instructions of Rob. Shamberg hadn't provided a studio budget to A&M, despite being asked to, but it did actually seem more logical and sensible to me that I provided it since the studio was in Manchester and he was in New York. The covert reason for the sacking, in my opinion: Tony was looking for a way of ousting me as he'd just become a father and, as he later told me, he'd fallen in love with his baby boy and out of love with me. I was an inconvenient reminder of his past from then on. '*Move on, darling,*' in other words. Can you imagine Tony sacking me if I had gone back to him and/or, if I was bearing his child? No way. I would rather have been congratulated for getting Marcel to record a song.

In later years, when Tony and I were on good terms again, I always referred to this as a grossly unfair dismissal. He wouldn't listen to my reasons and never once backed down, stubbornly saying it was justified. His version of 'praxis' – i.e. find a good reason for whatever you want to do?

Regarding Marcel, I'd tried in good faith to manage it the best way I could. It was a labour of love, nothing to do with silly politics. Tony's 'loyalty' to Michael Shamberg over this was rather petty really. It was only a studio budget, not a record deal. Plus, Marcel didn't have a manager and had specifically asked me to phone Nancy Jeffries on his behalf. Furthermore, what I was doing in the studio with Marcel would have only given Shamberg product to sell.

Marcel and his friend happened to call into the Factory offices on that awful day, saw my tears and accompanied me to my car. I offered to give them a lift home to Wythenshawe and then, Marcel's friend, sitting on the back seat, produced a bottle of champagne from under his coat that he'd taken from Factory's fridge. It had been there for years, and I'd often wondered who was going to drink it. It turned out to be we three musketeers in my car that day.

The following year, I had it in mind to release a record by Marcel myself, on my own label, and he agreed. Doubtless because I was paying him, he happily came along to the recording studio. We put the track down but unfortunately I lacked the funds to make the label happen. The shame was that Marcel never did release anything else and died of a brain haemorrhage, aged 38, in 1995. A great pity that the politics of who talks to who, and who is sleeping with who, came before the creative work itself.

Overall, I have to laugh at someone who'd worshipped at the shrine of punk rock sacking me for disobedience. Upon calling an industrial tribunal for an unfair dismissal, Tony turned up with Rob, Lesley, and Alan Erasmus. I thought it cowardly and unfair of Tony not to face me one to one. As noted earlier, punishment was Tony's modus operandi when people didn't behave the way he wanted them to. I felt this dismissal was intrinsically that – his punishment to me. I hadn't conformed to 'what he wants of a wife' and hadn't gone back to him. So really, I felt strongly that this case was just between the two of us.

I was so hurt and angry I certainly did swear badly in the office, but Tony swore all the time, so could hardly talk. It was wrong of me to be abusive, but I'd felt betrayed, since support for the sacking just went one way – towards the boss – with no interest in the reasons behind it. Doubtless they all planned to corroborate Tony's account of this, as it was probably the only valid reason for my dismissal. The tribunal case didn't get heard that day and I had to endure listening to the four of them laughing and joking in the next room from 9–4 p.m. as if this was a Factory outing. For me, it was deeply upsetting and painful, but there seemed little point postponing the case when it was four against one. My legal aid lawyer advised there wouldn't be much compensation even if I did win, as I was so badly paid. Money wasn't my purpose though; this was about justice.

My lawyer literally begged me to sue for half of Factory Records and half of the house on Old Broadway. He said our divorce was still open to settlement as we'd never had lawyers and it was less than two years since the divorce. He even said I had a 'moral obligation to do it'. Despite being left literally with nothing, I refused. Quite *why* I refused, I'm unable to explain. Was it because the *I Ching* had told me that 'the superior man does not go to the law'? Was it that money was never my goal in life? Also, because I'd been the one to break it up between us I didn't feel entitled to it. Or was it my low self-esteem that didn't credit myself for what I'd given to Factory? Tony didn't recognise it, particularly as I'd hated his total enthusiasm for the organisation so soon after the death of Ian. Or could it be that I believed I still had everything to play for? There were myriad reasons, but I've sometimes regretted my decision to walk away empty-handed, as well as not going back to Tony when I could. If I had, my life would have been entirely different. I was at a real crossroads and took the turning towards anonymity, impoverishment and independence. I'll never know if we would have been happier, but I do know I would have been seen as an important co-founder of Factory – instead I've been written out of my own history. Other people, usually male, are chosen for consultation on early Factory when they weren't even there.

Paul Morley, in his biography of Tony, *From Manchester With Love*, managed to write two pages about Orchestral Manoeuvres in the Dark without even mentioning me. Even Tony always said their debut release on Factory was entirely down to the fact I played their demo tape to him and enthused about it. This was echoed by the band themselves, who dedicated 'Electricity' to me when they performed it at the Rewind festival in Cheshire in 2018.

Another thing I'll never know is if revenge would have been sweet if I'd sued. I doubt it somehow, for revenge rarely is, although the money would certainly have come in handy. But I'm glad that the bitterness felt was only mine. If I *had* sued, Tony would have been the bitter one and we would never have made our peace. Factory would have suffered and struggled to continue but, as it was, both Tony and I were yet to have a second main act, musically and emotionally.

I observed in later years how the Factory partners' wealth grew as mine diminished. While I was unable to buy a home and either struggled to pay rent or had to live with my parents, it became obvious that monies were being splashed around by the directors of Factory. To rub salt in the wound, most of the money seemed to stem from product that was already in existence at the time of my departure, mainly Joy Division and New Order.

The last time I saw Rob was in 1997 at Tony's father's funeral in Eccles. I'd been pretty close to Tony's dad Sydney, and to his partner Tony Connolly, and so I attended with my mum, who also knew them both well. There was no animosity between Rob and I after so much water under the bridge, although his expression was one of bafflement when he looked at me. He was in a flash new car; Tony had his posh Jaguar, Tony's girlfriend Yvette looked like Jackie Onassis under a large hat, and my mum and I trailed behind the expensive black cars in her battered old Ford Fiesta, looking like a stray addition to the cortège.

CHAPTER 15
Phoenix and Ashes

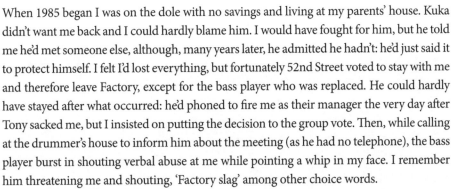

When 1985 began I was on the dole with no savings and living at my parents' house. Kuka didn't want me back and I could hardly blame him. I would have fought for him, but he told me he'd met someone else, although, many years later, he admitted he hadn't: he'd just said it to protect himself. I felt I'd lost everything, but fortunately 52nd Street voted to stay with me and therefore leave Factory, except for the bass player who was replaced. He could hardly have stayed after what occurred: he'd phoned to fire me as their manager the very day after Tony sacked me, but I insisted on putting the decision to the group vote. Then, while calling at the drummer's house to inform him about the meeting (as he had no telephone), the bass player burst in shouting verbal abuse at me while pointing a whip in my face. I remember him threatening me and shouting, 'Factory slag' among other choice words.

Things improved when 52nd Street got a deal with Virgin/10 Records five months later. This put an end to the dole and created a great deal of activity from then on with recording and promoting. But in those early months, I was furious with Tony and unimaginably hurt. Despite refusing to sue him, I felt so angry one night my mum had to almost physically restrain me to prevent me from severely slashing the tyres on his posh car. I hated him and I hated the people who ran Factory. I'm glad I didn't slash his tyres and also, in a way, that I did walk away without suing. Someone once told me that a thing isn't really worth having if you have to ask for it. Also, I would have missed what happened in 1988 between Tony and me, and that was truly special and important.

I don't exactly remember how our reconciliation came about, but there is no doubt that time does heal all wounds – or, if you prefer, time wounds all heels, as the old joke goes[1]. I think Tony was secretly impressed that I'd survived in the music business without him, not only working with 52nd Street – who were up to their second album release in 1987 – but also what I achieved with The Stone Roses.

---

1 'Heel' being US slang for a person who behaves reprehensibly; the phrase – attributed severally to John Lennon, Groucho Marx and others – promises that such individuals will get their comeuppance in time.

Around 1985, I'd been invited to co-manage The Stone Roses by Gareth Evans, who was running a live music venue in Manchester called The International. Initially, the Roses seemed to have a bit of a goth presence and, years earlier, they hadn't sounded good to my ears when I'd heard them practising next door to 52nd Street's rehearsal room in Chorlton. Gareth got them to play a private set for me in The International. When I heard them play the material that would eventually become the eponymous debut album, I instantly recognised they had great songs. Though I was unsure of trusting Gareth, I agreed to co-manage the band with him and work to get them a deal. At a similar time but a different place, Tony was getting excited about Happy Mondays, who were to enjoy many prolific years and releases on Factory. These two bands really epitomised the upcoming Madchester scene of the late eighties. 'Madchester' was a term to describe the indie/dance/acid house/rave scene that was taking off around that time.

We arranged for the Roses to record some songs on eight-track in Spirit Studios so I could take demo cassettes round to various companies in London. The cassette offered two versions of 'Elephant Stone' and 'The Hardest Thing in the World'. Getting them a deal was nearly the 'hardest thing' in itself, as most A&R departments rejected them. However, I did get Rough Trade founder Geoff Travis and Roddy McKenna from Zomba[2] to come to a gig we arranged at Dingwalls in London. Geoff told me he'd give the group a deal when they were halfway through their first number. Roddy got Andrew Lauder to check them out afterwards and he would then form Silvertone Records under the umbrella of the Zomba Group, specifically for the Roses' first release. Unfortunately, Gareth Evans turned out to be the most inveterate liar I've ever met. I once told him this and he was actually flattered. He had a certain charisma about him, coupled with a manic madness. Most of his speech was peppered with extravagant lies, which I soon saw through. It was good at least that he never made a pass at me: he was purely focused on making the band the next big thing and saw me, or rather used me, solely in terms of achieving that.

Gareth knew I had contacts in London, but he deceived the band to make it look as if he had got them their deal. He asked me to work on the Rough Trade deal and all the while went behind my back to Zomba/Silvertone. This was one lie I hadn't seen through, as the indie label of Rough Trade did feel right for them. This deception was Gareth's way of keeping me out of the loop. He cheated Geoff, and me, by taking the band into Rough Trade in London to discuss the marketing for their planned single release and then, on the same afternoon, driving them all round to sign their contract with Silvertone. Geoff, at least, got guitarist John Squire's original artwork for the single sleeve out of it. He told me: 'I felt double-crossed by both the band and also RT distribution for not sending our

---

2 52nd Street had their published with Zomba.

contract offer quickly enough/if at all. Yet another lesson in the wonderful amoral ways of some in the music business. I keep it on my wall to remind myself what not to do when attempting to sign a band.' And here it is:

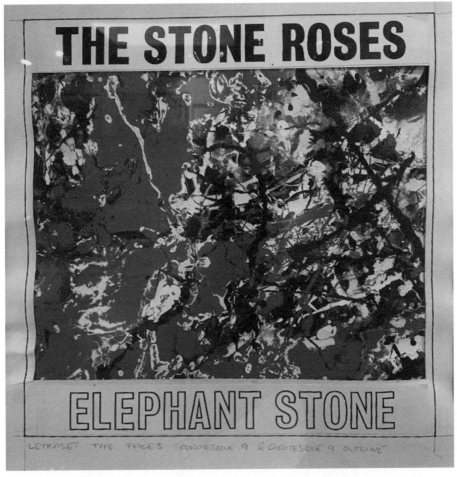

Geoff's reminder of what not to do when attempting to sign a band

I was gobsmacked that Gareth could be so unscrupulous and refused to work with such a dishonest man, abruptly ending my association with him, and *ipso facto* the group, before their first album was released. In terms of my contract with Gareth, he never paid me what he owed me (£7,500) but yet again, I didn't go to the law. It took me ages to receive just £1,000 for months of hard work arranging their demo, trawling it round London and putting on two showcase gigs. The band remained with Gareth until they eventually sacked him years later. It wouldn't be long, though, until I met Gareth again. I briefly worked in A&R for Hollywood Records in London, owned by Disney in LA. They were interested in acquiring the Roses' second album, and I attended their initial meeting with Gareth in Knutsford. The sums of money being bandied about by American companies in those days and for this particular group, not just by Disney, seemed to be all Gareth was interested in. He had no loyalty to Silvertone, and no doubt enjoyed a lengthy legal battle with them for the sake of the mighty bucks the US labels were offering. The group eventually signed to Geffen in America, but the second album inevitably wasn't as good as the first. There'd been too much focus on greed and the group, blocked by their contract from working when they were at their peak, seemed to have been misled. They soon disbanded.

It would be Oasis that took the crown in the early nineties that I thought could have belonged to Roses if they hadn't been blocked from working. But maybe there is some poetic justice now that John Squire has teamed up with Liam Gallagher.

The Haçienda had been losing money since its opening night, but I was a regular visitor and enjoyed meeting friends there, chatting and listening to music, usually sitting in the Gay Traitor bar downstairs (named after Anthony Blunt, a Soviet spy and art historian). There was also the Kim Philby bar and another bar called Hicks, named after Guy Burgess (codename: Hicks). All three men were part of the Cambridge Five spy ring and the fact that they'd been to the same university as Tony doubtless held appeal. While at Cambridge, Tony had been a member of the Kim Philby dining club, where wine and cheese were consumed while discussing how to smash the system.

I clearly remember the night The Haçienda changed; once half empty, it was suddenly packed to the rafters. I've never been a fan of 'explosions' though, and stopped going regularly from then on. It went from being a half-empty occasional live venue to a fully-fledged rave scene, fuelled by the popularity of the drug Ecstasy, and everyone who came seemed to be on it. The Mondays, the Roses and The Haçienda had all been around for years, but they suddenly found their niche around the surge of this drug's popularity and the club/dance scene that worked so well with it. The Haçienda had previously felt like my private club, the bouncers knew me and rushed me through with no charge, and I was always guaranteed to meet friends and associates who usually made up the bigger proportion of the attendees. In 1988 it was bursting at the seams with young ravers, all strangers who were having a wild time as if they'd known each other for years – the effects of Ecstasy.

Prior to this I'd occasionally bump into Tony at The Haçienda. Presumably this was how we got talking again. What I'd thought was dead ash turned out to hold hidden fire. Hate isn't the opposite of love but proved to be its near neighbour. There must have been some music-related, business reason for our meeting in private and that was when we realised our connection hadn't died. It still astonishes me that I forgave him, but I did.

Where or when our renewed love affair exactly began, I don't recall. But it was our long weekend in upstate New York that remains especially significant as the time our real reconciliation took place. Tony was to attend the New Music Seminar in New York, and so he booked his first-class ticket through Factory, buying me an economy ticket on the same flight. His note reminded me of the details:

FRI 15th July

BA 7267

MAN   JFK

1245   1455

By now Tony's son was 4 years old and the love of his life. He didn't want to break up his family and neither did I. So perhaps I shouldn't have got so hurt and upset when he stayed in the first-class lounge until the plane was boarding. He was known (from *Granada Reports*) and didn't want people to talk. My diary note of the day reads:

Plane to New York was delayed approximately three hours. I began to panic when people were boarding, and he still hadn't showed up – decided he definitely wasn't coming. Wondered what to do, whether to still go or not, went to the phone, maybe he'd got a message to my mum about why he couldn't come. Just then spied him walking as cool as you like – dashed to a seat and imitated calm, picked up a book but I was breaking down just like a little girl. He said he'd been watching the cricket in the lounge but seemed to be concerned about standing with me as we boarded the plane, which further broke my cool and the tears began to flow – so I put dark glasses on. He went up the stairs to first class and I took my place in the centre of the downstairs bustle. When I got to my seat I cried my eyes out. For once I felt grateful for the conversation of the two Americans on either side of me – otherwise I probably wouldn't have stopped.

I've wondered since why Tony didn't think to give up his first-class seat to me and take the economy for himself. Not that it crossed my mind back then. I was more astonished at him staying in the lounge for three hours without a word of communication to me. In these days of mobile phones, it's hard to imagine – a simple text would now suffice. I was really pent up and imagined all sorts of dramas. I hadn't even *known* there was a first-class lounge at Ringway airport! And then him not wanting to talk to me after I'd been waiting for hours on end, I was mortified. I was broke, with barely enough for a cup of tea, and there he was swanning about spending Factory money that I technically had rights to myself.

I hated Tony's play-acting when we got there. 'Can I offer you a lift?' he asked in the luggage reclaim, but most of the tension seemed to dissolve once we got in the car, a stylish, dark blue Mercury Cougar with leather seats, which he drove fast and expertly on the freeway.

We arrived at Lake George soon after midnight (5.00 a.m. to us) and checked into the Lake Crest Motel. Once our weekend began, all sense of separation dissolved, we were still young, still in love and we were happy.

The two days that followed were magical and proved beyond doubt that, where there is love, nothing, however outwardly damaging – the worst betrayal, even death – can ever truly destroy it. I learned that as long as there is love, forgiveness is always possible. There is a sweet, nostalgic sadness when I look back at that precious time. It even crossed my mind to revisit Lake George and that same motel, but then I realised how awful being there would be, with him dead and all my youth fled.

On the Saturday, Tony went windsurfing on the lake and I sat by it reading *The Passion* by Jeanette Winterson. Then, back in our room in the late afternoon, we took Ecstasy (as was the wont of Madchester/Haçienda people). My diary notes: 'Sat on the balcony listening to New Order. He watched Jesse Jackson at the convention and compared him to Martin Luther King. Slowly meandered down to a bar.'

When we were about to leave for the bar, there was a beautiful sunset and, as we set off, Tony took my arm and said, 'Let us go then, you and I'. But then he added something about the evening being spread out across the sky like a patient on a table. It was good to have the vivid colours across the sky pointed out. Turned out he was misquoting T.S. Eliot's 'The Love Song of J. Alfred Prufrock'.

In Manchester, we could only ever be secret lovers, but here, in upstate New York, it went beyond that. The next morning we attended the local Catholic church and it felt like we were husband and wife again. Anyone in the congregation would have thought so and I wished we could remain in this foreign country. We could make a new start, as he'd once suggested, but, alas, it was too late. My diary note for Sunday:

Went to mass. How odd – were we husband and wife or adulterers? I became very emotional during the service, the reading was, 'The Lord is my shepherd' – 'He leads me beside tranquil waters where He resteth my soul' etc'., and there was another reading about uniting after a period of division. It all seemed apt and beautiful, but I had to control my tears as they weren't the order of the day. Finished with a sweet song about peace. The heat was terrible, and we were longing to jump into the car and blast on the air conditioning but, even so, if I could keep one moment from the weekend it would be when we walked away from church, hands entwined, with the others. I could feel the time we had slipping away. Maybe that's why I remember so well how happy I felt then. We drove to The Sagamore – a nice hotel – and had lunch on the terrace. I had just finished the last strawberry when the heavens entirely opened. He left me in a gift shop while he phoned home. I had to laugh when he went to get the car – barefoot with trousers rolled up to his knees.

It was almost as if, sitting together in church, the veil of ordinary, day-to-day life had lifted, and I could see beyond it to something more significant. The alchemy of time had united us once more. He'd written to me once that 'beyond the games of Granada or Factory ... the personal life is something holy, and that throwing it away by negligence and ignorance...is my biggest mistake'. Actually, I knew, in the sanctity of this church, that it had been *our* biggest mistake. Tears were, perhaps, happy as well as sad. Despite our feelings for one another, this was just a moment in time, the life we could once have shared was finished. We'd wrecked everything, there was only arid desert from now on but, here, beside one another and for the whole of that Sunday, we could rest beside the tranquil waters the priest spoke about. It felt as if we were forgiven and that something precious had been preserved.

Back in New York we stayed at separate hotels; people were already arriving for the New Music Seminar and the networking these events entail. Tony didn't want us to be seen together and so I stayed for just one night at the Sheraton Squire Hotel while Tony was put up at the more stylish Morgans hotel. This wonderful picture of him in his room there was taken by Kevin Cummins.

Actually, it's my favourite picture of all of those I've ever seen of Tony. He looks so completely happy. He loved life and lapped it up. He was a relaxed, well-dressed man in his prime, with a 4-year-old he adored and not one but two wives, effectively. He had New Order, Happy Mondays and a revived Haçienda, so Factory was also riding high at that point. He deserved his success. Around him you can see all the typical accoutrements that generally went along with him: the phone, the pen in his hand, notepad, newspaper, list of things to do, cigarettes with equipment to make a joint and, of course, his Filofax. His expression reveals the nice boy his mum wanted him to be and who he was underneath his sometime 'nasty twat' exterior.

The next day I clearly remember our parting. Leaving him to fly home while he stayed on for the seminar, we said goodbye in the subway through a grill that resembled prison bars. I knew instinctively that these bars were symbolic of a greater barrier, that although we would still meet and spend short times together, we would never again share a length of days like those just passed in which we were incognito and free to be together. I left Tony the following note in pencil to read. He enclosed it with the letter he wrote me on Morgans paper while flying back to England. Presumably he didn't dare keep my note in case it was incriminating.

Memories fade like the red of an old eastern carpet washes pink after years of daylight. The times we shared – funny – they all seem happy now, as sweet as the days just passed – your soul in retreat with mine by a tranquil lake – and the only pain I can remember now was this one – the sadness for loss of you – mixed with a terrible fear that a day would come when we would no longer wake up together

– except by chance

– there is no sense in either of us

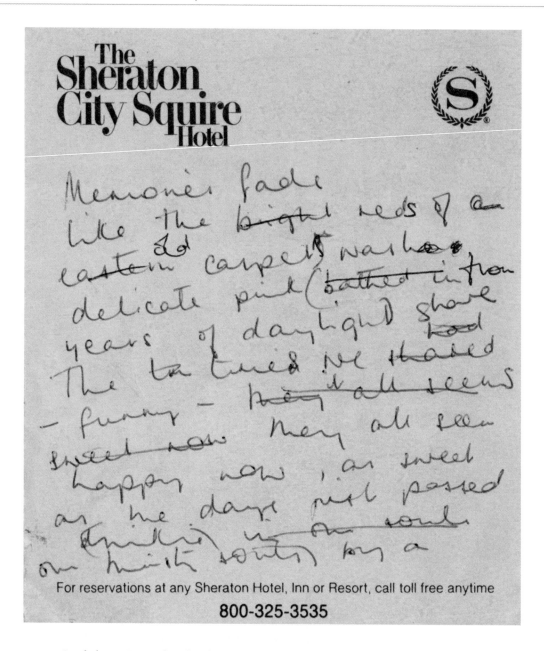

The Sheraton City Squire Hotel

For reservations at any Sheraton Hotel, Inn or Resort, call toll free anytime
800-325-3535

I only know I stayed at the Sheraton Squire because I kept a rough copy of the same note. It's strange that over 30 years later, this note still rings true. For all our rows, betrayals and bad behaviours, the failure of our marriage, the lack of money – everything – the only pain I feel now is sadness for the loss of him.

And then Tony sent me the following letter, written on his hotel notepaper, that he must have penned on his flight home.

MORGANS

Wed/Thurs
20/21st July
1988

I have been crying. In Mr Curtis's words, there are still "tears in my eyes". How well you write. How simply and how powerfully. And how right I have been to love you through these years for all those subtler reasons, beyond your sex and your "moments of glad grace".

Thankyou for these days. Though framed by sadness they give a fine shape to my life and I think they do to yours too. Our kinship is of this life and all this life. Of course "all this life" will not be for waking up together; but some of our life, from San Francisco to Lake George; from Charlesworth to some other place – the room is not yet booked. Really, can we ask any more. I am happy. You have made me happy. Though there are still those tears in my eyes and talking to you like this is making them well up just a little. You say

2

the past seems — all happy. For me, glorious; and yet your first lines, the words of a carpet dealer remind me that those days were as near to unbearable as any I can remember. My mum dead in Manchester & I in California — my wife dying in London and I in Manchester — and her changing her name.

Such And for all the past, I cannot recall before the tenderness in your eyes — through those 42nd St. Bars — at today's last kiss. Easy symbolism there, but welcome in it's way, and our love has not just grown older — it has also grown. When we have so much — a crime to ask to have it all.

And you were right; I was wrong to deny when you said 'you love Hilary don't you'. Of course, in my way, I do. For my way is to add that word "enough" and indeed I love Hilary enough to stay with her. Be cynical, and yes, I do not love my Lindsay "enough" to leave my new wife and son. But then do I really not love you. My tears — oh yes — I have been crying a little while writing this. I'm careful the stewardess doesn't notice. They're so tact-ful in CUB class anyway — my

3 / **MORGANS**

tears say something quite different. Till Death do us part, I think. We both had a fairly good go at parting but our twinned souls don't really allow it. For better or worse kid — it was a sacrament.

So what's next. What's now in for me a slightly overflowing soul and it wasn't just the Drambuie. You've made me glow — and your letter made my cheeks wet and my eyes heavy. You're right, I suppose, next time that we may wake 'by chance', I will have to defer to your next affair. How understanding we are both having to be — we who were so abject at 'understanding' when waking was 'by habit'. There's a fitting irony to end on.

I love you — if not 'enough' — at least as much as my heart can hold. And whether it be a month or five years before we wake together again — it does not change the fact that we are merely "turned aside to sleep." And in that continuous dream we must imagine my hand

on your right buttock – for in our sleep
that is where it always is.
I know its crazy
but I know it makes sense

for us perhaps the life of chance, like
Winterson's heroine – is natural – could
we ever succeed as creatures of habit.

I love someone whom I will
only wake up to by chance.

Fine.

Thank you.

Yours. Anthony. X

Wed/Thurs

20/21st July 1988

I have been crying. In Mr Curtis's words, there are still "tears in my eyes". How well you write. How simply and how powerfully. And how right I have been to love you through these years for all those subtler reasons, beyond your sex and your "moments of glad grace".

Thank you for these days. Though framed by sadness they give a fine shape to my life and I think they do to yours too. Our kinship is of this life and all this life. Of course "all this life" will not be for waking up together; but some of our life, from San Francisco to Lake George, from Charlesworth to some other place – the room is not yet booked. Really, can we ask any more. I am happy. You have made me happy. Though there are still those tears in my eyes and talking to you like this is making them well up just a little. You say the past seems – all happy. For me, glorious; and yet your first lines, the words of a carpet dealer remind me that those days were as near to unbearable as any I can remember. My mum dead in Manchester and I in California – my wife dying in London and I in Manchester – and her changing her name.

Such, and for all the past, I cannot recall before the tenderness in your eyes – through those 42nd St. bars – at today's last kiss. Easy symbolism there, but welcome in its way, and our love has not just grown older- it has also grown. When we have so much – a crime to ask to have it all.

And you were right, I was wrong to deny when you said "you love Hilary don't you". Of course, in my way, I do. For my way is to add that word "enough" and indeed I love Hilary enough to stay with her. Be cynical, and yes, I do not love my Lindsay "enough" to leave my new wife and son. But then do I really not love you. My tears – oh yes – I have been crying a little while writing this. I'm careful the stewardess doesn't notice. They're so tactful in CLUB class anyway – my tears say something quite different. Till death do us part, I think. We both had a fairly good go at parting but our twinned souls don't really allow it. For better or worse kid – it was a sacrament.

So what's next. What's now for me is a slightly overflowing soul and it wasn't just the Drambuie. You've made me glow – and your letter made my cheeks wet and my eyes heavy. You're right, I suppose, next time that we may wake 'by chance', I will have to defer to your next affair. How understanding we are both having to be – we who were so abject at 'understanding' when waking was by habit. There's a fitting irony to end on.

I love you – if not 'enough' – at least as much as my heart can hold. And whether it be a month or five years before we wake together again – it does not change the fact that we are merely "turned aside to sleep"

And in that continuous dream we must imagine my hand on your right buttock – for in our sleep that is where it always is.

I know it's crazy but I know it makes sense for us perhaps the life of chance, like Winterson's heroine – is natural – could we ever succeed as creatures of habit.

I love someone whom I will only wake up to by chance.

Fine.

Thank you.

Yours, Anthony

X

There are always, of course, moral implications in an affair, especially when a child is involved. But this sweet reconciliation was vital to our story. I'd hated him with a vengeance but was able to give him unconditional forgiveness and love, as he also gave it to me. Our troubled past was healed. Our aim was not to hurt anyone else but to undo all of our past hurts to one another.

I left my economy hotel and flew home on my economy flight to my parent's house. I felt I really belonged at that seminar but at least I got the badge.

The Joy Division track Tony referred to in the opening line of his letter, regarding the tears in his eyes, is 'Wilderness' from *Unknown Pleasures*.

Tony also refers at the end of the letter to Jeanette Winterson's heroine. I suspect this is Villanelle from *The Passion* as I was reading it while with him. He'd been a fan of *Oranges Are Not the Only Fruit* and I think this more recent book of hers was a gift from him to me. It felt especially significant because Villanelle, like me, defied true commitment. I wonder if Tony had a particular soft spot for Winterson partly because she was born in Manchester? He had a special place in his heart for talent made in Manchester, and the city itself of course.

If this book were a film, the weekend in New York and Tony's tender letter, and mine, would be a fitting end. In some ways, I wish it had been the end. But life isn't a film, and this wasn't the end of our story, which would continue until Tony's death. However, other than cards, there was to be only one more letter.

CHAPTER 16
'Nice Boys' Were Never My Cup of Poison

Despite our recently shared happiness, the parting at the subway bars had a finality about it. Our feeling of being married again, borrowed though it was, was over. It was a short break from reality with a fantasy of what our lives could have been, but which had now slipped away and was forever lost. We would never again find that same togetherness. That was why I'd looked at him so tenderly through the bars of the subway, a little death before the true one. Yet again we were moving away from the light. Our longest day had been spent.

Our affair though, such as it was, ambled on a short way further and even made its way from New York to the opposite coastline. Tony liked to plan trips away and, as it turned out, we both had reasons to be there and to meet at the city we'd visited twelve years earlier, on our honeymoon. My group, 52nd Street, were recording their second album in Los Angeles and I needed to fly out to lend support: as ever there'd been ructions. Tony, meanwhile, had some Factory business to attend to there and, by a fluke, we were both able to fly out on the same day, although not on the same plane this time, as Tony was travelling from London.

Tony refers to this occasion in his very last letter. He mentions our rendezvous at The Haçienda hotel, situated in a suburb beyond LAX airport. He'd suggested we meet there because of the name, spurred on by his delight at the overnight success The Haçienda club was now enjoying after years of losing money. Tony had an ability to create memories and it seemed poetic… until I got there, that is. Arriving first by shuttle from LAX, I found the two-star decor and surrounding neighbourhood disappointing, if not depressing. It was what you might call 'affordable', and would have been acceptable but it was rather an anticlimax after Tony had built up our meeting there into something really special – ever the fantasist. The hotel had opened in 1960 as a stopover for travellers going to and from the airport but would close permanently in 2022. I was glad to discover we weren't to stay here but travelled on to share a short weekend before going our different musical ways. Tony recalls our night in Santa Barbara before our separate work commitments began in West Hollywood, LA. We spent the last evening of the weekend in his room at the infamous four-star Chateau Marmont on Sunset Boulevard, where he was staying for the duration of his visit. The building's design was inspired by a French chateau; it looked like a castle and was incredibly romantic. I wasn't aware then that so many Hollywood stars had stayed there, such as Jean Harlow and Katherine Hepburn. I crept away before morning as Tony was worried about corporate colleagues, or maybe musicians, seeing me. My group, meanwhile, were recording on trendy Melrose Avenue. With its long line of interesting shops, eateries, bars and unusual buildings, it put me in mind of the Kings Road in Chelsea.

We shared another snatched day in LA later on; I was staying with Diane Charlemagne in a small apartment and, being skilled at applying make-up as well as being a superb vocalist, she duly made my face up in preparation for my tryst with Tony. Tony took me to Watts, where the riots had taken place in the sixties, and described what had happened there as we sat in the car. Six days of major civil unrest, initially triggered by the violent arrest of a young African-American man and his family. Anger at this racial discrimination was felt by thousands, and Martin Luther King soon spoke up about the riots being due in part to a recent repeal of a fair housing act, making discrimination on ethnic grounds now allowable for selling and letting properties. Sadly, thirty-four people were killed, mostly black citizens, but Tony enjoyed telling me about this uprising against an oppressive system and, as ever, the day was interesting. From there we toured the Queen Mary at Long Beach. It was still a ship then but has since been turned into a hotel.

Delightful as it was being with Tony, it was never the same. There was always a residue of guilt because of it being hidden, plus I felt I had to break with Tony for any chance of having my own now longed-for family with a partner on more equal terms. I was better suited as Tony's mistress than his wife – I was only able to fully embrace what we shared in more fleeting, romantic moments. Pablo Picasso said there are only two types of women, goddesses or doormats. As Tony's lover I felt like a goddess and as his wife, a doormat. I imagined the role of a wife to hold great appeal but failed spectacularly in the part. Despite believing I was looking for marriage and children, I subconsciously chose men that couldn't or wouldn't commit – relationships that had no future. Stations on the road. The other part of that was choosing the bad guys, because rows and difficulties felt familiar from my childhood. With nice guys the lack of conflict felt, at some deeply rooted subconscious place, unfamiliar and therefore, oddly uncomfortable. Tony, despite leading with his chin in a public arena, was uncomfortable with domestic rows, having had a childhood with doting parents and little obvious conflict. He wasn't entirely without his own damage though, but then who is? The poem by Philip Larkin springs to mind, about the way your parents inadvertently 'fuck you up'. They're damaged themselves, and so can't help it.

Despite Tony's apparently charmed childhood, there had been an undercurrent of tension. He'd grown up feeling ill at ease with his gay father without understanding why, and rejected him early on as a role model. It must have been awkward for Tony, identifying more with his more masculine uncle – his mother's brother – who also lived with them. Tony once queried his mother about why she'd married such a weak man like Sydney (he wasn't weak, incidentally, just effeminate) but she sternly told Tony that he must never, ever speak like that again about this man who'd been so very kind to both of them. Tony was very spoilt growing up with three attentive adults, none of whom had thought they'd ever have children. He continued in adulthood to be spoilt and I noticed he developed two methods of handling problems: one was by manipulation and, if that failed, the second was punishment for the supposed offender.

Tony was perceptive in noting in this letter that 'nice guys were never your cup of poison.' This was so eloquently apt, in fact, that it was the working title of this book, and now this chapter. (My publisher, David Barraclough, found a more appropriate title from Yeats' *Ephemera*.) The 'nice guy' Tony mentions was Peter Walmsley who ran Rough Trade International, with whom I'd had a relationship in 1986. Peter was hugely intelligent and an archetypal nice guy, so I was inevitably obliged to end our short relationship. Far from being sulky or antagonistic, even then, he sent me a package of good wine and a book by Pablo Neruda: *The Captain's Verses*. His enclosed card quoted from Neruda poem 'Your Laughter' – 'laugh at this clumsy boy who loves you'. He was too nice for me, and too nice for this world in fact, which may partly explain why he left it early. He died in 2010 of cancer.

Tony and I met again on 21 December 1988, which turned out to be the night of the Lockerbie bombing. We saw the dreadful news on the TV together. We were staying overnight in a London hotel for our Christmas tryst, our last, as it would turn out. I think most affairs take a toll at Christmas if children are involved. Whatever we shared, however lovely, it was second best to being together on Christmas Day. Of course, he'd want to be with his child and family, I wouldn't have expected anything else. But his unavailability on that day – the day he'd proposed to me because it was so special to him – was a painful reminder that our marriage had disintegrated into a dishonest affair. Even the photograph on the following page that I took of him somehow, to my mind, smacked of an adultery that I was not comfortable with.

By 1989 I'd decided enough was enough. I was 37 and felt driven to have the chance of a family. This was obviously ironic given Tony's earlier urgent desire for a child with me, but time was now beginning to run out for me.

If I'd known then that I was destined to be childless, I may not have ended things so abruptly with Tony. It saddens me that I did but Tony, as a loving father, understood. It was a case of the biological body clock running out of time. Tony offered to give me a child if we were still lovers after a year but being a single mother didn't appeal to me. Nor did the idea of any residue of shame or deceit around an innocent child.

Back in LA in early 1989, the producer John Barnes decided to send home all of my band, 52nd Street, except for Diane, who was an unrecognised diva with the voice of an angel. John felt that sufficient instrumentation had been recorded and wanted to spend a body of time finishing off tracks with Diane alone. There'd been too many rows amongst the band, and he saw Diane as the main talent. John was also a skilled keyboard player who worked with Michael Jackson.

I was summoned to join Diane and stayed in Los Angeles with her for three months. Because of my decision, I began dating someone from the studio, imagining that this American guy could give me the family I thought I wanted. Pure illusion again. In the first place, he wasn't the settling down type (and he never did become a father). Plus, he lived in Los Angeles, and I was essentially rooted in Manchester (even if my dad did wonder if I'd be applying for naturalisation through being there that long). The relationship ended as soon as I was back on English soil.

Tony wrote to me at the end of that year, in December 1989, from his travels. We'd become just friends by then. The letter was sent from Tahiti of all places. Tony would find any excuse to travel, and Factory gave him every opportunity he ever needed. He could visit the licensees and here he mentions visiting Sydney where he met the

ROYAL PAPEETE HOTEL
TAHITI

Boulevard Pomare • P.O Box 919 • Papeete, TAHITI • cable : ROYALPAP • tél : 42.01.29

N° T.A.H.I.T.I. : 067.066 - R.C. PAPEETE No. 1240 B - Telex : ROYAL PAP 384 FP

B.T. 01.31570 6 010 00
B.I.S. 052096 B 21

N/Réf^{ce} :
V/Réf^{ce} :

PAPEETE, le 9th December
                    1989

Hi kid,

This time last year it was sunny Santa Barbara for my weekend off 'before descending on L.A. Sunny Santa Barbara, log fires, and a rendesvous at the Hacienda. See — you don't believe it — but I think our ability to keep creating memories is marvellous — as in 'to be marvelled at — and inviolable.

This time this year, its a little boy on his own in the rain. I've never seen so much rain. It was raining in Singapore last weekend. It was raining in Sydney all week as I played the part of the appetitive record exec. And then I got to the Southern Seas. 6,000 km out from Sydney. 6,400 km to go to LAX — and all the water in between has been falling from these hot grey skies ever since. I'm not complaining, mind, after all I'm just resting up for another bout of selling and one hotel room is as good as another; and the collector in me values the luggage tags, and Oliver will dig the stamps.

— And still we collect memories. The rain

drives me back to my folofox and a line that sits therein.
Let me find it. Ah yes - "Into each life some rain
has to fall." I'm sure I've shown you the page. It
was late 80 or 81 - sitting in the driver's seat of an econoline
van - early evening in the shopping district of Philadelphia.
Listening to sad Country + Western songs on the radio - and
there wasn't a song that didn't go to the heart of my
problem. You. Looking at the page now - at the end
of the decade - I note - and it's trite - but you
can see how it got me;

"I gave you my soul on a silver platter,
And I found out, that it didn't matter."

Screws W. B. Yeats huh.

Well, darling - all my talk of memories - even the
fresh ones. I know it's easy for me - with family,
home, + jobs. And I know how tough it is for
you. And I know how "helpless" feels - it feels
like I can't help and it hurts the most. You should
have married Walmsley. Nice boy. But then "nice
boys" were never your cup of poison.

Don't know when you'll get this - maybe I'll
beat the Polynesian Air Mail and this will be
an opening letter for the 90's. It is written with
love and sent with love. And as for W.B. Yeats;

"When you are old and grey,

Can't quite remember - I think "love" hid his
head among the clouds - loads of clouds here.
love you. Anthus. x

Australian one, Base. He was ever hungry to make the most out of life, to experience it to the full and to see as much of the world as he could. He always liked to combine business with pleasure and would tag on short holidays and sightseeing, often by himself. Always the self-confident one, he'd never had qualms about taking himself on holiday alone. Because of Factory, he was able to enjoy the glamour of flying business class and staying in swish hotels. He had an interesting life, and I'm glad he did, because sadly it was shorter than most.

Royal Papeete Hotel,
Tahiti 9th December 1989
Hi kid,

This time last year it was sunny Santa Barbara for my weekend off before descending on L.A. Sunny Santa Barbara, log fires, and a rendezvous at the Haçienda. See – you don't believe it – but I think our ability to keep creating memories is marvellous – as in to be marvelled at – and inviolable.

This time this year, it's a little boy on his own in the rain. I've never seen so much rain. It was raining in Singapore last weekend. It was raining in Sydney all week as I played the part of the appetitive record exec. And then I got to the Southern Seas. 6.000 km out from Sydney. 6,400 km to go to LAX – and all the water in between has been falling from these hot grey skies ever since. I'm not complaining mind, after all I'm just resting up for another bout of selling and one hotel room is as good as another; and the collector in me values the luggage tags, and Oliver will dig the stamps.

And still we collect memories. The rain drives me back to my Filofax and a line that sits therein. Let me find it. Ah yes – 'Into each life some rain has to fall'. I'm sure I've shown you the page. It was late '80 or '81 – sitting in the driver's seat of an econoline van – early evening in the shopping district of Philadelphia. Listening to sad Country and Western songs on the radio – and there wasn't a song that didn't go to the heart of my problem. You. Looking at the page now – at the end of the decade – I note – and it is trite – but you can see how it got me;

"I gave you my soul on a silver platter
And I found out, that it didn't matter."
Screw W.B. Yeats huh.

Well, darling – all my talk of memories – even the fresh ones. I know it's easy for me – with family, home & jobs. And I know how tough it is for you. And

I know how "helpless" feels – it feels like I can't help and it hurts the most. You should have married Walmsley. Nice boy. But then "nice boys" were never your cup of poison.

Don't know when you'll get this – maybe I'll beat the Polynesian Air Mail and this will be an opening letter for the 90's. It is written with love and sent with love. And as for W.B.Yeats;

"When you are old and grey

- - - - —————————- ———————

Can't quite remember – I think "Love" hid his head among the clouds – loads of clouds here.

Love you.

Anthony

X

The line about souls and silver platters is an adapted quote from a song entitled 'What Will I Do?' by The Whispers, a group from LA who actually formed in Watts in 1963. The song itself is somewhat mediocre, not one of their best but the line Tony chose does stand out.

A year later Tony met Yvette, twenty odd years younger, and became so enthralled that he eventually broke up his family for her, leaving not just his young son but his 1-year-old daughter. He told me it nearly broke him, that he was able to relate to Ian Curtis who saw suicide as the only way out, given the dilemma of choosing between the children you love and a woman you love. I wasn't sympathetic, whereas with Ian, I had been. Having made his move, Tony was prone to invent reasons why it had been the right decision – a case of his version of praxis again.

Tony always kept any contact with me hidden from Yvette. I saw this as a weakness of the first order. Once she telephoned him on his mobile when he'd called round at my mum's house for coffee; his mobile was the size of a brick and was something very few people had then. Tony panicked, didn't dare pick up and then ran outside to speak to her from his car. I saw this as cowardly, especially since we were platonic friends then and had nothing to hide. Feeling disenchanted with him, I rather lost interest in seeing him if it was to be like that, and decided my time would be better spent on my quest to find a partner. But the men I chose were always in some way unavailable for commitment, a subconscious defence mechanism mentioned before. I hadn't then worked through the reasons for this, nor was I even aware of it operating.

I wasn't exactly an attractive proposition for the right man either. Struggling to take care of myself, I owned nothing, had zero savings and was scraping a living in the music business which, by the early nineties, was ready to spit me out. In 1994, after a failed venture in America trying to launch a CD Rom called 'The Women's Disc' (for which I was told by male executives 'Women don't buy CD Roms'), I was back living with my mum (father dead) and penniless.

As time moved on, Tony became more daring about meeting me. He was there when my mum died, and at crucial times when I was in a dark place. He was there when I got the first house of my own two years later, a small cottage not dissimilar to the one we shared in Town Lane. In happier times he would drive up to see me and take me to Pizza Express. We'd made our peace and there was no judgement anymore, only acceptance of one another.

Then, in January 2007, I was visiting him at his apartment in town when he told me he had kidney cancer. I burst into tears in front of him. I remember seeing my mum do the same when my dad told her he'd got cancer. I realised then that my mum must actually have loved my dad in spite of his terrible treatment of her. She was able to see through his damage to the person underneath and able to forgive. When my own tears fell over Tony's announcement I realised the same thing. None of his flaws came into play anymore, I simply loved him and didn't want him to die.

In the months before Tony's death we saw a lot of each other as, by then, Yvette was no longer living with him. Technically, and in the public eye, they were still a couple and he remained committed to her. I stayed with him every weekend in the three months of his illness up to his death, but she never knew this, as she usually saw him on weekdays. Tosh Ryan and I had recently broken up, so I was free to devote my spare time and emotional energy to Tony. His last week or so was spent in Christies hospital, which was down the road from Old Broadway in Didsbury. I was alone with him the evening before the day he died. Everywhere was quiet. He didn't seem to be suffering, but he was tired. I held his hand, and he kept hold of it as he drifted into sleep. It got later and later, and I thought I'd better leave. I gently let go, checked he was still asleep and tiptoed out of his room. Outside, a nurse asked me if I'd like her to arrange bereavement counselling for me. Did she think I was his wife? The day he died he sent instructions that I wasn't to visit, as Yvette was going to be there for the duration. I felt a bit hurt by that and wondered why he cared about such a thing on his very last day on earth. Then, as described, even at his funeral I was sent upstairs by Bruce Mitchell to be out of sight from her. He stood at the door like the nicest bouncer you could ever meet. Again, Tony had deliberately arranged this, a showman to the end.

I felt I hadn't really been able to properly say goodbye to Tony, not being allowed to visit him on his last day and not knowing, the night before, that I'd never see him again. So, I went to the Chapel of Rest to do it. His hair had been washed and, the struggle now over, he looked restored somehow. I wept, of course, but, because he didn't like snivelling, tried not to. Since he was so quiet I started talking to him. Feeling silly, I got up to leave but I simply didn't feel ready to, and asked the man outside if I might have a chair and also take a lock of Tony's hair. He said he'd need the permission of Tony's next of kin and went off to make telephone calls. I looked at Tony and said, 'I'm causing trouble again, aren't I?' 'Yes,' he seemed to silently reply while casting his gaze heavenward. It transpired that the next of kins' mobiles were switched off, so I just put my hands through Tony's hair instead. It was a gesture I'd made a thousand times before, but the sadness of this last time was too much. I began to cry again, and said out loud, 'It's only a lock of hair, I don't think anyone would notice.' The man heard me and went to get the scissors. He left me to it, but I did notice him peering through the window slightly anxiously, in case I had it in mind to give Tony a crew cut or something.

I bear much guilt for the failure of our marriage. After all, I was the volatile one who finally walked away from it, the one who broke it up. Tony really meant it to be for life, as evidenced by his letters. My regret is enormous; it was my own insecurity that led to the rows, my infidelity and onwards destruction from there. He might have been a self-confessed twat, he might have treated me appallingly many times, punishing me severely for my offences, but there it is. And underneath it all, he was really the nice boy his mum wanted him to be, he just went astray, as we all do in one way or another.

And our marriage wasn't entirely a failure, since we did have good times and sustained love for one another throughout, even if it was mixed sometimes with hate. Sitting with him in the final stages of his illness, he aged alarmingly in front of my eyes, but I felt as if I had aged along with him. We sat watching television and it was as if we really had grown old together after all.

And besides, a lot of so called 'successful marriages' could be deemed failures. Kierkegaard, an existential philosopher, once wrote that, 'people settle for a level of despair they can tolerate and call it happiness.' Maybe I'm incapable of truly loving any man.

Fifteen years after Tony's death, I spoke to a medium about him. You, the reader, may – as he would have done – consider such 'communications' to be half-baked, fantastical nonsense. However, here's what she told me: she said that his life was not what he wanted it to be. I immediately responded with, 'but people regard him as some kind of hero of Manchester.' 'No,' she replied, 'People used him. He didn't find love.' I have to agree that people used him. My mum used to refer to some in Tony's circle as always having 'an eye on the main chance' with him. But regarding him not finding love, I wasn't convinced. I told the medium, 'I loved him.' 'No,' she said again. 'You left him.' Incidentally she didn't know my story about Tony, or who he was. I said he would have left me for a younger woman eventually in any case, but she said he wouldn't have, his commitment to me would have been for life. I think I cried at that point, if not before. The medium said he was still healing in the spirit world; it was taking time and that his mother was helping him with it. Also, that his mother truly loved him but admitted she put him on a pedestal. Indeed, said I, and all I did was try to knock him off it at every turn because I felt he was an arrogant egomaniac. I repeated that I loved him in any case but again, apparently, I wouldn't have left him if I had. But she did say that Tony knew I deeply cared for him.

It was fitting personally, and for this book, that Tony's last written letter to me ended with a reference to his favourite author's bittersweet poem, 'When You Are Old'. Did he have some kind of presentiment that I would 'take down this book' while dreaming of our youth together? The last verse in which 'Love flees and hides his face amid a crowd of stars' is particularly poignant and pertinent. Tony imagined it was clouds, rather than crowds and yet his version is similarly poetic. W.B. Yeats's appeal is to think ahead to the time, when old, that the young addressee may sadly regret having let go of the true love of this young man. The poet's own great love for the actress and suffragette Maud Gonne was largely unrequited and, to his dismay, she became involved with other men. They both had children with other people.

But the poem works just as well by looking back, when old, how it was to be loved and how regretful it still is that it fled. Now older age is upon me, it was fitting to do that, and an appropriate closure to this story, of a boy and a girl, to recite the full poem.

When you are old and grey and full of sleep,
And nodding by the fire, take down this book,
And slowly read, and dream of the soft look
Your eyes had once, and of their shadows deep;

How many loved your moments of glad grace,
And loved your beauty with love false or true,
But one man loved the pilgrim soul in you,
And loved the sorrows of your changing face;

And bending down beside the glowing bars,
Murmur, a little sadly, how Love fled
And paced upon the mountains overhead
And hid his face amid a crowd of stars.[1]

1 Yeats, W. B., *The Collected Poems of W.B. Yeats.*, New York, Macmillan, 1956.

ACKNOWLEDGEMENTS

Writing this book began as a lockdown project, initially out of my own interest, but it wouldn't have entered the public domain without the support of other people. Of course, my main thanks must go to Tony who was such an excellent writer and it is his letters that frame it all. Anyone who wants to write a romantic letter should take note of his skill, even if there's also a glimpse into the twat side of his nature on reading his dismissal letter to me.

Amongst the living, special thanks go to the publishing director of Omnibus, David Barraclough, who could see the value and is also a decent and lovely man. Another one is Stephen Lea who helped bring the baby out of the womb as it were. Then the letters themselves are published with the kind permission of A.H.W Archive 2023, © 0 and I Wilson, so special thanks to them. The above are all the *sine qua non*, otherwise this might have remained forever on my computer.

Bob Dickinson helped during the birthing process with his astute observations, and rock writer and editor, Zoë Howe, who asked me great questions which improved the story immensely. By the end of the process she also felt like a friend, (definition of a friend being someone who is on your side). I needed every bit of encouragement while holding more guilt (gilt) over the contents than King Midas. My other editor at Omnibus, Claire Browne, deserves a medal for all the visual copies she's had to sort out, not to mention the words and emails. Others at Omnibus who have and will be helping include Greg Morton, Giulia Senesi and Neal Price.

Then my thanks go to the following (in alphabetical order): Lawrence Beedle, Howard Devoto, Jan Hicks, Shan Hira, Steve Hopkins, Jonathan Kebbe, Jez Kerr, Pam Lee, Seamus Lennon, Gary McMahon, Thelma McGough, Nathan McGough, Mick Middles, Bruce Mitchell, Susanne O'Hara, Maggie Greatbanks, Phil Rainford, Tosh Ryan, Ross Shelley, Kuka Steiner, Linder Sterling and Geoff Travis. And huge thanks to Lawrence Beedle, Howard Devoto, Thelma McGough, Stuart Murray, Phil Rainford, Neville Richardson, Tosh Ryan, Les Thompson and Geoff Travis for supplying visual material.

Then there's my family, friends and workmates for continuing help and support. You know who you are.